AMERICAN FURIES

AMERICAN FURIES

**CRIME, PUNISHMENT, AND VENGEANCE
IN THE AGE OF MASS IMPRISONMENT**

SASHA ABRAMSKY

**Beacon Press
Boston**

Beacon Press
25 Beacon Street
Boston, Massachusetts 02108-2892
www.beacon.org

Beacon Press books
are published under the auspices of
the Unitarian Universalist Association of Congregations.

10 09 08 07   8 7 6 5 4 3 2 1

This book is printed on acid-free paper that meets the uncoated paper
ANSI/NISO specifications for permanence as revised in 1992.

Composition by Wilsted & Taylor Publishing Services

Library of Congress Cataloging-in-Publication Data

Abramsky, Sasha.
   American furies : crime, punishment, and vengeance in the age of mass imprisonment /
Sasha Abramsky.
      p. cm.
   Includes bibliographical references and index.
   ISBN-13: 978-0-8070-4223-6 (paperback : alk. paper)
   ISBN-10: 0-8070-4222-6 (hardcover : alk. paper)   1. Criminal justice, Administration of—
United States. 2. Punishment—United States. 3. Imprisonment—United States. 4. Sentences
(Criminal procedure)—United States. I. Title.

   HV9950.A334 2007
   364.973—dc22   2006031105

To Rose Uren,
for knowing when to laugh and when to cry,
and for living life well,

and

to Natalie Bimel,
who always had the courage to smile and the strength to dream

CONTENTS

FROM OUT OF TARTARUS

Moundsville, West Virginia, is a sleepy little town deep in the heart of Appalachia, a ninety-minute drive south of Pittsburgh. The otherwise drab town center is dominated by the crumbling but still formidable visage of the old state penitentiary. Since the mid-1990s, when a new prison was built, the town has hosted an annual Mock Prison Riot, run by the federal Office of Law Enforcement Technology Commercialization and actively supported by West Virginia's congressional representatives, in the dank nineteenth-century penitentiary. Spanning several spring days inside the abandoned cellblocks, common areas, and yard, the mock riot has become a fixture on the social calendar of corrections aficionados from around the world.

"Freeze! Don't move!" Enforcement Technology Group (ETG) sales rep Aaron Dexter barks into an electronic gadget perched in front of him on the central lawn of the old prison, in April 2005. Immediately the public-address system translates the commands into Arabic, the harsh staccato voice amplified as it reverberates off the prison's massive turreted stone walls.

Clad in a T-shirt and gray slacks, the slightly bald Dexter keeps feeding in commands, and the PA system keeps broadcasting them across the yard in different languages. The hundreds of onlookers—mainly prison employees who have driven or flown in from around the country, many shivering in the damp early spring of Appalachia—applaud.

The command-translation machines were developed, Dexter informs me, with funding from DARPA (Defense Advanced Research Projects Agency), the shadowy Defense Department organization that has, over the decades, provided seed money for everything from the Internet to state-of-the-art biometric devices to bioweapons-detection technology. They were originally designed to control captured insurgents in Iraq and Afghanistan, as well as terrorist suspects in Guantánamo Bay. In all possibility, the brutalized prisoners who turned up in photographs from Abu Ghraib in 2004, some hooded and with electric wires attached to parts of their bodies, others being set upon by attack dogs, others bruised and bloodied from beatings, and still others naked and, under duress, performing various sexual acts, had at times during their confinement heard Arabic orders hurled at them through these sorts of machines.

Now, however, as the distinctions between American overseas military operations and domestic control policies for the country's burgeoning prison and jail population become more amorphous, translation systems are being marketed as must-have tools for high-security institutions inside the United States. For a mere twelve hundred dollars, a prison administrator can buy the device preprogrammed to simultaneously translate approximately one thousand commands into Arabic, Spanish, and Russian, with additional languages as optional add-ons.

———•———

Inside the exhibition hall—a blue and yellow prefab metal building erected in a corner of the yard—dozens of new technologies are on display, the salesmen and -women aggressively touting their products' benefits and demonstrating how their widgets work. Like quack medicine sellers of a bygone age, they promise that their wares will deliver wonderful, transformative results. There's a table with a picture of a fully armored guard, his eyes covered in thick goggles, pointing a gun straight at the observer. "Tactical & Survival Specialties, Inc.: Equipment Your Life Can Depend On," reads the sign. There's the Red-Man training gear, featuring a dummy decked out from head to toe in red armor plates made of some indescribably strong plastic-looking material, its face covered in a mesh guard. Another dummy is dressed in what looks like an updated version of medieval chain mail, the face protected by a Plexiglas mask, the hands covered in thick gloves, a cross between the Terminator and a knight of Camelot.

Then there's an unmanned miniature spy plane, marketed for use above prison yards. "We're partnering with a lot of companies in Israel, where the technology is now very commonplace," the sales rep explains matter-of-factly. "Correctional facilities really like this equipment. But," he continues somewhat mournfully, "they're considered the bastard child of law enforcement—and they don't have the funding to procure this."

Another marketer talks about the possibilities of the VeriChip, a microchip designed to be injected into humans with a syringe so that the controlling agency—be it the prison, parole, or probation—can monitor their whereabouts. Alas, this particular invention is not on display in the exhibit hall. Someone else hawks tiny black Lector Mark 2 tactical robots that roll around on little tank treads carrying spy and camera equipment into corners that guards cannot easily access.

Standing on one of the busiest aisles in the hall, a gray-bearded inventor fast-tracked into the United States from Britain by the Department of Homeland Security explains the portable system his company has developed for taking biometric readings from people and then feeding them, in real time, into databases to see whether the individuals are on lists of potential bad guys. It is being designed to augment airport-security systems; to protect vulnerable bridges and tunnels; even, he tells me with a touch of glee, to help Halliburton defend Iraq's oil pipelines. If cameras detect suspicious activity along the pipeline, he explains, the system will feed the suspects' biometric data into a database to see whether it matches those of known insurgents—whose data has presumably been taken in one or another prisoner-processing camp somewhere in post-Saddam Iraq. If it does, the information will be transmitted to a drone carrying Hellfire missiles that can take aim at the troublemakers before they have time to blow up the pipeline. One day, the inventor hopes, these devices will be standard law-enforcement equipment across the United States. Traffic police might carry them; prison guards might use them to screen visitors. Already, he tells me, his company is preparing to crank out tens of thousands of these gadgets in the coming months.

My favorites, however, are the bone-conductor headsets, aptly named Radioears, that convert vibrations of the skull, generated when a person speaks, into voicelike sounds that can be transmitted even in the noisiest of situations—the sort of inherently improbable and, yes, seductive creation periodically unveiled in a James Bond movie.

Of course, in addition to the sexy-technology showcases, there are more mundane exhibits: the various forms of stun-gun weapons; the new, super-lightweight batons; the acoustic grenades that disorient inmates with bursts of unbearable noise; the various dispensers of tear gas, pepper spray, and mace. There's the Numb John rubber dummy, being pummeled into oblivion by the demonstrator of a vicious-looking rapid containment baton. There's even a fold-up chemical toilet, complete with pop-up privacy tent, for those moments during a prison standoff when you've just got to go.

———•———

In its time, West Virginia State Penitentiary was intended to awe the populace with its impenetrable façade and its portcullis entrance, from the beams of which were hung capital defendants in the period before the introduction of the electric chair. "One man, the rope was too long and it was a very painful hanging," explains the woman who registers me for the mock riot event. "And one man, his head come off, which wasn't fun." The prison was intended as an architectural presence suggesting the invincibility of the state and the insignificance of those serving out their sentences inside. Until 1995, prisoners lived in these dank, lung disease–inducing cellblocks, with their chicken-wire fences and tomblike cells (five by seven feet, with ceilings barely high enough to allow a man to stand up and virtually no natural light). Now that West Virginia houses its miscreants in newer, more sanitary facilities, the penitentiary is at once a tourist destination for those looking for glimpses of the "bad old days," and a venue for large correctional gatherings.

Every spring, fifteen hundred people descend on Moundsville—named for the large Native American earthen mounds dotted around the region, its small clapboard houses built to house workers during the heyday of American industrialism—to attend the event, swap stories about the latest technology, watch teams of correctional officers enact simulated riots, and observe the latest control techniques developed by state, federal, and privately run prisons in response to unruly inmates. Replete with large dinner buffets, fist-pumping speeches, opportunities to show off buzz cuts, muscles, and physical prowess (there are speed competitions in such categories as hostage rescue), and an abundance of machismo energy even in the quieter moments, the mock riot is one of the correctional world's undisputed annual highlights. It is, claims the narrator of the promotional video created out of footage from the 2004 mock riot, "one of the most spectacular events known to the corrections community." As he talks, film rolls of prisoners being "taken down" in a cartoonish, almost computer game–like way; of SWAT teams; and of armored officers wielding stun guns, all while space-war music swells out of the speakers.

"The Office of Law Enforcement Technology Commercialization strives to get market-driven technologies into the hands of law enforcement personnel," the narrator proclaims in stentorian tones. "Technology should, technology can, technology will save lives."

I enter a glassed-in observation area with dozens of correctional officers to watch a team from the Michigan Department of Corrections prepare to take back control of a dining area occupied by hostage-holding inmates. (The "inmates" are volunteers from a local Jesuit college, dressed in short-sleeved orange shirts and formless orange-and-white-striped pants. Some are made up with fake gore.) Unlike real inmates in real prisons, they are given protective goggles and earplugs. And then the fun begins.

At 1:06 p.m. the correctional officers, dressed in black paramilitary uniforms and helmets, mass outside the dining room, one group on the left, another on the right. Four minutes later, the teams enter, throwing noise grenades as they come. They line up in a row, their bodies shielded by thick Plexiglas shields. And then they advance, step by step, left feet forward, their flanks protected by gun-toting officers, bellowing in unison with the crunch of their boots on the floor, each step a choreographed exercise in intimidation. It is like watching the shock troops of a disciplined Roman legion advancing against a barbarian horde.

The inmates are shoehorned into a progressively smaller corner of the room, unable to break out beyond the line of shields. Some begin throwing food; others try to run the gauntlet of officers.

"There you go, get that stick on him!" a correctional officer in the observation room yells, as the members of the Michigan team begin to swing their batons.

"Do what you got to do to go home," another cries.

"Last year, they let us shoot them at their feet," says a third nostalgically. "Easy being an inmate when you know they're not going to hurt you."

By 1:21 p.m. all the inmates have been marshaled into a tiny space, where they are lying flat on their bellies in surrender. Then they are ordered to back up, one at a time, on hands and knees, toward the line of officers. While one officer provides cover with a shield, pairs of guards run toward the inmates, drag them back out by their legs, handcuff their wrists behind their backs, and pull them out of the action. If the inmates resist, officers jump on their backs, batons swinging. Each hog-tying takes about seven seconds. By 1:39, the hostages have been rescued and all the inmates removed.

An hour later, in the bitterly cold prison yard, West Virginia correctional officers enact fights between inmates in the exercise area. Dressed in bulky purple body armor that completely covers his body and his head—Humpty Dumpty meets Darth Vader—one of the "inmates" absorbs repeated blows and kicks from fellow "prisoners" before the guards rush the yard, screaming and firing gas at point-blank range. Within seconds all the inmates are on the ground and the officers are speedily cuffing them. Then they regroup for another go, this time with Darth Vader as the instigator; the guards fire a volley of rubber bullets at his armor-protected legs and abdomen. Finally, in scenario number three, Darth Vader is lying on top of another inmate, pummeling him. The guards rush him, fire pellets at him, and literally blow him off the other inmate with the force of whatever it is they hit him with.

As of mid-2006 approximately 2.2 million Americans were incarcerated in local jails and in state and federal prisons. The United States has far and away the largest penal population in the world—larger both as a percentage of its total population and in absolute numbers than that of any other nation. And that includes countries such as Russia, the various other republics of the former Soviet Union, and China, notorious for their casual use of incarceration and their brutal, exploitative treatment of prisoners. Buoyed by tough mandatory-minimum sentencing regulations for drug offenders, which have disproportionately affected racial minorities; by habitual-offender laws designed to throw away the key on people convicted of several crimes over the course of their lives; by policy changes that treat growing numbers of juvenile offenders as adults; and by a strong move away from parole in many states; and bloated by a failing mental-health system that channels hundreds of thousands of mentally ill people into jails and prisons, the United States' engine of incarceration has been running at full throttle for a generation.

In states such as Louisiana, Texas, and Mississippi, almost 1 percent of the total population, and a considerably higher percentage of the adult population, now live behind bars.[1] Throughout much of the country, one in three young black men is either in prison or under the control of parole and probation services.[2] Studies show a correlation between the massive expansion of California's prison system and huge cuts in state funding for higher education.[3] In midwestern states such as Minnesota, which not long ago ran model prison systems catering to a relatively small number of prisoners, based on a Scandinavian-style rehabilitation system (in addition to developing inclusive social-welfare models, Scandinavian countries have pioneered some of the world's most progressive, rehabilitation-based penal systems), the vast numbers entering prison in recent years have, tsunami-like, swamped these time-tested programs. In the early 1970s, according to Pat McManus, former director of the Kansas Department of Corrections and deputy director of corrections in Minnesota, Minnesota adopted a Community Corrections Act specifically intended to divert offenders into local programming, from drug treatment to job training, rather than prison, and the director of corrections said on the record that it might be possible to close a state prison—indeed, that closing a prison should be seen as a mark of success rather than as a failure to defend one's bureaucratic turf.

"It gave the community some clout," McManus said when I talked with him in 2005. "[But] now we've joined the rest of the U.S. Being tough on crime is an incredibly popular political position." When the Community Corrections Act was passed, about two thousand Minnesotans were incarcerated; by the early twenty-first century, that number had risen to twelve thousand.[4]

"The enthusiasm and optimism in Minnesota that we can close a prison was shattered," McManus acknowledged. "We always blame politicians. A sense of meanness. A loss of optimism. I don't know what caused it, but certainly the change occurred."

Nationally, said New York University's David Garland, a renowned historian of criminal-justice practices, the federal system and the tough-on-crime culture fostered in recent decades has acted as a magnifier to state systems, creating between the fifty states "a race towards the most intensive punishments."

How stark this change is from the not-too-distant past can be seen in the raw numbers, the relentless march toward mass incarceration. In 1972—the last year the United States' incarceration rate remained at levels that represented the norm throughout the twentieth century—roughly 340,000 inmates peopled the country's jails and prisons, giving the Nixon era an incarceration rate of about 165 per 100,000.[5] This was a level roughly comparable to those of other large industrial democracies, and far below that of the Soviet Union and its satellite states.

Then, in the 1970s and 1980s, while western Europe, Canada, Japan, New Zealand, and Australia kept their imprisonment rates roughly constant and a bankrupt Russia and its neighboring states began reining in their prison populations, the United States started devoting more and more of its resources to locking its miscreant classes away. This was due in part to public fears in the face of rising violent crime and the pervasive use of Class A narcotics such as heroin, powder cocaine, and eventually crack. The optimism associated with the Great Society and the antipoverty programs of the 1960s gave way to a more punitive, more moralistic mindset that, all too often, assigned to the poor the responsibility for their own misfortunes and crafted social policy accordingly.

"Criminality is the most extreme manifestation of the unsocialized young male," opined conservative author Charles Murray in the immediate aftermath of Hurricane Katrina's destruction of New Orleans in 2005, writing specifically about the breakdown of law and order in the city. "Another is the proportion of young males who choose not to work.... Large numbers of healthy young men, at ages when labor force participation used to be close to universal, have dropped out." Murray, whose work has influenced a generation of conservative thinkers and politicians, continued with a question that he then immediately answered. "Why has the proportion of unsocialized young males risen so relentlessly? In large part, I would argue, because the pro-portion of young males who have grown up without fathers has also risen re-lentlessly."[6] In other words, the chaos in New Orleans didn't come about because tens of thousands of desperate, utterly destitute people were stuck in a city that was in the process of being destroyed; rather, it was the all-too-predictable result of promiscuity and a collapsed work ethic.

Blame the broader society, or the social and economic relationships that underpin a society, for the pathologies of urban poverty, and you're likely to endorse social interventions—literacy programs, job training, slum clearance, the creation of a first-rate community health network, and the like. Blame the urban poor for the pathologies of urban poverty and you're unlikely to want to throw good money after bad by crafting doomed-to-fail social programs. Instead, you're likely to endorse spending more money on law enforcement and incarceration so as to insulate the wider community from the mayhem generated by dysfunctional low-income communities. In his 1975 book *Thinking about Crime,* James Q. Wilson, one of the country's most influential crim-inologists, wrote, "Punishment is not an unworthy objective for the criminal justice system of a free and liberal society to pursue. The evidence supports (though cannot conclusively prove) the view that deterrence and incapacita-tion work, and new crime-control techniques ought to be tried in a frankly ex-perimental manner." Later, in *Crime and Human Nature,* he upped the ante still further, arguing in favor of altering "permanently and for large numbers of people the expected disutility of crime."[7]

———•———

In ancient Greek mythology, the Erinyes, or Furies, rose periodically from out of the dark, cavernous underworld of Tartarus to avenge wrongs and hound unpunished criminals. Ironically nicknamed Eumenides (well-wishers) by the populace, the Furies were usually portrayed as three wild-haired, robed fe-male goddesses whose names, in Greek, meant "unceasing," "grudging," and "avenging murder." So feared were these goddesses, these incarnations of hu-manity's elemental need for retribution, for the shedding of blood when wrongs have been done, that those pursued by the Furies were generally driven insane.

When Orestes killed his mother, Clytemnestra, in revenge for her murder of Orestes' father, Agamemnon, Clytemnestra's soul conjured up the Furies to track her son down and persecute him. In Aeschylus's immortal theatrical tril-ogy dramatizing these events, the *Oresteia,* Orestes is chased around the Greek world until he is finally tried and acquitted by the Council of Areopagus, the ancient Athenian judicial tribunal. Fusing mythology and history, Aeschylus defines the struggle over this ruling, and the Furies' eventual acceptance of it, as the point in time when Greece was transformed from a land of blood feuds to one in which courts of law would prevail. "This day, a new Order is born," says the leader of the Furies, and the goddesses, at least temporarily, fade away into the background.

But goddesses as potent as the Erinyes never really die. At most, they go into hibernation, reawakening periodically to rise from the depths and wreak havoc. When Inquisition-era Europe whipped itself into a frenzy believing that witches, in league with the devil, were conspiring to bring down the Christian order, tens of thousands of people were burned at the stake, hung, drowned, beheaded, crushed, and otherwise mutilated and killed. In some towns in Germany, hundreds of men, women, and children were publicly dispatched on specified execution days. The death cult lasted into the seventeenth century and beyond, famously infecting colonial America in the town of Salem, Massachusetts. When early Tudor England felt itself besieged by thieves, vagabonds, and otherwise idle poor, judges across the land responded by instigating an era of hanging that, the Elizabethan chronicler John Stow estimated a century later, cost the lives of seventy thousand people over four decades—an extraordinary number, considering that the country's entire population was barely in excess of 5 million at the time. Similar hysterias against putative threats to the existing social order appear with almost cyclical regularity across the continents and millennia.

And so it was that in the 1970s the wild-haired ones began rubbing their eyes and stretching their arms as, once more, they shook themselves out of their slumbers. By the 1980s they were fully awake and ready to enact their unforgiving punishments. They were no longer in the Mediterranean; now they were hovering over the United States of America, a land so consumed by its desire for revenge, its willingness to subjugate other social goals to this overriding end, that the politics and rhetoric around crime and punishment had assumed an almost mythic quality. Because sensibilities had changed since the witch trials, and the wholesale shedding of blood was not acceptable in the ostensibly more civilized environs of late-twentieth-century America, the Furies channeled their energies into a carefully constructed, bureaucratic prison system.

In 1980 the incarceration rate was just over 200 per 100,000, somewhat higher than it had been in 1970, but still not too far off the historic norm. By

1990, however, it stood at 461 per 100,000. By 2000 it had risen to an astronomical 703 per 100,000. In the years since, it has gone up still further: by 2005, the Bureau of Justice Statistics was estimating that over 2.13 million people were living in the thousands of prisons and jails now dotting the country. In absolute numbers, the United States went from being a country that incarcerated just under 475,000 people in 1980 to one with well over 2 million inmates.[8] Nearly 5 million more were on either parole or probation. All told, by the end of 2004, 7 million Americans were under the supervision of one or another criminal-justice agency, up from 1.8 million a mere quarter century earlier.[9]

Increases in incarceration that in the 1970s and 1980s could have been partially explained by concomitant rises in crime—an attempt to put a lid on escalating social chaos—continued on into the 1990s and 2000s, a period when crime rates were plummeting year in and year out. The Furies, once unleashed, were on a mission: to sweep up the riffraff, to lock away the addicts and the bumbling, impoverished neighborhood nuisances, the mentally ill and the simply antisocial. By the turn of the twenty-first century, approximately 1 million Americans were in prison and jail after being convicted of nonviolent crimes.[10]

It is hard to overstate the implications that this surging prison population has for American culture and politics, on local economies and on community structure. At any moment in time, more than one in a hundred American adults are living behind bars, with the numbers even higher in the southern states. If current trends continue, tens of millions of Americans will spend a significant portion of their adult life as prisoners. In some neighborhoods and in some racial and economic categories, more young men now go to prison than attend college; and in many states, since the mid-1990s, more tax dollars have been diverted to the criminal-justice system than to public universities. In the post–World War II era, the GI Bill massively expanded access to higher education and fundamentally transformed the American economy and job market, creating the conditions for a dramatic increase in prosperity and access to middle-class lifestyles. More recent legislation, such as the 1986 Anti–Drug Abuse Act and the 1994 Omnibus Crime Bill, has had the reverse effect, ramping up popular involvement with the criminal-justice system, paving the way for large-scale and overwhelmingly negative economic changes, and cementing into place a growing American underclass. Incarceration takes many breadwinners and taxpayers and converts them into prisoners, and their families into clients of the welfare system and charities. Those who were unemployed and had cost taxpayers a few thousand dollars a year through the welfare system, once behind bars require shelter, food, and health care at a far higher cost. Moreover, ex-prisoners face numerous restrictions on access to employment, residency, and government programs. Perhaps most disturbing, studies indicate that spending time behind bars reduces workers' earnings for the rest of their lives.

———

"People were impatient to see results [in the 1980s and 1990s], and so they said, 'The absolute answer is lock 'em up and keep 'em locked up,'" averred Mary Ann Saar, Maryland's secretary of public safety and a onetime prosecutor, when we met in the summer of 2005.

"I think we could have done much better diverting the low-level people [into non-prison environments]. . . . You need a very holistic approach. All of the churches involved, and whatever groups are out there, whether it's the Shrivers or the Rotarians. You've got little kids out on the streets, untended, it's just so overwhelming. [But] ten years ago you couldn't say this. Diversion was a no-no. If you said anything like that, you were soft on crime and nobody wanted you."

There is no doubt that many correctional professionals are honorable and caring people. The guards and medical personnel, the administrators and counselors have extremely hard, often unpleasant jobs, and many of them go beyond the call of duty on a regular basis. But to a large extent they are performing a Sisyphean task. For by warehousing so many people behind bars, conditions have been created that, all too often—even when lip service is paid to rehabilitation, to preparing convicts to return to life outside—make violence the default mode of dealing with inmates and allow for the sadistic impulses of a few to gain disproportionate influence behind prison walls. Despite the tens of billions of dollars channeled into corrections, there simply aren't enough human resources to provide for 2 million prisoners the intensive counseling, monitoring, education, vocational training, and drug-treatment programs that could form the core of a less coercion-based penal system. Increasingly, then, as the Mock Prison Riot demonstrated, prison systems flush with state and federal funds in an era of the twin wars on crime and drugs have deployed high-tech gadgets and weapons as first-response methods of prison control, discouraging human contact and dialogue between inmates and guards, and relying mainly on overwhelming force to deal with problems as and when they erupt.

"Life in 1981 to life today is entirely different in the Arizona Department of Corrections," Denny Harkins, the warden of Perryville women's prison, explained to me in the spring of 2005 at his facility west of Phoenix. He was dressed casually, in black jeans and a checkered shirt, his upper lip sporting a mustache, his eyes lively behind thin-rimmed spectacles. On his office wall was a framed poster of a huge wave and the words "Attitude: A Positive Attitude Is a Powerful Force." Harkins, who had worked in several prisons over a three-decade career, was one of a new group of top prison administrators hired to run Arizona prisons by a correctional director who, along with a handful of other reform-minded correctional administrators around the country in the first years of the new century, wanted to return to the days in which "rehabilitation" was not considered a dirty word. After twenty years of endless one-upmanship in toughness on crime, however, Harkins believed the director still had a mountain to climb.

"In '81 inmates were called 'residents.' Perryville was called the Arizona Correctional Training Center. As a correctional officer, we were almost encouraged to be the buddies of inmates. For example, I've taken inmates on escorted leave. One inmate, I took out to a private residence so he could have a private conversation with his daughter about why he and his wife were getting divorced. Totally unheard of today. I've taken an inmate to see his sick mother. Our relationship as staff with the [inmate] population was much more friendly. And we've lost that. The rules began tightening up and things began to change. Step by step, we began to take away from the population, take away from the population, take away from the population. We got to where the needed security changes had been implemented and then we started becoming more punitive. And we began to take things just because it was politically correct to take things. It seemed like we were always working on, 'What else can we take away from the inmates?' Tensions rose. We literally divorced our staff from contact with the population. We locked our staff up in the control room. Hostility began to rise. We started depending on concrete and steel for security and not just good old-fashioned, 'What's going on in the yard?'"

Treated as de facto war zones, prisons, and especially the crop of supermaximum-security institutions—supermaxes—that have opened up since the 1980s, become war zones, with prisoners and staff engaged in a perpetual, albeit unequal, arms race. Treated as enemy combatants, even many initially nonviolent inmates end up getting swept into the culture of brutality. When prisoners don't come out of their cells after being ordered to do so, or don't return their food trays, extraction teams gas them and drag them out with overwhelming force. When gangs fight on the prison yards, entire prisons can be locked down for weeks or months at a time, their inmates allowed out of their cells for less than an hour a day. When mentally ill inmates disobey orders or behave in the erratic, bizarre, self-destructive manner typical of people suffering from diseases such as schizophrenia and bipolar disorder, guards frequently respond with beatings, the firing of TASER stun guns or other "nonlethal weapons," and the use of four- and five-point restraint devices to hold down these individuals. Often when this happens, prison administrators hold hearings and decide to place the disruptive inmates into secure housing units—prisons-within-prisons where inmates are held for long periods of time in virtual isolation. The conditions inside these buildings have been described by psychiatrist Stuart Grassian as producing a "devastating psychological impact," somewhat akin to the mental collapse experienced by many prisoners of war when kept in solitary confinement for extended periods of time.[11] They are, in many ways, hidden Bedlams operating virtually outside the moral and behavioral codes that govern the broader society.

"There is no kind way to explain how a 24 year old rapist who was raped and turned out in prison could take a single-bladed razor and cut his penis off," one middle-aged prisoner in Indiana, serving thirty-six years for armed robbery, wrote me. "Throwing it out on the range. While 4 guards argue over who will pick it up!!" The inmate continued, "I have no love for guards or the system they represent. But, at the same time, I see often they are as much a victim as we are. The bottom line is this. No matter what side you're on, prison does not work! In rare cases it has. But, as a general rule, it only makes mean people meaner, weak people weaker, and crazy people crazier."

Another man wrote from the maximum-security prison in Florence, Arizona:

> I live in my cell 24-7 a day. My food portions are small cause the dept. said since we don't work or move around that we don't need the regular serving general population gets. We also cannot order food items from the inmate store. I'm on psychiatric meds Prozak. When we're giving cleaning supply's to clean 3 x a week the stuff in the bottle that is supposed to be disinfectent is pure water. The guards are to lazy to fill the bottles so they give us water. I have caught staff infection 5 x since I've been here 3 years. We are given toe nail clippers to do our nails once a week and are shared among other inmates which majority have hepatitis C.

From the Kinross Correctional Facility in Michigan, another prisoner wrote about guards who "urinate in prisoners food without repercussions," and "guards who have been caught spitting in prisoners food."

The anecdotes in this book—the letters from prisoners (their often idiomatic spelling and grammar left intact), the in-person interviews with individual inmates—do not prove anything in and of themselves. Many of the prisoners' allegations are just that: allegations, not proven mischiefs. Yet, taken as a whole, they form a part of a broader pattern. When a prisoner wrote me with allegations that seemed simply off the wall or delusional, I filed the letter away and didn't quote from it. When the incidents described gelled with trends identified in lawsuits and judicial rulings, by special masters hired by courts to oversee correctional systems, by large-scale studies and hearings conducted before blue-ribbon commissions, I included these stories of abuse and neglect.

For, hearing the voices of these men and women helps to answer fundamental questions: In cycling so many millions of Americans through this increasingly regimented, dehumanized prison environment, what kind of society is being created? What damage is being done both to these individuals—the vast majority of whom are released and return to the community at some point—and to the United States' broader sense of self? How did the world's preeminent democracy become, in the years since the Cold War, the world's preeminent jailer, incarcerating more people than do coercive, totalitarian political systems such as China and the strongman dictatorships in many parts of the former Soviet Union? And how did a country so preoccupied with the rule of law and with setting in place administrative regulations to control governmental institutions become a country that uses administrative rules and regulations not to eradicate violence meted out by institutions of state, but instead to formalize and codify and bureaucratize such violence behind bars?

———

Told by a generation of politicians to be ever more afraid, encouraged by a sensationalist media in an era of instant reporting to fear the chaos and bloodlust lurking just beneath society's surface, Americans became progressively more hyped on prisons toward the end of the twentieth century. Electorates obsessed with the next wave of drug addiction, the next random murder, the next gang-related atrocity, the next teenage psychopath, increasingly voted for politicians preaching a lock-'em-up-and-throw-away-the-key approach to punishment, and correspondingly tolerated, even welcomed, an extraordinary diversion of public funds into criminal justice. Incarceration, along with the various feeder institutions that channel such a high percentage of Americans into jail and prison, is today a very big business.

In 1982 the United States spent $19 billion on policing, $7.7 billion on the judicial system, and $9 billion on its prisons and jails. By 2001, according to Bureau of Justice Statistics data, it was spending $72 billion on policing, $37.5 billion on the judicial system, and close to $57 billion on corrections systems. While spending on the police had increased almost threefold, spending on incarceration had gone up more than fivefold.[12] In the five years from 1990 to 1995 alone, more than two hundred new prisons opened in the United States.[13] And in the two decades from 1982 until 2001, the number of people working in the criminal-justice system as a whole—including correctional officers, court workers, and so on—grew by nearly 1 million, to over 2.2 million.[14] Many people who in previous times might have sold patent medicine, or marketed miracle cures for stress, or developed gadgets to peel apples automatically, now go into corrections. It's not that they know much about criminal justice or care deeply about penal philosophy. It's just that at the moment, there's an awful lot of money floating around the world of incarceration.

"I got involved by chance," ETG's Dexter explained as the exhibition hall at the Mock Prison Riot filled up with potential customers. "I had a sales background and was working for [another] company. I knew this girl. She said, 'Yeah, we're looking for someone to market these batons.'"

None of this ought to be surprising. Correctional professionals always stress that prisons are simply a mirror of the larger society. They are, says Jim Estelle, onetime director of the Texas prison system, "a microcosm of the community." The United States today is a high-tech country with an extraordinary faith in techno-fix solutions. It is also a country that, alongside its democratic yearnings, has historically treated its poor and lower classes in ways harsher than those of many other contemporary democracies.

From the Reagan presidency onward, the United States' social policy has increasingly mirrored that of Victorian England; while the overall society has gotten wealthier, the divides between haves and have-nots have multiplied. Access to welfare programs has been restricted, as has the Food Stamp Program; state agencies that administer aid to the poor have come under increasing rhetorical attack from legislators, conservative cultural commentators, and radio shock-jocks; religious charities have become first responders to a homelessness crisis that local, state, and federal agencies have proven unable or unwilling to grapple with; the mentally ill, removed en masse from state mental hospitals during decades of deinstitutionalization, have been left without adequate community mental-health facilities; public schools have been underfunded; and the progressive tax base upon which a vibrant public culture, capable of tackling deep-rooted societal problems, rests has been denuded.

In Idaho, during these years, somewhere in the region of three-quarters of welfare recipients were cut off from state aid following "reform" of the welfare system. Not surprisingly, by 2003 close to 14 percent of Idahoans told researchers that they worried about how to put food on the table, and fully 3.9 percent reported actually going hungry at times. The numbers suggested that Idaho's food problems had worsened during the years when it was most aggressively dismantling its social safety net, with about 25 percent more state residents reporting that they were hungry in 2003 compared with two years earlier.[15] At the same time, the state's prison population rose from fewer than three thousand in 1990 to almost seven thousand in the early years of the new century,[16] increasing by more than 60 percent between 1996 and 2003 alone. A similar combination of dramatically rising hunger and escalating prison numbers prevailed in the neighboring state of Utah, which has historically had some of the lowest incarceration rates in the country.

An array of other data suggests that, as the poorest, least-educated Americans fell further out of the economic mainstream, the growing prison system was overwhelmingly populated by members of this underclass. Estimates indicate that two-thirds of the United States' incarcerated population are significantly less literate than the populace as a whole, with many functionally illiterate. In 2004 researchers with the Dyslexia Research Foundation of Texas found that one-third of released inmates in the state were functionally illiterate, with half completely unable to read.[17] A few years before this report, a study by Columbia University's National Center on Addiction and Substance Abuse concluded that about 80 percent of prison and jail inmates were either incarcerated on drug convictions, were high at the time they committed their crimes, had committed economic crimes specifically to fund their addictions, or had long histories of addiction.[18]

Nationally, the real value of the minimum wage has declined by more than a third since its peak in 1968, at the height of President Lyndon B. Johnson's Great Society. In September 2005 the Center on Budget and Policy Priorities reported that the purchasing power of the $5.15 hourly minimum wage was lower than it had been at any time since 1955, with a short-lived exception in 1989. Also in 2005, the Forum on Child and Family Statistics reported that fully 18 percent of all children in the United States were living in poverty.[19]

The Victorians feared the nascent power of "the Great Unwashed" multitudes, and built an entire prison philosophy around the notion of less eligibility—the idea that, in a survival-of-the-fittest society with already unpleasant ways of treating the free poor, prisons would have to create conditions manifestly worse than the worst of the free world, to avoid being seen as desirable resting places for the destitute. It is no accident that the idea of make-work, of prisoners running on a treadmill, not to produce anything tangible but simply to keep them busy for hours at a time, was pioneered in the state-of-the-art prisons of mid-nineteenth-century England.

In the United States today, the language might not be quite the same, but the underlying philosophy is. We need our prisons, because our increasingly unequal society generates tremendous levels of addiction, mental illness, violence, and other social dysfunction, and we aren't willing to invest enough resources in social programs to tackle these problems and preserve societal order. At the same time, we don't want our prisons to be seen as a soft touch, as tax-supported rest stops or hostels for the poor, hungry, or unemployed. In a society with generous public-assistance programs, the principle of less eligibility can still result in prisons with humane living conditions. In a society with corroded community-welfare systems, the principle of less eligibility demands a race to the bottom within correctional settings. And it is this race that, in recent times, has largely determined the direction of criminal-justice policy. At the local, state, and indeed the federal levels, electorates have demanded "toughness," and politicians have thrived by out-toughing opponents with ever more punitive policy proposals.

PART ONE

———

A MINDSET MOLDED

CHAPTER 1

THE HOLY EXPERIMENT

Just to the north of Moundsville stands one of the most secure high-technology prisons in the United States. From the outside, the State Correctional Institution at Greene, or SCI Greene, in the southwestern Pennsylvania coal-mining hamlet of Waynesburg, looks like a quiet place. Pilots who take off from the small airstrip next door could be forgiven for thinking they were flying over a prefab industrial warehouse, albeit one with an awful lot of rolled razor wire on its fences. Visitors staying at the Comfort Inn, Waynesburg's premium hotel, just down Route 21 and up a dumpy hill, generally wouldn't know that behind the screen of trees visible from the lobby stands one of the largest supermax prisons in the country. Wal-Mart, planning to open a superstore adjacent to the prison in fall 2007, clearly assumes that shoppers won't be put off by the store's proximity to thousands of criminals, including the journalist Mumia Abu-Jamal and more than 120 others on death row.[1]

After initial concern from locals, when the prison plan was first floated in the early 1990s, that the facility would endanger this sedate little community, interest subsided when it became clear that prisoners would not be routinely seeping into the nearby streets from the Orwellian-named Progress Drive. (So far, not one has escaped.) Many locals aren't even aware of the prison's existence, a somewhat surprising state of affairs given that it is by far the largest institution in this town of fewer than five thousand nonincarcerated people. The prison, Tara Kinsell, the town's thirty-eight-year-old tourism officer told me in the summer of 2005, is largely invisible. "After you've driven by it so many times, you don't even give it another thought. It's just another business."

When a messy prisoner-abuse scandal erupted at SCI Greene in 1998, with dozens of inmates filing suits alleging routine beatings by guards within the Restrictive Housing Unit—a form of hazing for men just admitted to the unit —the town, like so many others faced with prison-abuse scandals in the 1990s, greeted the allegations with stony silence. Waynesburg College, a (recently turned) fundamentalist Christian campus, hosted no teach-ins, and the community held no public forums even after several guards were dismissed and the prison administration, which had signally failed to clamp down on the abuse, was overhauled. There was simply no public outrage that systemic human-rights violations might be occurring in the heart of Waynesburg.

"I do not remember people talking about it, no," recalled county commissioner Pamela Snyder. "The concerns here are the concerns that truly affect people's daily lives: it's jobs, it's health care, it's quality of life."

In 2004, as the macabre images and reports from Baghdad's Abu Ghraib prison hit the headlines, Waynesburg again found itself in an unwelcome spotlight. For it soon emerged that army reservist Charles Graner, the man implicated most directly in coordinating the violence at the cellblock level in Abu Ghraib, was, in his civilian incarnation, a correctional officer at SCI Greene. Like Graner, who served for several years in the Marines in the 1980s and early 1990s, most guards at SCI Greene had previously served in the military, employed by the Department of Corrections as part of a preferential hiring process for veterans that turned Pennsylvania's new prisons, like the new prisons throughout much of the country, into virtual preserves for retired military personnel. In the years after 9/11, dozens of SCI Greene staffers were reactivated into National Guard and Army Reserve units and sent to Iraq and Afghanistan.

In hindsight, I'm not sure exactly what I was looking for when I visited Waynesburg. I suppose I was hoping to find a visible mark of Cain, an identifiable image of evil. I wanted something that would immediately mark Waynesburg as a place where brutal correctional officers could terrorize prisoners, and where a colleague of those same officers could, when sent off to Iraq, wreak havoc on the bodies and souls of Iraqi captives. I wanted to understand how Abu Ghraib, and by extension the beatings at SCI Greene in the late 1990s, could have happened. Perhaps I ultimately wanted reassurance, wanted to see how Waynesburg was different, wanted a cast-iron guarantee that its residents weren't like the rest of us.

Of course, that's not what I found. Instead, I encountered something far more disturbing: ordinariness, the mundane insularity of the everyday, a profound indifference to the broader world, even as the United States sought to reshape much of that world. At most, there was a quiet embarrassment that failed to translate into outrage or activism. In Waynesburg, there seemed to be almost a cultural resignation—an acceptance that, in the post–September 11 world, torture, at least of the lite variety, would have to be commonplace and the best response was to turn a blind eye and get on with daily life. Indeed, this must have been how ordinary Joes coped with institutional horror, how they insulated themselves from historical currents, in the totalitarian regimes of other countries in bygone decades.

Waynesburg wasn't a right-wing bastion. It was, in fact, a Democratic town, part of the hardscrabble coal belt of southwestern Pennsylvania that once played host to radical unions and rabble-rousing class warriors. When I visited, however, it was resolutely apolitical, its good folk mainly concerned with the annual fair; the annual bet (the prize, a hat) between the mayor and one or another celebrity as to whether it would rain on Rain Day; and the myriad local beauty pageants (one recent teen queen had made good by moving to New York and getting a job with Donald Trump).

"I'd say the major phrase was 'It was blown out of proportion,' " a thirty-one-year-old SCI Greene guard told me over beers late one night at a local tavern, about his colleagues' reactions to the Abu Ghraib revelations. "Basically, all that was done was a couple degrading photos and a little bit of mistreating. They're cutting people's heads off on TV, we're taking pictures of people nude with our thumbs up. So, the perception was that it was blown out of proportion. I work in the Restrictive Housing Unit, the Hole. These guys throw piss, shit on trays, put sperm in cups. That's a health hazard. But it's not okay to take a photo of a prisoner nude and strapped up? There are worse things going on in the system. The whole war and Graner issue isn't even in our minds anymore."

"It's Greene County," said one of Kinsell's colleagues in the tourism office. "What do we care what they do to I-raqi people?"

There was, according to Lucy Northrup, co-owner and general manager of the *Observer,* one of two local papers, "more of a protest about the fact we published some of the pictures on the front page than about the acts themselves. In town, you go to meetings, people are really talking about small-town scandals rather than larger issues."

———•———

America's fascination with the science of incarceration began three hundred and thirty miles east of Waynesburg, in the city of Philadelphia. There, the Eastern State Penitentiary still towers over Fairmount Avenue, its massive stone perimeter a reminder of the historic origins of prisons such as SCI Greene.

The building presents at least as imposing a vision as that of the West Virginia State Penitentiary at Moundsville. A vast stone construction, its impenetrable front stretching along several city blocks, its entrance bookmarked by gothic, castellated towers, Eastern State was, at the time of its opening in 1829, the most state-of-the-art building in America. It was widely hailed as an architectural marvel: seven spokes emerged from a central observation area, with each spoke housing fifty-six prisoners, twenty-eight on each side of the hallway. From the central hub, guards could see down the length of each hall, providing comprehensive oversight with a minimal number of staff. So confident of prison security were the wardens in those early years that they would lead visiting luminaries—from John Quincy Adams, whose presidency had ended the year the prison opened, to President Andrew Jackson to Charles Dickens—into the innermost core of the prison to observe how it functioned.[2]

In an era when the White House itself relied on chamber pots, each cell in the Eastern State Penitentiary contained a flush toilet, made of stone and attached to the corner wall in order to minimize the amount of time inmates spent outside their cells but not subject them to unendurable odors behind their locked doors. The entire building was ventilated and heated using cutting-edge technology that pumped and circulated air through a complex system of pipes. Exploiting the great engineering advances of the nineteenth century—in particular the development of effective sewer systems and the use of steel in creating large vaulted structures—the building allowed the use of extensive isolation techniques without compromising inmates' health with fetid, germ-ridden air, freezing them to death in winter or stifling them in the humid Philadelphia summer. When the inmates had to be brought out of their cells, they were hooded, with only slits in the head coverings for vision. Etchings and early photographs make them look somewhat like the infamous Abu Ghraib prisoners under U.S. coalition oversight in 2003. That way, the overseers reasoned, the captives, depersonalized by physical anonymity, their names replaced by numbers, couldn't get to know one another. This would both limit their ability to conspire against administrators and force a greater degree of self-reflection. So obsessed were the prison's designers with the theory of silence that they attached individual exercise yards to the back of each cell, so that each inmate could get about an hour of fresh air each day without speaking to his fellow prisoners. About the only communication tolerated was that of the chaplains, who walked up and down the cellblocks preaching the gospel to their captive audience.[3]

Decades later, in the middle of the nineteenth century, similarly ambitious engineering in Victorian London led to the construction of Pentonville prison, a gargantuan, cavernous space crisscrossed, at various levels between floor and ceiling, with massive steel walkways, its blurred windows sealed shut and its air circulated using ventilation techniques specially developed for the building. The lessons learned from the building of Pentonville—known to Victorians as the Model Prison—and its innovative uses of steel were later applied by the great bridge designers and railway engineers whose work so permanently altered the landscape of nineteenth-century Britain. "No other prison or penitentiary had ever been so meticulously contrived," wrote the historian Robin Evans in 1982. "All services and transactions had been depersonalized, mechanized, centralized, and integrated." In much the same way as research-and-development programs for the military have, over the last century, provided enormous impetus for scientific developments such as jet travel, laser surgery, and, of course, the Internet, so in the nineteenth century prisons served as a driving force for architectural innovation and the invention of new heating, plumbing, ventilation, and structural techniques for use in large public buildings.[4]

As at Eastern State, Pentonville's prisoners were referred to by number rather than by name, and were fed their meals through slots in their cell doors. None of this was done surreptitiously; on the contrary, these methods of controlling criminals were held as glorious advances in the understanding of human behavior. To a degree that is hard to understand today, prisons such as Eastern State and Pentonville were as much a source of civic pride and wonder as the Eiffel Tower would be to Parisians several decades on, and later still, the Empire State Building to New Yorkers. In the most tangible way possible, they represented the intersection of science, modern thinking, and power.

Sealed within their cells, inmates at Eastern State worked at making shoes, dying fabrics, sewing tapestries, and crafting furniture, their tools and raw materials provided by the prison staff—who hoped these exertions would make the prison largely self-funding—and their labors monitored by guards who patrolled the cellblocks in wool- or felt-padded shoes to camouflage their approach. (By contrast, the authorities at Pentonville eventually put their wards to work on the utterly unproductive but exhausting treadmill: early photographs show hooded men running up and down the steps of the mill, their energies focused solely on keeping up with the machine.) If Eastern State's inmates broke the rules of silence, they were punished. Records from the 1820s and 1830s detail the gagging of talkative prisoners with an iron mask, a bizarre object that was attached to the tongue and pulled around the back of the neck, serving both to limit the tongue's movement and to constrict the flow of blood to the organ. Unruly or insane inmates were literally sewn into primitive straitjackets, and some were taken out into the cold yard in winter, stripped naked, and doused repeatedly with bucketfuls of icy water—a process known as "ducking," which, on at least one occasion, according to a state legislative investigation from the period, had fatal consequences.[5] For reading material, they were allowed only the Bible. Letters from home were prohibited.

Over weeks, months, and years, the solitude and silence and labor were supposed to work miracles on the inmates' souls, converting the most hardened of criminals into reliable, work-accustomed citizens. "Give this system a fair trial, and the commonwealth will be amply compensated by the restoration of the wayward and law-breaking classes to industry and social order," wrote the Reverend John Ruth, "moral instructor" at the penitentiary, in 1877, half a century into the Eastern State experiment.[6] Twenty years later, with a new generation of prison reformers once again arguing that the solitary model of confinement drove many prisoners insane, warden Michael J. Cassidy offered a stirring defense of the institution in which he had worked for close to three decades. "The individual prisoner, when not surrounded by associates whose ridicule is more powerful than his better nature, is more susceptible to reformatory influence than in the presence of those who look upon obedience to the demands of authority as cowardly weakness," he wrote. Yes, there were insane prisoners, he went on, but they weren't driven insane by the system over which he presided.

> *In years gone past, one of the objections made to the cellular system, as it was then called, was it was likely to impair the mind of the persons under its treatment. That theory has been abandoned long since for want of facts. There are insane people in all prisons, and more in proportion than in the same number of the community at large, for many of the crimes committed are such that only insane persons would conceive.*[7]

Despite Cassidy's reassurances, however, the evidence wasn't nearly so sanguine. In practice, many inmates did go insane (at both Eastern State and Pentonville) and began to self-mutilate—cutting themselves, swallowing sharp objects, gouging at their limbs—or attempted to commit suicide. The prison authorities, thoroughly convinced of the humane attributes of their solitary system, blamed the mental deterioration on an epidemic of masturbation. Not until 1913 did the last vestiges of the pure isolation model wither away, ultimately replaced by a more communal, less coercively silent system of imprisonment.

Not least because of problems such as rampant self-mutilation, the historian Norman Johnston titled his definitive history of the prison *Eastern State Penitentiary: Crucible of Good Intentions.*

———•———

Like Moundsville, Eastern State housed prisoners well into the latter half of the twentieth century, the structure being continually enlarged—and the integrity of its ingenious architectural layout undermined—to meet the needs of a growing prisoner population. It was originally designed to house about 250 inmates, but by the early 1900s over 1,700 prisoners were living behind its walls.[8]

Eastern State Penitentiary finally closed its doors to inmates in 1971, by which time Pennsylvania had eight prisons and slightly more than 5,000 inmates. A year later, the nation's year-in-year-out prison boom started, and Pennsylvania's inmate population soared. By the early part of the twenty-first century, the state's prison population was climbing toward 40,000. The state now had more than two dozen correctional institutions, most of them, like SCI Greene, sited in small, out-of-the-way communities far removed from Philadelphia and the state's other large cities.[9]

Pennsylvania's penal transformation was in keeping with countrywide trends. Nationally, the number of state prisons in the United States went up from 592 in 1974 to 1,023 in 2000, with hundreds of additional facilities for state inmates run by private companies and dozens more operated by the federal Bureau of Prisons. Much of this institutional expansion took place in just ten states: in Texas, the number of prisons went up an almost unfathomable 706 percent from 1979 to 2000, with 137 new prisons built in the Lone Star State during these years. Colorado more than quadrupled the number of institutions it was operating; Missouri, Ohio, and Illinois trebled the size of their systems; and California, Florida, Mississippi, Georgia, and New York more than doubled theirs.[10] But significant growth also occurred in the number of prisons run by the remaining forty states, as corrections departments struggled to house the endless prisoners that courts were sending their way. In Louisiana, an unprecedented 814 per 100,000 residents were living in prison by 2004, with many more serving time in parish jails. In Oklahoma, 684 per 100,000 were in prison, and in South Carolina the number was 555.[11] Even the traditionally liberal state of Maine—which, at a mere 149 per 100,000 residents, had the lowest incarceration rate in the country in 2004—now had a higher rate of incarceration than virtually any state in America had at the start of the incarceration binge.[12]

While only 24 of the 556 inmates admitted to Eastern State Penitentiary in 1877 had been sentenced to over ten years, the Pennsylvania Prison Society calculated that the average stay of Pennsylvania's inmates was sixty-nine months by 2001, with many thousands of the state's prisoners slated to spend over a decade behind bars. Conversely, while eighty-six of the admissions to Eastern State in 1877 were for one-year sentences, making that the most common sentence length, by the twenty-first century only a lucky few of those sentenced to prison could expect such leniency. The average stay at the prison in the nineteenth century, curators at Eastern State have calculated, was between eighteen months and two years. Rare longer sentences reached eight years and more. Life sentences were all but unknown.

———•———

Today, like its West Virginia counterpart, Eastern State Penitentiary is a bustling tourist destination, its cavernous brick and stone interior hosting everything from run-of-the-mill tours (complete with headset guides) to a Halloween ghost-and-ghoul spectacular. On a good day in the summer, as many as 350 people descend on the building, coughing up the nine-dollar admission fee (four dollars for kids) for the privilege of walking along the granite-slabbed hallways of the vaulted cellblocks and peering into the cells, many of which, behind their thick wooden doors reinforced by bolted-iron slats, now have crumbling paint and semicollapsed ceilings. Some of these cells have trees growing up their walls and snaking up through the tiny skylights—referred to by prisoners as the "eye of God" or "the dead eye"—that provided the only natural light to those inside. If prisoners misbehaved, guards could, and did, cover the skylight up, leaving the troublemakers in almost absolute darkness for days on end, with nothing to do save lie on the woolen bedding atop their metal frame beds or pace back and forth; the cells were six paces long and three or four paces wide. Later, in the twentieth century, troublesome prisoners were thrown into an underground hole, colloquially called "Klondike," and fed only bread and water for days on end. "It'd be common for inmates to come up not even knowing their name," my guide tells me as we walk around the yard one particularly humid, cloying summer morning. "They'd be driven completely insane." Guards continued to throw unfortunate prisoners into Klondike until 1959, when, in the face of ongoing criticism that the facility was unfit for human habitation, the prison finally opened a newer, aboveground punishment cellblock.

The faces of the visiting tourists, and their conversations, suggest that they are repulsed by these spectacles, yet repulsed in much the same way as are rubberneckers at a fatal accident. There is something compelling about the nastiness, something almost exhilarating. That's why shows such as HBO's *Oz*, set in a supermax prison, achieve something akin to cult status; that's why the multitude of cop-chase TV dramas, all of which dangle the promise of physical confrontation and possibly even bloodshed, get such stellar viewing numbers. Perhaps that's also why the theatrics and staged mayhem of the World Wrestling Federation appeal to tens of millions of viewers. So long as we don't feel personally at risk, most of us seem to be titillated by these glimpses into the darker recesses of our collective psyche.

Out by Eastern State's death row cellblock, added to the building in 1954 during the last wave of expansions, a couple and their two young children gawked at the exhibits. "Could you tell me where the electric chair is?" the woman asked my guide excitedly as we walked by. The guide explained that Eastern State had no electric chair; inmates were transported to the prison at Rockview for their executions. "Do they do tours?" the woman continued in a breathy tone. "Do they have an electric chair? That would be cool!"

———•———

Close to two centuries after Eastern State's principles were delineated, the practice of throwing recalcitrant prisoners into tiny cells completely isolated from normal human interaction is again in vogue. Since the 1980s, state and federal correctional systems have invested billions of dollars to create secure housing units deep within high-security prisons and, increasingly, to build entire supermax prisons based on the isolation model. Not content simply to establish zones of absolute security, surrounded by state-of-the-art defenses from which no prisoner can possibly escape and into which no unwanted intruder can possibly penetrate, some prison systems have built supermax wings underground. The Estelle Unit at the sprawling penal complex in Huntsville, Texas, looks like nothing so much as a wartime bunker, a subterranean labyrinth of echoing concrete, lit by fluorescent ceiling lights. Every feature seems to have been carefully crafted to minimize all sense of normalcy.[13]

Anyone who's visited these supermax facilities knows how hermetically sealed they really are. Knowing this, it's also fairly obvious that when the Bush administration argued that the terrorism suspects it was holding after 9/11 were so dangerous that they had to be housed in a specially created camp, at Guantánamo Bay, they were clearly not being honest about their motives. Whatever the arguments for creating a detention facility in a remote part of Cuba, outside U.S. constitutional jurisdiction, might be, security concerns could not have been paramount. The supermax prison model developed in America—concrete buildings divided into small pods of individual cells and saturated with security cameras, the entire facility ringed with electrified fencing topped by razor wire and separated from the free world by numerous security gates, computer-controlled exit points, and motion sensors—is the most securely sealed prison or camp system ever developed. It is more than adequately able to keep trained terrorists behind bars. Before his execution, Timothy McVeigh, the Oklahoma City bomber, was housed in a federal supermax in Colorado, as is Theodore Kaczynski, the Unabomber. The notorious thrill-killer Charles Manson resides in a supermax in California, his view of the world restricted to the few square inches he can see through the rectangular Plexiglas window in his cell. Nobody escapes from these overwhelmingly fortified institutions. Even the larger communities' fear of escapes has largely disappeared, as evidenced by the fact that some of the most dangerous prisoners in the country are housed close to population centers (albeit usually small towns) rather than in pure wilderness areas, miles from the nearest human habitation.[14]

Hardly surprisingly, as occurred at Eastern State, prisoners in these isolated facilities—many of whom are mentally ill to begin with, many others of whom develop signs of mental illness while in lockdown—routinely hurt themselves as a way to get attention, or to get sent to the marginally less unpleasant environs of the prison hospital or psychiatric ward. In 2002 and 2003, during the course of my research for Human Rights Watch on how prisons treated mentally ill inmates, I encountered women who repeatedly stuck pens and staples (reaped from the bindings of magazines) into their arms; men who cut at their own genitalia; prisoners who spent days and weeks covered in their own feces; and others who had made a virtual hobby out of slashing their arms and legs with razors or banging their heads against their cell walls.[15] Over the years that I have reported on America's criminal-justice system, I have even heard stories of mentally ill prisoners who scooped out their own eyeballs, and one who pulled his testicles out of his scrotum.

The practice of incarceration, and America's centuries-long prison experiment, goes to the heart of what the United States is and what it has historically stood for, though perhaps not in ways that a critical modern audience would anticipate. Delve into the origins of America's prison system—at least as it evolved in the northeastern states after Puritanism loosened its grip on the region—and you rapidly arrive at some of the core values that shaped revolutionary and postrevolutionary America. Look for the founding fathers of American penology and you start to find some of Enlightenment America's most illustrious and radical citizens—individuals who, when they weren't designing prison systems, were busy signing the Declaration of Independence and writing tracts on liberty and tomes on republican government. Ask what single institutional innovation of the early United States most effectively captured the imagination of the rest of the world, and you could make a powerful argument for the ringing declaration: "Its prisons!"

Today, prisons are such an integral part of state infrastructures around the world that it is hard to imagine just what a revolutionary concept they originally were. Only a few generations back, however, a prison—used primarily to house people awaiting trial as well as debtors—was often simply a castle, or a series of rooms inside the gates of a town wall, or a disused church or warehouse with a few extra locks, reinforced doors, and a handful of poorly paid and untrained guards. In the annals of human history, the notion of specialized buildings designed solely to house, and ostensibly rehabilitate, sentenced criminals over prolonged periods of time—architecturally laid out to maximize security and minimize the element of surprise, to put on dramatic display the might of the state without resorting to the spectacle of public floggings or executions—is a recent development.

In fits and starts the notion of the prison evolved in Britain, Ghent—in what is modern-day Belgium—Rome, and a handful of other locales in the seventeenth and eighteenth centuries; yet it was not until the nineteenth century, when the newly independent United States opted to build a system of justice centered around incarceration, that it became commonplace, acknowledged as a central institution of state power and a critical part of the criminal-justice apparatus of any self-respecting country.

Theorists such as Michel Foucault, and historians of punishment such as David Garland and Lawrence Friedman, have argued that the growing use of incarceration was an almost inevitable by-product of the rise of the modern nation-state; that it wrested the notion of revenge from private individuals and capricious local lords and allowed impersonal state bureaucracies to set up shop as interpreters of the law. Imprisonment permitted the state to control not just the bodies but also, through a supposedly scientific implementation of imprisonment, the minds of inmates. It served to pacify not only individuals but, through the spectacle and fear of prolonged punishment and humiliation, entire classes of people. For Foucault in particular, the emergence of criminal classes and the subsequent creation of what he called, in his classic book *Discipline and Punish,* a "carceral system"—a web of laws and institutions that worked to channel social discontent into demands for the punishment of miscreants, rather than broader political activity—went hand in hand with industrial society's needs for a regimented, disciplined populace.[16]

In a way, prisons became symbols of national prestige in industrial nations: examples of the forward-thinking attitudes of their rulers, the bureaucratic and administrative prowess of the state, and the willpower of ruling groups to dominate and crush the chaotic elements bubbling up at the edges of society. Imperial Britain, flush with self-confidence and a sense of historic mission, determined to reshape the world according to the moral and economic strictures of its rising middle classes, began devoting an increasing amount of attention and money to incarceration.[17] From the 1780s onward, Britain not only built more prisons, employing some of the country's top architects and engineers in this pursuit, but also created new bureaucracies to marshal the full force of the modern state in pursuit of crime control and the rehabilitation of errant individuals. Prisons would, according to the logic of the times, not merely secure criminals away from the society upon which they preyed, but also deal a deathblow to the propensities of the great unwashed toward inebriation and idleness. In 1878 a celebrated Prison Commission, chaired by an energetic, if rather colorless, bureaucrat named Sir Edmund du Cane, urged the creation of uniform standards in prisons across the land: they would, he declared, house prisoners in isolation cells with uncomfortable plank beds, force them to work at such tasks as picking oakum or exhausting themselves on the tread wheel, and feed them bread, potatoes, and low-grade meat.

France, too, in a slightly later period, opened a network of state-of-the-art prisons. So did Prussia, Italy, and other European nations seeking to bolster their claims to great-power status.

And then, of course, there was the United States. From the earliest days, American penitentiaries were seen as symbols of a New World breaking from the past. As the country began asserting itself on the world stage in the nineteenth century, its social-control mechanisms, most notably its vast prisons, became poster children for a buoyant, dynamic, innovative American culture. "The experiment which was to be made, promised to be decisive," wrote the French aristocrats Gustave de Beaumont and Alexis de Tocqueville, after touring America in 1831 on a fact-finding mission about the country's penitentiaries. "No expense was spared to construct these new establishments worthy of their object, and the edifices which were elevated, resembled prisons less than palaces."[18] David Garland told me that in the United States, "there's been an engagement with crime and punishment that's much more intense than in other countries. Populism drives American criminal justice in a way that's not so forceful anywhere else."

Even before the first large prisons were built in the postindependence United States—in Pittsburgh, in Philadelphia, and in Auburn, New York—the Quaker commonwealth of Pennsylvania had, since the earliest days of its founding, been moving away from the lash, the noose, and other eye-for-an-eye punishments. While it didn't yet have centralized prisons, by the late seventeenth century it was increasingly using local jails to house convicted criminals. Indeed, in 1682, close to a century before the colonies gained independence, William Penn, one of London's leading Quakers, arrived in America, bringing with him the Quaker ideals of redemption and forgiveness. Penn was instrumental in getting his Commonwealth of Pennsylvania—land personally granted to him by Charles II in a charter signed the previous year—to adopt the most humane, least violent penal code on earth. While England applied the death penalty to more than two hundred crimes, Pennsylvania's First Frame of Government reserved capital punishment for murder and treason only. The democratic structures and concepts of citizenship codified in the Frame, the protections for private property, the creation of a free press, and the notion of religious tolerance—in marked contrast to the realities of Puritan New England to the north—along with the visionary penal policies, all added up to a new social system that Penn grandiosely termed "a holy experiment."[19]

The center of this holy experiment was Philadelphia, which in the eighteenth century emerged as America's largest metropolis and the center of Enlightenment thinking in the New World. Penn's Quaker vision of societal responses to crime stood in counterpoint both to seventeenth-century Puritan notions of vengeance and eternal damnation and to later fundamentalist understandings of crime and punishment, influenced as they are by the fire-and-brimstone idea that crimes are not simply social transgressions but sins against the word of God. Throughout the century leading up to American independence, and in the decades following, Quaker scholars viewed the shaping of punishment policies as a central function of any political system. "Revenge we know in its utmost extent is the universal and darling passion of all savage nations," wrote Benjamin Rush, one of the Quaker signers of the Declaration of Independence.[20] A leading antislavery advocate, a famous medical doctor, an early psychiatrist fascinated by the ways in which humans functioned and were affected by their environment, and a prison reformer, Rush was unignorable: in his heyday, he was acclaimed on both sides of the Atlantic as a figure on par with George Washington, Benjamin Franklin, and Thomas Jefferson. "The punishment of murder by death, is contrary to divine revelation. A religion which commands us to forgive and even to do good to our enemies, can never authorise the punishment of murder by death."

Before the Revolution, and during the years of the War of Independence, when it was still a common sight in the colonies to see convicts paraded through the public streets while chained to wheelbarrows, dressed in rags, their heads shaven, Rush, an elegant man with a long, thin face, poetic eyes, and carefully brushed-back hair, wrote pamphlets and made speeches urging the humane treatment of prisoners. Shortly after the Revolution, he became a founding member of the Philadelphia Society for Alleviating the Miseries of Public Prisons. Anticipating the practices at Eastern State Penitentiary, an institution that was in no small part his legacy, Rush advocated a regimen of enforced silence (to focus criminals' moral faculties) and prolonged solitude, interrupted only by religious tutoring. He also preached the virtues of hard work. "Labor of all kinds favors and facilitates the practices of virtue," the Quaker told a gathering of the American Philosophical Society in Philadelphia in 1786.[21] "The bridewells and workhouses of all civilized countries prove that labor is not only a very severe, but the most benevolent of all punishments, in as much as it is one of the most suitable means of reformation." And how to organize such a system of solitude, silence, and labor? Build prisons.

Correctional institutions today are all too often violent, psychically dark places, but in eighteenth-century Pennsylvania—birthplace of the American prison system—they were held up as a great leap forward into an era of rational, humane, rehabilitative responses to crime and to criminals. At a time when the default responses to crime were generally corporal punishment, deportation, or death, the creation of vast institutions in which to house those convicted by the courts was applauded as a great triumph of Enlightenment thinking. Such an approach brought compassion to pervasive social problems and dramas that went to the heart of the human condition, compassion combined with the inquiring, rationalist, scientific mindset being utilized in physics, chemistry, and the other burgeoning natural sciences. Indeed, the penitentiary was nothing if not a vast scientific experiment, founded on half a century of intellectual speculation, with criminals as raw material.

———•———

By the mid-eighteenth century, with Europe's ancien régime under attack from political radicals, the onset of the age of science and the accompanying explosion of social ideas and theories began to reformulate the age-old drama of good versus evil, God versus Satan, heaven versus hell, in more subtle and sophisticated ways. In 1764 in Milan, a young nobleman by the name of Cesare Beccaria wrote an essay titled *On Crimes and Punishments,* the first great treatise formulating modern notions of criminality: specifically, what traits and circumstances help create the criminal mind, and what actions society can best employ to reclaim these wayward souls. Beccaria felt that punishment could only be justified as a deterrent, never as revenge. He declared the use of torture to be both immoral and functionally useless in generating reliable confessions. He argued that the death penalty was unjust, and that the good of society was best served by certain and swift punishment following the committal of a crime, rather than needlessly harsh retribution; and he called for more humane conditions within the jails and prisons used to house debtors, defendants awaiting trial, and increasingly, those convicted of noncapital offenses.[22] The impact of Beccaria's work was explosive, and it was rapidly translated into French and English, assuring it a large readership among Europe and America's growing intelligentsia.

A generation later, amid the intellectual and social ferment generated by the American and French Revolutions, the English philosopher Jeremy Bentham turned his pen to the issue of crime and punishment. It was a subject that had been dear to the heart of English progressives in recent years, following a series of comprehensive and damning surveys of the state of English prisons and jails by the prison-reform campaigner John Howard. After several years of research, Howard had detailed a haphazard prison system in which the way prisoners were treated largely depended on the caprice of individual jailers and the prisoners' own financial resources; in which men, women, and children, convicted criminals and those waiting to be tried, were all housed together, often in beyond-squalid conditions; in which everything from liquor to sex could be bought and sold in broad daylight; and in which no serious efforts were made to rehabilitate prisoners. In large part because of Howard's almost messianic fervor, a series of prison-reform bills, some successful, others ultimately failing to win passage, had recently been pushed in the two houses of Parliament, seeking to allot more funds for prison construction and to create the rudiments of a modern penal bureaucracy. Given added impetus by the burning of the famous Newgate prison in 1780 (by rioters led by the mad aristocrat Lord George Gordon), prison reform was a hot-button issue by the time Bentham started addressing it.

Bentham was already acknowledged as the father of the school of thought known as utilitarianism, a behavioral system famously summarized in the idea that social policy should be aimed simply at creating the greatest happiness for the greatest number, and generally equating happiness with pleasure and unhappiness with pain. When he turned his intellectual eye to prisons, it was with the intent of applying this equation within the realm of punishment. In 1787, while sojourning in Russia, Bentham, thirty-nine at the time, began jotting down ideas for a model prison that, he argued, could so precisely regulate the behavior of its inmates as to essentially reduce these individuals to programmed automatons. He filled up notebook after notebook with scribbled ideas and increasingly complex diagrams.

Bentham's words represented the philosophical side of the equation: the notion that, through precise adjustments in the disbursement of pleasure and pain in response to inmates' behaviors, their behavior could be entirely regulated to make them productive and respectful. Ultimately, the prisoners' desire to avoid pain would coincide with the guards' desire to run a safe and orderly prison, which, in turn, would mesh neatly with society's need for criminals to go through the prison system and return to the community as law-abiding citizens. The diagrams represented Bentham's fusion of architecture and philosophy: the revolutionary concept that the structure of a building itself could be an essential part of a massive experiment in what is now known as behavior modification.

Bentham wanted to create a building in which every nook and cranny was accessible to a warden from his central command post. He wanted the inmates to know that, wherever they were, they were always being observed; and, conversely, he wanted to be able to hide the warden so that his wards never knew where he was or to whom he was paying attention. Such a system would, Bentham believed, give almost godlike powers to the warden, making him as close to omnipotent within his fiefdom as any man could reasonably hope to be. Day and night, the limitless spying would continue. The design was remarkable in its simplicity: a circular building centered on a central command tower with windows on all sides. Several levels of cells were ranged along the circumference, facing in toward the central tower. Even the door of the tower had windows; for the occupant of this tower, there were literally no blind spots.

On top of this, the philosopher began laying on additional details: systems of pipes, so that verbal commands could be transmitted into each and every cell from the central observatory; complex screening systems so that inmates could never see other inmates nor could they see the guards; elaborate chapels that seated each inmate in a miniature prayer cell so that preachers could communicate with their congregants without ever allowing them to see one another. "The essence of it consists, then, in the centrality of the inspector's situation, combined with the well-known and most effectual contrivances for seeing without being seen," Bentham wrote.[23]

In its entirety, the Panopticon, a name devised by the philosopher to emphasize the significance of the visual arrangements, was a unique fusion of philosophy, morality, and architecture, all intended to marshal the full force of the state in a massive effort to recalibrate the souls, or at least the behavior—Bentham, an avid materialist, was decidedly skeptical about anything as ethereal as "souls"—of society's miscreants.

Over the next several years, Bentham grew more and more obsessed with his Panopticon. It was, he came to believe, a panacea for many of society's most intractable ills. He began designing modified Panopticons that could function as workhouses for the idle poor, asylums for the insane, hospitals, and even schools. After all, he reasoned, any place in which large numbers of individuals were in daily contact with agents of the state ought to be designed so as to maximize the state's control over, and knowledge of, those individuals. And what better way to further this than an entire network of Panopticons spread out around the country?

———

Beccaria and Bentham's ideas had stout sea-legs and they traveled well across the Atlantic. The intellectual leaders of the new United States were firmly committed to the ideals of the Enlightenment, and in much the same way as notions of citizenship, democratic political participation, and the Rights of Man occupied center stage here, the topic of crime and punishment soon came to the fore.

Eastern State and the myriad other penitentiaries that sprang up in nineteenth-century America were not, in the literal sense, Panopticons. (In fact, around the world, only five genuine circular Panopticons, using Benthamite designs rather than later high-tech alternatives, were ever built: the Illinois State Penitentiary, constructed between 1916 and 1924; three prisons in Holland; and one in Cuba.) Despite the apparent simplicity of the idea, building enormous circular prisons with cellblocks ranged against the perimeter, with contraptions inserted to prevent inmates from seeing or communicating with other prisoners in the facing cells, proved too expensive a proposition for most penal architects and state legislatures to accept. Jeremy Bentham's ideas were ingenious, but in many ways they were far ahead of their time, too reliant on embryonic or not-yet-existent technologies. Like Leonardo da Vinci's sketched designs for bicycles, helicopters, and parachutes, they were doodlings destined to be left mainly on paper, until a time centuries later when technology finally caught up with the vision. In the case of the Panopticon, the idea of central observation decks that could effortlessly spy into every corner, deliver instructions to every cell, and gather all-encompassing information on what the inmates were doing and where they were doing it—all while preserving the invisibility of the guards themselves—would have to wait until the age of computers, video imagery, advanced eavesdropping technology, remote-controlled electronically operated doors, and so on: in other words, the late twentieth century, at which point supermax prisons emerged in answer to Bentham's challenges.

Eastern State took Bentham's core premises and studiously adapted them to fiscal and technological realities. Splendid though the prison's architecture might have been, it was essentially a poor man's Panopticon, one that sacrificed much of the subtlety of Bentham's vision for overarching control in the name of affordability.

And yet, even if Eastern State was a creature of compromise, to early-nineteenth-century observers the creation of humane, ordered penitentiaries built at least partially with the Panopticon philosophy in mind—in contrast to the overcrowded, verminous dungeons, fortresses, and makeshift jails of previous epochs, in which rotted debtors, paupers, and defendants awaiting trial and physical or financial punishment for their sins—was a signal to the rest of the world that America was breaking with barbaric medieval practices still in use elsewhere. Control techniques that seem harsh, even "cruel and unusual," today were then trumpeted as representing the most forward-thinking virtues of the age, in particular the use of solitary confinement and the imposition of a regimen of silence, frequently enforced by the whip and other coercive devices. Proponents might differ in the type of silent system they supported—debate was particularly fierce between advocates of the Eastern

State Penitentiary model of keeping inmates in solitude around the clock, and boosters of New York's "congregate system," which allowed inmates to work in common areas during the day—but all agreed on the therapeutic value of silence combined with hard work.

In England, Bentham had been concerned mainly with creating self-contained systems, calibrated with scientific precision, that could restructure prisoners' behavior. In Catholic France, Belgium, and papal-ruled Rome, prison reformers had begun positing that the spiritual regimen of silence that governed monasteries and cloisters could also be useful in reforming the souls of criminals. In the United States, the materialism espoused by Bentham came to be combined with these religious musings: not only were early prison reformers concerned with changing outward behavior but, by consciously adopting the "penitent" model of Christian cloisters in their "penitentiaries," they were also hell-bent on remodeling their wards' inner souls.

CHAPTER 2

A RISING TIDE OF VIOLENCE

Despite the utopian rhetoric surrounding prisons on both sides of the Atlantic, the realities were always far messier. Virtually from the get-go, allegations surfaced of guards taking advantage of their positions to intimidate, sexually molest, and wreak violence upon those in their custody.

At Eastern State in Philadelphia, the intimations of torture, deprivation of food to rule breakers, and guards abusing their power reached a crescendo barely five years after the penitentiary was opened, leading to state legislative hearings in December 1834. "However guilty they [prisoners] may have been, and however just may be the sentence of the law under which they suffer, the feelings of our nature revolt at the infliction of torture not authorized by a judicial tribunal," wrote one legislator who participated in the hearings, in a book published anonymously. "Man is invested with power over his fellow man only to the extent of self-preservation and the good order of society: vengeance and mercy belong to the Deity." Writing about the infamous iron gag, the author declared that "the pressure consequently act[s] on the chains which press on the jaw and jugular veins, producing excruciating pain and a hazardous suffusion of blood to the head. The Spanish Inquisition itself cannot exhibit a more fearful mode of torture." He described straitjackets being sewn so tight that the necks and faces of the victims became black with congealed blood. "When undergoing this punishment, men of the stoutest stock will shriek as if on the rack." And he referred to inmates wasting away on punishment rations of only eight ounces of bread a day.[1] (Today, one of the ways that inmates in secure housing units and supermax prisons are punished for rule violations is by being fed "food loaves": coarse, almost indigestible bricks of food in which are amalgamated mashed-up versions of the day's ingredients from the prison kitchen.)

Despite the high-flown rhetoric surrounding Pennsylvania's trophy prison, there was still, it seemed, ample room for abuse. And so, like air rushing to fill a vacuum, creative forms of torment began to flourish.

———•———

In hindsight, perhaps it wasn't a surprise that Eastern State Penitentiary became a "crucible of good intentions." In 1960, a young psychology professor
at Yale University, in the town of New Haven, Connecticut, organized what
would become one of the most famous psychology experiments in history.
Fifteen years after the end of World War II, and more than a decade after the
Nuremberg war crimes trials, in which numerous Nazi functionaries had offered the excuse that they were "only obeying orders," Stanley Milgram wanted
to know how people in a nonfascist environment would respond to orders
from authority figures when those orders conflicted with basic moral values.[2]

Through advertisements in local newspapers and a direct mailing to thousands of New Haven residents, Milgram's team asked people to come forward
to participate in an experiment on different learning techniques. Over a period of time, they gathered several hundred individuals into their study, each
paid $4.50 for a few hours of their time.

When the volunteers—adults of all ages and both sexes, of varying racial,
educational, class, and economic backgrounds—arrived at the laboratory, they
were told that the goal of the experiment was to see whether people memo-
rized things more effectively when they were threatened with punishment for
failing. Ostensibly, volunteers were paired off into teams, both members of
which drew lots to see who would be the "learner" and who would be the
"teacher." In reality, only one member of each team was a volunteer; the other
was a paid actor. The drawing was rigged so that the real volunteer was always
the "teacher" and the actor was always the "learner." Then the experimenter
explained that the learner was going to face a series of word-combination
questions. Whenever the learner got an answer wrong, an electric shock would
be administered, ascending, in 15-volt increments, from a starting shock of
only 15 volts all the way up to 450 volts. Learners were taken into a room and
strapped into an electric chair, where their wrists were painted with a paste
(designed, said the experimenter, to keep the subjects' skin from burning) and
electrodes were attached to their bodies. The volunteer teachers were then led
to a control room, separated from the learners by a panel of glass, and were
seated in front of a console with thirty switches, each labeled with its respec-
tive voltage and appropriate warning signs. For the strongest shocks, the warning labels read "danger: severe shock," followed by "XXX."

The actor strapped into the electric chair was to give three wrong answers
for every correct answer, and each time an incorrect response was given, the
man in charge of the experiment was to order the teacher to administer an-

other shock. In reality, no shocks were given, but the teacher didn't know that, and the actor screamed and howled and begged for mercy in a convincing-enough manner that the volunteers never caught on to the ruse.

As the shocks increased in intensity, most often the volunteers' moral confusion grew. The teacher would look to the authority figure—the experimenter —for guidance, and, when ordered to continue with the experiment, frequently would do so, even though the experimenter was not making physical threats against the volunteer teachers. A few stopped giving the shocks as soon as the learner asked for the experiment to be brought to a close; others stopped at a higher level, when, for example, the learner ceased to respond verbally to questions. More than half of the volunteers, however, continued all the way up to the 450-volt level, seemingly unable to break with the orders that they had been given by the authority figure—even when their team members in the experiment repeatedly begged to be saved, some even giving indications of suffering heart attacks.

Repeated, with slight variations on the original experiment design, at a number of institutions around the country over the next several years, the Milgram experiment redefined how psychologists understood the concept of obedience and the power of authority to get ordinary people to engage in utterly inhumane actions. "The results of the experiment are both surprising and dismaying," Milgram wrote in his book *Obedience to Authority.*

> *Despite the fact that many subjects experience stress, despite the fact that many protest to the experimenter, a substantial proportion continue to the last shock on the generator. It is the extreme willingness of adults to go to almost any lengths on the command of an authority that constitutes the chief finding of the study. . . . Ordinary people, simply doing their jobs, and without any particular hostility on their part, can become agents in a terrible destructive process.*[3]

In the late summer of 1971, close to a decade after Milgram's results hit the headlines, another research team, this one led by Philip Zimbardo at Stanford University, in northern California, gathered a host of students willing to participate in a prolonged psychology experiment for fifteen dollars a day. With some of the students acting as prison guards and others as prisoners under the absolute control of their captors, the research team wanted to see what sorts of interactions would unfold over the course of several days.

As the experiment progressed, the "guards" increasingly resorted to brute force to control their wards—and the "prisoners," who had been publicly arrested in front of their neighbors, taken to a real-life jail for booking, and then driven, blindfolded, to the site of the university experiment, began behaving in ever more antisocial, manipulative ways, thus justifying, in the guards' minds, their own brutal responses. Gradually, the violence shifted from being functional—with the ostensible purpose of controlling the prisoners—to being straightforwardly sadistic. The guards began humiliating and psychologically breaking down the inmates simply because they could: making them clean toilets with their bare hands, tripping them in hallways, stripping and sexually abusing them, mocking them as they were transported, their heads covered by paper bags, to the showers or out into the yard. "They steadily increased their coercive aggression tactics, humiliation and dehumanization of the prisoners," Zimbardo told a student reporter at Stanford more than a quarter century later.[4] Two years after that interview, in a 1999 lecture titled "Transforming People into Perpetrators of Evil," he explained that "it is especially important to hear how the worst of our guards justified his evil as wanting to see how far he could torment them before they stood up for [their] dignity, and rebelled against the brutality of the guards. They did not, and thus they deserved what they got. And suppose they did rebel? Would that have pleased him, and then would he say he was glad to see they had spunk and dignity, and so would no longer torment them? I doubt it, they lose no matter what they do."[5]

Within days of the start of the experiment, the makeshift cellblock in the basement of the Psychology Department at Stanford had morphed into something resembling a modern-day Bedlam, a place where those guarded and those doing the guarding both had ceased to function as normal, morally conscious members of society. Some of the prisoners had begun dissociating, obeying orders with the blank stares of zombies; others had become so emotionally volatile that the researchers had to release them for fear of long-term psychological damage. The entire experiment was brought to a premature end after Zimbardo's girlfriend and future wife, Christina Maslach, convinced Zimbardo that the experiment was inflicting immense emotional pain on its participants.

———

In the annals of university research, the Zimbardo and Milgram studies have become familiar and infamous examples of the excesses and potential ethical morasses to which unregulated research can lead. It was in their wake that universities adopted far more stringent human-research codes governing and limiting such projects. But, while both experiments raised ethical concerns, they also became feted examples—factual counterparts to William Golding's *Lord of the Flies,* about the descent into barbarism of a group of stranded children—of how easily moral restraints can be shed, shucked off like the husks on corn, to reveal something far more primal, far more brutal, lurking beneath our civilized veneer.

Milgram's experiment showed not so much that people were inherently brutal, but rather that, in certain circumstances, they would act brutally under orders. Establish a clearly defined hierarchy—as exists, for example, in a prison setting—develop a rationale that authority figures can fall back on to justify the infliction of violence, and chances are pretty high that many workers within that hierarchy will come to act in a vicious manner. Zimbardo's experiment showed that, within the prison setting, individual guards come to see themselves as authority figures with absolute control over their prisoners; they come to, in a sense, rationalize sadistic, humiliating acts by reference to the setting in which those acts take place.

Taken together, the Milgram and Zimbardo results show the toxic possibilities inherent in the institution of the prison, which by definition is a place delineated by strict hierarchies; a sphere in which obedience is inculcated as the highest virtue; and a miniature social system characterized by extremes of power and powerlessness, control and subordination. As such, they stand as reminders of the dangers of locking away huge numbers of people under the absolute control of uniformed officers of the state. These officers act in the certain knowledge that their cause is just, that their means will ultimately be justified by the ends—a safer society and the behavioral transformation of the prisoners under their control.

Add the pressures and horrors of war into the mix, and the warped realities of, say, the Abu Ghraib prison in Baghdad become not just understandable, but altogether unsurprising. "It's not that we put bad apples in a good barrel," Zimbardo explained to reporters in the wake of the Abu Ghraib revelations. "We put good apples in a bad barrel. The barrel corrupts anything that it touches."[6]

———————

While experiments such as Eastern State enjoyed mixed success in the mid-nineteenth century, returning some inmates to the community cured of their criminal habits while physically and mentally destroying others, in much of the country the philosophy of rehabilitation and the accompanying investments in large, structurally and administratively complex new prisons simply failed to take hold. Chaotic, crowded, antiquated, violence-prone buildings functioned as prisons in states such as Maine and Rhode Island into the latter part of the century. Inmates, wrote the historian Blake McKelvey in his 1936 book *American Prisons: A Study in American Social History prior to 1915*, were kept in "wretched structures," in the "worst makeshift jails."[7] Observers chronicled stories of prisoners chained at the ankles in subterranean rooms; of guards demanding sexual favors from their prisoners; of strong inmates terrorizing weak ones; of beatings and whippings and shootings and maimings; and of punishment rooms known as "doghouses"—updated to "heartbreak hotels" more than a century later, in the age of Elvis Presley—in which inmates were kept deprived of light and fed only starvation rations of bread and water. In short, they found similarly sorry conditions to those the late-eighteenth-century English prison reformer John Howard had encountered on his tours of Britain more than a half century earlier. "There are prisons," Howard wrote in the opening chapter to his celebrated book *The State of the Prisons,*

> into which whoever looks will, at first sight of the people confined, be convinced, that there is some great error in the management of them: their sallow meager countenances declare, without words, that they are very miserable. Many who went in healthy, are in a few months changed to emaciated dejected objects. Some are seen pining under diseases, "sick, and in prison"; expiring on the floors, in loathsome cells, of pestilential fevers, and the confluent smallpox; victims, I must not say to the cruelty, but I will say to the inattention, of sheriffs, and gentlemen in the commission of the peace.[8]

Elsewhere, lacking the tax base to maintain and staff even the most mediocre penal institutions, younger states began leasing out their prisoners to local businesses. It was a practice not too different from that in Europe hundreds of years earlier, when felons were frequently branded and condemned to years of galley slavery manning merchant ships and naval vessels.

The first state to embark down this road was Kentucky, in the 1820s. Soon it was followed by Indiana and Illinois, Missouri and Alabama. In Mississippi, from 1829, unclaimed runaway slaves were briefly jailed before being handed over to county authorities, who would then use them to build highways and bridges, often literally working them into their graves. In the decades after the Civil War, as bankrupt former Confederate states with a historical aversion to raising taxes tried to restore their public finances, prisoner leasing became standard practice across the South. Not only did it negate the need to build large prisons but, since private companies essentially bought the rights to prisoners' labor from the state, it also served to generate revenue. Within a few years of the end of hostilities, gangs of prisoners—the vast majority of whom were ex-slaves—were working the mines and farms and building roads and railways, with wardens advertising their "hands" in local newspapers and charging a range of fees based on the physical prowess of the prisoners. Company representatives chose their chattel in much the same way as plantation owners had chosen theirs in the antebellum slave markets.

While prisoners in the North were generally sentenced to a few months, or at most a few years, behind bars, long sentences became the norm in the post–Civil War South, with courts in states such as Georgia routinely sentencing men to more than ten years of hard labor for low-end, often economic crimes. Fed starvation rations, housed in camps made up of leaky wooden shacks with over one hundred men per building, or simply forced to sleep in the open air, guarded by trigger-happy overseers, clothed in skimpy black-and-white-striped uniforms and worn-through shoes, and provided no medical services despite epidemic levels of typhus, tuberculosis, and other poverty-induced diseases, the convict workers died in droves.

Crusading journalists such as Enoch Cobb Wines and George Washington Cable documented in some of these labor camps mortality rates that would have been familiar to later denizens of Soviet or Chinese camps. In 1882 researchers estimated that across the South as a whole the annual prisoner mortality rate was 41.3 per thousand, nearly three times the rate in northern prisons.[9] In Mississippi, according to the historian David Oshinsky, mortality rates rose as high as 16 percent a year in some camps.[10] In Florida, McKelvey quotes a Captain J. C. Powell, who was in charge of labor camps in the state for fourteen years, as saying that conditions were so barbarous, so corrupt and cruel, that they could only aptly be described as "the American Siberia."[11] If they didn't work hard enough, prisoners were whipped, "watered" (a process in which prone inmates had water forced down their throats, not dissimilar to the notorious "waterboarding" reportedly carried out by twenty-first-century interrogators against senior Al Qaeda suspects), and set upon by trained attack dogs. So cavalier was convict leasing, so indifferent to the lives of the convicts, that Cable, in his classic book *The Silent South* (1885), denounced the institution as "worse than slavery."

No matter how deadly the system was, however, proponents could always point to its cost-effectiveness. In 1880s Alabama, wrote McKelvey, "full hands" were rented out for $5.00 per month, "medium hands" for $2.50, and "dead hands"—the old and the infirm—given away for free, in exchange only for a bare minimum of food and, in theory, the provision of housing from the companies who bought their labor. So lucrative was this system that, some historians say, into the 1890s the bulk of Alabama's (admittedly small) state revenues were raised through prisoner leasing. Prisons in Alabama, says Birmingham drug-treatment program administrator and prison reformer Ralph Hendrix, in an accent so deliberately exaggerated that it could etch itself in stone, have always been related to the state's broader economic needs. "It's such a genetic institution in this state and this part of the country. Prisons are as important as education, as cornbread." And so, despite the well-voiced repugnance of men such as Cable, the leasing system continued into the twentieth century, stuttering to a close over decades, as southern states gradually moved toward a "penitentiary farm" system, in which inmates would be housed in large prisons on old plantations, and would work the fields for the state instead of for private enterprises. In Florida, the last state to abolish convict leasing, examples of the practice continued until 1923—the year in which Governor Cary Hardee also abolished the practice of hanging capital defendants in public—providing an unsavory overlap between the forced labor system of the American South and the then-embryonic gulag network being set up in Soviet Russia.

———•———

But something more was going on, in the southern states in particular, than mere reluctance to release scarce tax dollars to create model penitentiaries. In many parts of the United States, the cultural values and goals underpinning institutions such as Eastern State had notably failed to gain traction. In Pennsylvania and elsewhere in the Northeast, the Quakers and Episcopalians might have largely succeeded in replacing age-old codes of private honor and tribal vengeance with a more dispassionate vision of justice informed by the age of Enlightenment, but, as documented by the historian Grady McWhiney in his 1988 book *Cracker Culture: Celtic Ways in the Old South,* in parts of the country largely peopled by migrants from the Celtic fringes of the United Kingdom, those codes continued to shape much of everyday life. With weaker state institutions and stronger notions of revenge, much of the South's response to crime remained the purview of private individuals and mobs until the recent past.

At the same time, southern religion was far less forgiving than the religion of the Quakers, the Episcopalians, and other northeastern sects. The southern God demanded eye-for-an-eye retaliations and imposed order through fear, rather than encouraging his flock to turn the other cheek. There was, longtime Alabama prison warden Oscar Dees told the journalist Ray March in the 1970s, a biblical imperative to impose physical punishment on rule breakers. "Use the rod, don't spare the rod," March quoted Dees as saying, in his 1978 book *Alabama Bound.* Dees matter-of-factly explained how he frequently beat men with a thick leather strap, sometimes administering as many as fifty lashes, in order to force compliance with his officers' orders—or, more prosaically, simply because they were black and he felt they needed to learn their station in life. "Of course, I'm still for the strap, and I think the time is fast coming back now where you're going to see the courts, the courts get tighter. I think the time's coming, and it's coming mighty fast, where you're going to see stricter discipline through your country," the old warden predicted. "The Bible says it, it says you got to have discipline. It plainly says, 'Use the rod.' "[12] Perhaps not entirely surprisingly, the warden, disgruntled by the fact that the courts had restricted the rights to inflict violence upon inmates, also advocated electrocuting repeat offenders.

Dees's views, offensive to the point of caricature to a liberal mindset, had a long pedigree in the South. For Michel Foucault, punishment was always at least in part about organized public spectacle, about terrifying yet exhilarating audiences by breaking the bodies and souls of those caught on the wrong side of the law. Indeed, in France, Foucault's home country, the public guillotining of murderers continued, albeit with increasing rarity, into the late 1930s, the bloodied heads of the victims dropping into baskets, the bodies rolled off the execution plank into shapeless coffins. And while the need for spectacle had largely been tamed by the competing modern sensibilities of squeamishness and a desire for punishments proportionate to the crimes—what the historian Norbert Elias famously labeled in his 1982 book of that title "the civilizing process"[13]—support for bloodshed and violence in the name of justice remained extraordinarily strong in the American South.

In the late nineteenth century, the crusading African American journalist Ida B. Wells documented hundreds of lynchings, some involving crowds of thousands of people, around the region. Victims were burned, shot, hung, stabbed. Sometimes their bodies were literally ripped apart by the frenzied mob, and morsels of flesh and bone distributed as grizzly mementos among participants.[14] According to former Texas prison warden and historian of the state's criminal-justice system Lou Bennett Glenn, 335 mob lynchings were carried out in Texas between 1889 and 1918, with even higher numbers in Georgia and Mississippi.[15] Glenn—who, like Dees, expresses in his writing a disconcerting nostalgia for the good old days, when physical violence was un-questioningly accepted as a routine way of controlling prisoners—records that nine black men were lynched on a single day in June 1908 in the town of Hemphill; that three black men were burned to death on May 6, 1922, in Fair-field; and that the last recorded lynching in the state was carried out in 1929. When executions were legally enacted by local and county authorities, they were, he noted, not much different from those performed by the mob, "at-tended by not only the local riff-raff, but also all manner of polite society, who considered the executions a high-toned form of entertainment."[16] His de-scription of the festivities could equally well have described public hangings carried out at the Tyburn gallows in London in earlier centuries.

Why did the lynchings stop? Not because of any change in Texans' sensi-bilities, Glenn wrote; but rather because the state usurped the function of lo-cal executioners and mobs by introducing the electric chair—"Old Sparky"—at Huntsville prison in 1924, and itself dispatching to eternity an increasing number of convicted criminals in a dramatically painful manner.

At the same time that the South became a petri dish for lynch culture, it also remained a bastion of the old European hobby of dueling. Throughout the first six decades of the nineteenth century, urban elites in southern towns such as New Orleans, Savannah, Vicksburg, and Charleston, as well as aris-tocratic planters, adhered to the "Code Duello," the formal honor code of eighteenth-century Europe, which mandated that gentlemen avenge attacks on their reputations by challenging their enemies to duels. In New Orleans in particular, contemporary records indicate that pistol duels were practically daily occurrences, the protagonists' techniques often honed in "dueling acad-emies" located throughout the region. At a time when the countries from which dueling had been imported—England, Ireland, France, and Prussia in particular—were abandoning the practice, it remained central to the social code in the American South. Governors, senators, attorneys, bankers, wealthy planters, and newspaper editors all partook. President Andrew Jackson was known to have been involved in at least fourteen duels.[17] Only with the onset of the Civil War, and the resultant collapse of the southern aristocracy, did the institution gradually fade into the history books, and even then it took some time to die. As late as 1880, the practice was so common in South Carolina that the legislature felt the need to pass a law specifically banning dueling.[18] When dueling, like lynching, finally did run its course, its demise had as much to do with a stronger state usurping the revenge function as with the coming of a more tender moral sensibility.

The honor code of the South—the notion that a gentleman once insulted must seek satisfaction on the dueling field, and that a community as a whole, when faced with a challenge to its social code, should seek justice by lynching —was, as the twentieth century progressed, increasingly replaced by state action. The aggrieved gentleman-dueler became the tough-on-crime politician advocating draconian sentences for those who had insulted the majesty of the state through their actions; the lyncher became the vengeful citizen, the supporter of capital punishment, the gawker come to see Old Sparky.

Always a distinct beast, the American South, when it came to criminal justice, had generally turned its back on Enlightenment theories of imprisonment and rehabilitation in the years surrounding the War between the States. While western European nations such as England and France, Holland and Italy were busy emulating radical Yankee penal innovations that the Quakers had initiated to set themselves apart from the Old World, the South instead adopted a brute-force approach.

———•———

By the post–Civil War period, the parameters of America's criminological debate had thus been firmly set, defined around a series of overarching questions: was incarceration about rehabilitation and redemption, as the Quakers believed, or revenge, including God-sanctioned, often bloody punishment, as many other strains of American Christianity and the southern heirs to the Celtic blood-feud culture advocated? Was everyone potentially redeemable, as certain strands of Christianity had argued almost since the inception of the religion, or were some people doomed to eternal damnation? Was inmate labor best enforced in the privacy of the prison or through the spectacle of the chain gang? Should prison staff be something akin to armed missionaries, or simply musclemen for the state? Were the large, taxpayer-funded, public construction projects mandated by the "penitentiary" philosophy necessary, or would the public be served just as well by dumping its malfeasants into overcrowded, vicious, but low-cost jails and makeshift prisons? Was prison labor intended primarily to morally rehabilitate prisoners, or to generate profits for

private contractors or the state itself? Should prisons house only the most serious offenders, or should they be utilized to sweep up vagrants, addicts, and
impoverished laborers—especially blacks in the South—in much the same
way as European bridewells had been used to control that continent's destitute and hungry classes for several hundred years?

————•————

Violence, it seems, is nascent within most human beings. Put all except the
most resolutely pacifist individuals into conditions in which they have absolute control over others they believe to be "bad" or criminally minded, and
chances are that confrontations will escalate into violence; that cruel impulses
normally hidden deep below the surface will bubble up and find an outlet; that
the infliction of pain, and the giving of orders for others to inflict pain, will
become commonplace. There was, the sociologist Hannah Arendt came to believe after reporting on Adolf Eichmann's 1961 trial in Jerusalem for *The New
Yorker,* nothing extraordinary about the bureaucratic architects of the Nazi
Holocaust, nothing that could have marked them out ahead of time as people
capable of horrendous acts. To the contrary, Arendt argued, it was precisely
the ordinariness of Eichmann that was so compelling, so disturbing. He was,
she wrote, emblematic of "the banality of evil."

Time after time, in the centuries since the American prison experiment
was kicked off—a grandiose real-world venture far beyond anything Zimbardo or Milgram could have orchestrated—the Janus-faced nature of the
system, the schizophrenic divide between redemption and rehabilitation on
the one hand, and revenge and punishment on the other, has been hammered
home.

Many commentators purported to be shocked by the prisoner-abuse scandal at Abu Ghraib. The images of hooded, manacled prisoners being electric-
shocked, humiliated, set upon by dogs, and beaten by guards were, pundits
and politicians proclaimed, simply un-American. Yet over the decades many
of those very techniques have been used, with or without official approval, in
prisons throughout the United States, from Quaker penitentiaries to southern chain gangs. In much of the South, heavy leather straps were an official
correctional tool for beating prisoners until well after World War II. Stories of
crank-up electric-shock devices, colloquially referred to as "telephones," being used on suspects and inmates were legion into the recent past; indeed, in
the 1980s and 1990s, several men in Chicago were sent to death row on the basis of confessions they claimed were tortured out of them by officers on the

notoriously rough South Side using precisely this technique. (It was at least in part because of this scandal that Illinois governor George Ryan commuted the death sentences of everyone on death row in his state, and declared a moratorium on prosecutions in which the state sought the death penalty, in the opening years of the twenty-first century.[19]) Attack dogs are still commonly brought into prison settings to help control riot situations. Seriously mentally ill inmates continue to be placed in restraining devices. The use of gasses such as pepper spray and mace are commonly used to subdue recalcitrant individuals, despite the fact the gas might well choke, sicken, and burn prisoners in surrounding cells. Female and male prisoners alike are sexually abused by other prisoners and by staff; in 2000 *The Prison Journal* found that one in five male prisoners in seven prisons studied reported being coerced into having sex at some point during their incarceration.[20] In New York City, at a meeting arranged by the Fortune Society—a widely respected organization that helps ex-inmates navigate life after prison—I talked with forty-year-old Mark Klass, who had spent ten years behind bars. Klass recalled how an eighteen-year-old at his prison was deliberately celled with a serial sex offender. Not surprisingly, the teenager was raped. "It was so deliberate," he explained in disgust, "that another guard, angry about what happened, actually put the rapist in another cell with a real gorilla, who beat him up."

As in Abu Ghraib, so in Texas into the recent past. Lou Bennett Glenn explains how, in the 1960s, prisoners were handcuffed to rails for hours on end, their arms yanked above their heads, their toes barely touching the ground. He wrote of inmates being made to stand for hours at a time on a plank or barrel, sometimes alone, sometimes in groups, and being forced to restart the punishment every time one of them fell off. He testified to the allegedly therapeutic value of beating inmates. And he described, nostalgically, the regimen that isolated troublesome prisoners in dank, pitch-black holes for days on end, and conversely made "houseboys"—essentially domestic slaves to prison staff —out of prisoners who curried a high level of trust among their captors. "They were always on call and had to be ready to serve at the beck and call of the employee," Glenn wrote. "The inmates prized these jobs, and many inmates worked for the same families for generations."[21]

While Texas's prisons are far more professionally run today than they were when Glenn was a young guard, allegations of violence are still commonplace. In 2002, lawyers documented allegations by prisoners at the Gibb Lewis unit, a prison in the eastern part of the state, that a ring of guards in the segregation unit would "ritually abuse" black inmates. The abuse, testified to and independently corroborated by dozens of men, apparently included putting a broomstick on top of an inmate's feet and having a three-hundred-pound guard step down on it with all of his weight. "I remember a letter written in Spanish by one prisoner," recalled San Francisco attorney Donna Brorby, who spent years working in Texas as the court-appointed lead counsel in a multi-decade class-action lawsuit filed by prisoners against the Department of Criminal Justice. "It was really pitiable. This humiliating, dominating sort of thing. 'Who's your Daddy?' sort of stuff. They made people beg for things."

They would even, prisoners alleged—presaging some of the Abu Ghraib allegations about guards forcing captives to denounce or mock their own religion—make Catholic inmates pretend that a fat lieutenant was God. According to Brorby, "The guards would ask [the inmate] questions, and when he couldn't answer them, the correctional officers would hit him. The sort of stuff designed to demonstrate absolute power. The state purported to not really believe it. [Then] they said it was the sadism of eight to ten guards. But eight to ten is no longer individual. It's what reigns on an entire cellblock. When the staff has no rules, the abuse gets more extreme. The staff say to inmates, 'I don't care what you tell people. Nobody will believe you.' "

The twenty-one-year-old man to whom Brorby was referring told investigators that when he arrived at the unit in January 2002, he was escorted to an office, ordered to call an officer "Daddy," and kneed in the solar plexus when he refused. "As he fell forward, the officer behind him yanked him up by the cuffs," the investigator's notes recorded.

> His eyes teared. They told him to take it like a man. They told him again to call the ranking officer "Daddy." He refused. The kneeing and jerking up by the cuffs was repeated. He obeyed the next order to call the supervisor "Daddy." That wasn't enough, they wanted him to do it 5 times. He did. They told him that they cliqued on him in order to get the things they told him into his head. They told him not to tell his homeboys. They put him back in his cell. He cried in shame.

Another prisoner reported being slammed to the floor, placed in leg restraints, and having a female guard stomp on his legs. Afterward, a male guard stepped on his elbow and kicked him in the ribs. When, in anguish, he subsequently cut his arm with a razor, the guards gassed him, and the female officer who had hurt his legs informed him that she "hoped he would bleed to death."[22]

In Florida, in a part of the state with a long history of Ku Klux Klan activity, death row prisoners in the 1990s reported that correctional officers had wandered through their unit wearing white robes and hoods. Christopher Jones, a Gainesville attorney with Florida Institutional Legal Services, recalled a scandal during the mid-1990s when a gang of guards at Charlotte prison, north of Fort Myers on the state's west coast, were revealed to be Klan members; they identified each other by a certain leather tassel on their key chains. And at the Central Florida Reception Center, a warden reportedly referred to his difficulties hiring guards from the northern part of the state, because so many were Ku Kluxers. Meanwhile, at the Florida State Prison in the little town of Stark, guards allegedly formed "welcoming committees" to beat new prisoners who had been transferred to the facility after harassing or assaulting officers at other prisons. One man was beaten so badly that his jaw was broken. Another, on death row, was stomped to death.

More recently, Jones sued the Florida Department of Corrections after several mentally ill prisoners were gassed so severely that their bodies were covered in red blisters, the skin literally burned off of them. One of the men gassed was an elderly blind man with glass eyes. He was gassed while on the toilet, after guards decided his cell wasn't tidy enough for their liking. "He stumbles into the bunk bed and knocks out one of his glass eyes and the gas get into the socket, which becomes so inflamed he can't get the glass eye back in. The idea you'd need to pepper spray a blind guy who's already in lockdown is insane," Jones asserted when we met in his cluttered office, files spewing out of filing cabinets, in 2005. "It's not about rogue officers and bad apples. We've got a really sick system. It must be hard to be a good apple in Florida. There's always been this 'We're going to kick your ass' attitude."

After several hours of talking about prison-abuse scandals, Jones—a middle-aged man with a ponytail and a fast-talking persona—came up with one final anecdote. Over a period of time, he said, numerous inmates had, independently of one another, told him about Union prison in Raiford. Into the 1980s, according to these men, new inmates entering the receiving area had to walk past a jar filled with human teeth. On the jar was a label, and on the label were the words "Jacksonville Niggers."

———

Brought to the light of day by crusading prison reformers and periodic spasms of state and federal judicial activism, these sorry conditions momentarily improve; then, when public attention moves on, conditions generally deteriorate again. The pattern is sadly predictable. In the nineteenth century, journalists such as Enoch Cobb Wines and George Washington Cable wrote exposés of southern prisons, resulting in a series of congressional hearings and rapid-fire legislative reforms.[23] In the latter half of the twentieth century, the majority of state prison systems ended up with some form of federal oversight imposed by the courts, following a flurry of prisoners'-rights lawsuits.

Since the mid-1990s, prisoner-abuse scandals have ranged from guards at California's supermax Corcoran prison ordering rival gang members to fight it out on the yard and shooting them apart with rubber bullets, to staff at Red Onion and Wallens Ridge prisons in Virginia forcing inmates to run gauntlets of club-wielding officers; from guards at Pelican Bay, in the remote far north of California, almost boiling a mentally ill inmate alive, ostensibly to clean off the feces he had smeared on his body, to prison officials in several states being accused of turning a blind eye to epidemics of rape inside their institutions. The high-security facility in Youngstown, Ohio, faced so many allegations of wrongdoing that the state had to close it down. In California, the Youth Authority was shamed into reform after videos surfaced of teenagers in juvenile correctional settings being savagely beaten by bevies of officers: grown men pummeling pubescent boys. So frequent are the allegations of prisoners being hit, kicked, gassed, stunned, sexually molested, verbally humiliated, and racially abused that they eventually begin to merge into a vicious mélange. They become an appalling, unendurable cacophony: nails scratched across a blackboard, combined with the squeals of soon-to-be-slaughtered pigs.

———•———

In New York, the ex-prisoners I met at the Fortune Society detailed casual, almost reflective violence. One recalled getting into a shouting match with a guard who had thrown some of his legal papers into the cell's toilet. Later that night, he claimed, a gang of officers came back "and whipped my ass. When I woke up I was in the Box [the punishment cells], and the back of my head looked like a hot fire had been run over it. I finally worked it out. After they knocked me out, they dragged me by my feet to the Box." Another talked of how guards would strip prisoners naked before moving them to the punishment cells, order them to stand still in the corner of an elevator while taking them to these cells, and "beat the shit" out of those who moved without permission. A third detailed how, in winter, guards on the B Block of Sing Sing prison would deliberately break prisoners' windows in order to "freeze them up." The old-timers remembered how, in the middle of the night, in the years following the deadly Attica prison riot of September 1971, guards would savagely beat African American inmates who supported the radical black-nationalist Five Percent movement. Other prisoners, he said, would listen as the victims screamed out in pain. Finally, one mentioned that a newly arrived convict who objected to the mandatory delousing procedure "was pinned up against a wall at Downstate Prison like Jesus Christ and officers beating him so hard they eventually wore themselves out."

The prisoners didn't sound surprised by what they'd seen. They had, over the years, come to expect this sort of thing.

The violence, Donna Brorby believes, in effect repeating the Zimbardo experiment's conclusions, was largely a result of "the creation of an immoral code that becomes the moral code of the institution." She explained, "As soon as you get detached from the moral code we develop as a society, you lose one of the most important sources of restraint of conduct. And when that's lost, there are no rules. You can see it in the arrogance of the photos in Abu Ghraib, and you can see it in the egregious instances in domestic prisons. A lot of the things that happened in Abu Ghraib have happened in U.S. prisons. People are only *so* imaginative. There's only a limited number of ways to do things that are brutal and humiliating."

———

Despite the utopian motivations of many of the original penal reformers, in reality violence has been embedded in America's large-scale prisons since their inception, often emerging as a frustrated response to prisoners' failure to be "reformed" or to acknowledge the scope of their wrongdoings. Certainly there is nothing uniquely American about this; over the years, press reports and human rights activists have exposed routine torture in India's jails, extrajudicial executions in Brazil, South Africa, China, Russia, and many other countries, the massacres of rioting inmates that periodically occur in Latin American prisons, and the endemic violence meted out to those being interrogated in, say, Egypt or Saudi Arabia, as well as the harsh treatment of Irish Republican Army suspects in British prisons and jails and Bader Meinhof suspects in 1970s Germany. Almost by definition, prisons represent society's underside. Whatever violence or pathology is present in the broader community will be magnified in prisons, whether the initial levels are low—as in Scandinavia, Japan, and Canada—or more potent, as in the United States, South Africa, Russia, Brazil, and other societies defined, at least partially, by high levels of violence. Why countries differ in their initial levels of violence, and why populations in different countries tolerate differing levels of brutality meted out in their name by the state, are sociological questions largely outside the scope of this book; undeniably, though, whatever the initial level of societal brutality, prisons act as a magnifier.

What *is* unique about incarceration in early-twenty-first-century America is not per se the level of violence inside prisons—although recent technological and architectural advances may, perhaps, make that violence more profound and more regimented—but the *scale* of the modern incarceration system, the fact that so many millions of Americans have, since the 1970s, been caught up in it. That a social experiment as profound as that of America's penitentiary system has become so intertwined with America's complex system of race relations and its frustrated attitude toward poverty, and in so doing has expanded so vastly and at such extraordinary fiscal and moral cost, is what makes the topic today so powerful and so disturbing.

Today's massive prison archipelago is neither solely the descendant of the early-nineteenth-century Quaker penologists nor that of the latter-nineteenth-century advocates of the prisoners-as-slaves model. Instead it is a hybrid, combining the regimentation and obsession with detail of Eastern State's proponents with the harshness, greed, and callousness of those who designed the prisoner-leasing system. The resource-heavy Quaker system worked only by limiting prison admission to those convicted of the most serious crimes; the prisoners-as-slaves system, by contrast, functioned best by sweeping up lower-level offenders en masse and then trading away their labor. Today's solution to societal problems seems to be to expand the definition of "felony" beyond anything envisioned in the past: to sweep *all* offenders, from the lowliest drug addict to the nastiest killer, into the staggeringly expensive prison system and to subject them to a regimented existence that would have been all too familiar to Pennsylvania's nineteenth-century penological idealists. How much does such an all-encompassing program cost? The devil may care.

"The 1990s," said American Correctional Association president Gwen Chunn, when I interviewed her in the summer of 2005, "had a lot to do with straightforward punishment. In the nineties the notion of get-tough came from the very top and permeated the entire system. Resources for lock-'em-up were more available to the states than were resources for rehabilitation in the 1960s and '70s. The get-tough movement wasn't well informed. Many politicians who were making changes were often not very knowledgeable about their own systems. They were making policies based on anecdotes."

"The prison system," stated Joe Bogan, a retired senior-level employee of the federal Bureau of Prisons, "is a reflection of the larger society, generally speaking. The society has gotten more conservative, more harsh. It's an easy political sop to throw the book at the drug dealers and all the other bad apples. These people are The Other. They are *not* us."

CHAPTER 3

USING A SLEDGEHAMMER TO KILL A GNAT

A quarter century before the prison and jail population surpassed 2 million, in the spring of 1974, during a political season dominated by the burgeoning Watergate scandal, *Public Interest* magazine ran a long article by a Berkeley-educated sociologist named Robert Martinson titled "What Works?—Questions and Answers about Prison Reform." Unlike most articles by academics, which might make ripples among scholars but rarely cross into the popular culture, this piece was an immediate sensation. Martinson became an instant celebrity, quoted by politicians and invited onto some of the most-watched TV shows in the land.

Nearly a decade earlier, Martinson and two colleagues, Douglas Lipton and Judith Wilks, had been hired by New York State to conduct a large-scale investigation into the state's burgeoning rehabilitation industry, and the principles and success of rehabilitation programs between 1945 and 1967. Basically, the inquiry was to find out whether or not the cornucopia of treatment programs that had sprung up inside prisons in recent decades—from "skill development" plans and group psychotherapy to special-education classes, from "assessment counseling" regarding a person's work potential to specialized training in the use of IBM equipment—were actually changing inmates' criminal proclivities. By the late 1960s, in progressive systems such as California's and Minnesota's, some prisoners were being organized into "self-government" units within psychotherapeutic settings; others were being subjected to "authoritarian" systems of therapy.[1] Some reformers were focusing on creating "empathetic" environments within which to conduct their rehabilitation experiments. Others pushed for field trips and "community meetings" to be incorporated into inmates' routines. Massachusetts even embraced a program called Outward Bound, which taught teenage detainees survival skills, culminating, said Martinson, in "a final 24 hours in which each youth had to survive alone in the wilderness."[2]

Did these programs, their intent frequently obscured behind an alphabet soup of acronyms, lead to fewer released prisoners returning to lives of crime? Or were they simply expensive feel-good measures, pushed by professional cadres with their own agendas, that allowed manipulative inmates to fool parole boards into believing they'd had a Road to Damascus awakening and deserved to be released early? Given the resources devoted to rehabilitation by the 1960s, and judicial rulings making it likely that even more resources would be so earmarked in the future, these were by no means idle questions.

Many of the treatments and therapies offered to prisoners had not been rigorously evaluated before being implemented on a large scale. Reform-minded correctional administrators had taken advocates' promises as gospel, rather than with the healthy dose of skepticism they generally deserved. When Martinson's team did the legwork and crunched the numbers, they predictably found glaring mismatches between the hype and the reality; but, wary of the implications of these findings, New York State tried to sit on the results, refusing to publish the finished report and banning the researchers from releasing their findings independently. The conclusions, correctional officials feared, were simply too explosive to unleash into a heated political environment.

Eventually, the finished report was introduced as evidence in a court case in the Bronx, and the state reluctantly gave the researchers permission to publish their findings as a book. The volume, a mammoth seven hundred pages of statistics and highly technical analyses, was damning. The authors concluded that at best, the evidence of these programs' success was inconclusive, and at worst, many of them were outright useless.

While the team waited for their book to see the light of day, Martinson, an imposing, bearded figure, struck out alone, condensing the findings into a thirty-page article. In boiling down the arguments to their core themes, he helped set in motion a chain of events that would ultimately transform the United States' criminal-justice system. Martinson, described to me by long-time prison reformer Al Bronstein, of the American Civil Liberties Union's National Prison Project, as an "interesting, somewhat arrogant" man, posed his question as, "What works?" His pugnacious answer, modified by only a few caveats: "Nothing." While the original research had uncovered serious flaws in existing rehabilitation programs, Martinson went further in his *Public Interest* article. It wasn't simply that the programs were flawed; rather, the very idea of rehabilitation seemed incoherent. "It is possible to give a rather bald summary of our findings," he wrote. "With few and isolated exceptions, the rehabilitative efforts that have been reported so far have had no appreciable effect on recidivism. . . . The implication is clear: that if we can't do more for (and to) offenders, at least we can safely do less." It may be, Martinson went on, "that education at its best, or that psychotherapy at its best, cannot overcome, or even appreciably reduce, the powerful tendency for offenders to continue in criminal behavior."[3]

In the period preceding the release of Martinson's research, with the country plagued by rising drug addiction and violent crime rates, state governors had begun calling for harsher penalties for drug offenders. In the early 1970s, President Richard Nixon had started advocating a national war on drugs. Americans had watched in horror as prisoners in Attica and other penitentiaries seized control of prison buildings and yards, demanding better conditions and threatening to kill hostages unless they got their way. Anecdotes abounded of criminals with access to better living conditions and educational opportunities than working-class residents of the surrounding communities. In some California prisons, the libraries had grown so massive that they now rivaled those of the state's universities, presenting prisoners with a powerful opportunity for intellectual self-improvement. In 1968, no less a conservative than Governor Ronald Reagan had signed an Inmate Bill of Rights guaranteeing minimum living standards for the state's approximately twenty thousand prisoners. (Reagan also pushed the adult authority to release thousands of inmates at the early end of their indeterminate sentences so that the state could close one of its prisons. Ironically, it fell to Reagan's liberal successor, Jerry Brown, to reduce indeterminate sentencing and sign into law an amendment to the state's penal code, declaring that the primary purpose of incarceration was no longer rehabilitation but simply punishment.) And, in the years surrounding the publication of "What Works?" federal courts, responding to class-action lawsuits filed by prisoners and their legal supporters, were increasingly requiring overextended state prison systems to provide even more programs to inmates, including access to prison law libraries, education, and drug treatment.

At the same time, across the political spectrum from Nixon's increasingly resentful "silent majority," a growing number of political progressives were adding their voices to the chorus against rehabilitation, arguing that the very notion of "adjusting" an individual's fundamental behavioral traits smacked of totalitarianism. Moreover, they argued, allowing parole boards and prison administrations to determine when an inmate had served enough time was a recipe for racial and class biases, present in the broader society, to be replicated in correctional settings. In the late 1960s, groups such as the Black Panthers had begun to argue that prisons, home to a disproportionate number of black and Latino inmates, were political institutions intended to control not criminality but racial and economic underclasses. Because the definition of "rehabilitation" was so vague, parole boards could deny prisoners parole for any reason they saw fit, rational or irrational, and defend their action by saying they didn't think the inmates were sufficiently rehabilitated.

For radical correctional reformers in the 1960s and 1970s, looking at prisons as parts of a larger societal setting, one thing seemed clear: if prisons were going to continue to exist—and by the early 1970s, many radicals on the increasingly fractious fringes of American politics were moving toward a prison-abolitionist position—discretionary sentencing ought to be replaced by strictly defined, or determinate, sentences. The lengths of these sentences would be set by something akin to a grid delineating the appropriate punishment for various crimes. Now, Martinson's warnings about the futility of pricey inmate "treatment" programs added intellectual credibility to both the "Leave our personalities alone" school and the "We're mad as hell and not going to take it anymore" camp.

On August 24, 1975, slightly over a year after the publication of "What Works?" Mike Wallace interviewed Martinson on CBS's flagship news show *60 Minutes*. By now, perhaps infatuated with his own stardom, Martinson was willing to make the kind of sweeping, reductive generalizations his original research had shied away from.

"The prisoner who has been exposed to no rehabilitation programs—are his chances of going back to crime better, worse, or the same, as the prisoner who has had the whole treatment?" Wallace asked.

"They're the same. They're the same. I know it sounds astonishing, but they're the same," the sociologist replied.

"Is it conceivable that nothing works?" Wallace continued.

"Conceivable, certainly," Martinson replied with relish. "There's been literature written, as you well know, which suggests that this is—may well be the fact."[4]

And there it was. Despite the fact that many correctional experts around the country, not to mention many judges, were deeply suspicious of Martinson's strutting certainty, and despite the fact that Martinson, himself a political middle-of-the-roader, rapidly became uncomfortable with the politicization of his work, a phrase had entered the public consciousness that would ricochet through corrections for the next three decades: "Nothing works." Martinson's timing had been perfect, coming at precisely the moment when a post-Vietnam sense of national malaise was leading more and more political figures to find scapegoats for the fact that the country seemed to be heading to hell in a handbasket. The culture was scratching around for a new, more muscular approach to crime and punishment.

"What it did was to silence debate. It was well done, thorough, reputable, and his presentation of what it all meant was powerful," remembered the Australian-born criminologist Francis Cullen, who, in his capacity as a research professor at the University of Cincinnati, was a leading critic of the "Nothing Works" school in the decades following Martinson's article. "He was saying it may be that it's impossible to cure offenders in correctional settings. It would be like somebody saying, 'We spend all this money on cancer research and cancer's never going to be cured. It's beyond our capabilities.' My sense is he provided a finding that a lot of people already believed. There already were substantial numbers of people, including criminologists and political members, who already believed rehabilitation didn't work. It was just a weapon in their disillusionment with, attack against, rehab."

"His message and support in the media was so extremely strong," recalled Ted Palmer, a psychologist who headed the research wing of California's Youth Authority for over three decades and was one of the earliest critics of Martinson's work. "Almost everybody was afraid to challenge him and his strong, well-known supporters—both on the liberal and the conservative side." A generation after the publication of "What Works?" Palmer, a skinny old man with red eyes behind thick, plastic-framed spectacles, his mottled bald pate ringed by thin white hair, still resented Martinson's sensational rise. "I'm a strict scientist, as rigorous as they come—and from my position, he really wasn't ready for prime time in terms of his science. I'm sure he knew he was overgeneralizing and was overlooking a lot of data. He had to know it. But he chose to be dramatic. He was a dramatic fellow. I'm sure he thought he was doing a good service. It wasn't just that he sought glory."

Whatever Martinson's true motivations, in the years following publication of the *Public Interest* article his critique stuck. With judges aggressively intervening against shoddy state penal practices, ordering states to spend large sums to improve their inmate services—even the generally conservative Supreme Court chief justice Warren Burger repeatedly argued that the state had a moral imperative to try to rehabilitate prisoners through an intensive combination of education, job training, and employment—the media, politicians, and populace began inveighing against what many saw as out-of-touch activist courts. After all, why spend money on educating inmates, training them to rejoin the labor force and providing them with state-of-the-art drug treatment, when research suggested they'd still return to crime? Why give them a chance at early parole when the rehabilitation markers used by parole boards to determine whether an inmate was a good release risk were inherently unreliable or, worse, biased? Why try to divert convicted criminals into nonprison alternatives when those alternatives were doomed to failure from the start? Why not simply incarcerate more criminals for longer periods of time, removing criminals from society rather than trying to alter the way they behaved? Thus, at the very moment when the courts were best disposed to order prison systems to shape up or shut down, Martinson had, the famous conservative criminologist James Q. Wilson later wrote, "administered a highly visible *coup de grace*" to the notion of rehabilitation.[5] (One of the early advocates of an increased usage of incarceration, and later the coauthor of a famous *Atlantic Monthly* article urging more proactive policing in run-down urban neighborhoods, Wilson was another public intellectual whose writings on crime and punishment would help shift public policy away from rehabilitation and toward incapacitation.[6])

Although activists on the left and right had both been dissatisfied with the previous model, Martinson's frontal attack on rehabilitation was one that, in hindsight, could not help but benefit conservatives. While the full force of the philosophical transformation took time to kick in, by the 1980s and 1990s "Nothing Works" was driving correctional practice across the country.

"It's like a bidding war," explained Peggy Burke, of the Center for Effective Public Policy. Burke, who had in the course of her career worked on shaping parole guidelines for the federal system, Oregon, Washington, and Minnesota, believed that what replaced the rehabilitative model was a "tendency to inflate punishment, because in a sound bite it sounds good." Determinate sentencing, says Joe Bogan, a former warden in the federal prison system, was initially a liberal idea, but it got "hijacked by the conservatives, the people who believed in more severe punishment."

"I went in right after the Attica riots. After Attica, they gave us concessions—college, let us wash our bodies three or four times a week," explained Edmund Taylor, a man who spent twenty-two years in the New York State prison system during the years preceding and the decades following Martinson's study. In the 1980s, the rollbacks began. In the 1990s, after the state's political leadership embraced the Nothing Works philosophy, "You could *feel* the change, the way COs [correctional officers] responded to you. College programs literally disappeared. They didn't make any effort to better a person. It was all about punishment. Rehabilitation programs were wiped out. It was all about doing time. Angry people doing time."

"Today," says sixty-two-year-old Pablo Santos, who went through vocational training programs and got a community-college degree while in New York prisons in the 1970s and 1980s, "people have nothing to do in prison. So they're given make-work like picking paper in the prison yard."

———•———

Throughout most of the twentieth century, cutting-edge correctional theory in advanced democratic nations had been moving toward a treatment model, viewing prisoners as individuals who, through specialized programs, could be "cured" of the tendencies that had led them into criminal activities, and hence into involvement with the criminal-justice system. Viewed through such a lens, the challenge of reducing the cycles of crime, imprisonment, release, and return to crime became a professional problem, solutions to which mandated expanding ranks of specialists and layers of bureaucracy to structure society's response to criminals. In the late eighteenth century, Jeremy Bentham had largely sought to modify prisoners' behavior through physical controls and a one-size-fits-all regimen of silence and work. His successors had advocated frequent recourse to corporal punishment for those who broke the internal rules, and in nations with colonies that could be used as dumping grounds for convicts, harsh deportation policies that were generally more concerned with creating order through terror than with transforming character. So it was that England shipped thousands of convicts, men and women, young and old, first to the American colonies and then, after 1776, to the newly discovered territories that would come to be known as Australia. There they were bought and sold like slaves; sometimes starved to the point where stories of murder and cannibalism became somewhat commonplace; brutalized by whip and chain; frequently worked literally to death.[7] Twentieth-century models, by contrast —developed in the wake of psychoanalysis, in an era when the medical community was beginning to understand the role of genes in shaping personality and behavior—emphasized, at least theoretically, the individuality of prisoners and the importance of tailoring "treatment" models to the psychological makeup and personal history of each inmate.

At the back end of the prison system, parole and probation services were created to, in a sense, chaperone felons during the difficult days following their return to society after a felony sentence. The parole and probation officers were, in many ways, more social workers than law-enforcement personnel, helping clients find housing, employment, and other requirements thrown out by the free world. At the front end, inside the prison buildings and reformatory schools for teenage delinquents, armies of psychiatrists, psychologists, social workers, drug-treatment experts, teachers, classification specialists, and vocational trainers labored to transform their wards into productive, law-abiding citizens. They led anger-management classes, therapeutic communities, group counseling, individual counseling, parenting classes, correspondence-college courses, and numerous other programs.

"If we handle things right—and that is a considerable 'if'—if we handle things right, rehabilitation is going to be a key word in corrections. It is going to be the watchword," E. B. Whitten, the executive director of the National Rehabilitation Association, told a seminar in Washington, D.C., hosted by the Joint Commission on Correctional Manpower and Training, in December 1967. Whitten's colleague Mary Switzer, commissioner of vocational rehabilitation, was, if anything, even more enthusiastic. "Research in correctional rehabilitation can help solve one of the most serious problems facing our society today," she asserted. "One of the foremost correctional researchers has referred to correctional research as 'an elusive paradise.' If this is so, it is time to capture this elusive paradise." Not to be outdone, Myrl Alexander, director of the federal Bureau of Prisons, talked of a "ferment in corrections rising around the world," with the U.S. Peace Corps providing teachers for the children of prisoners in the Philippines, and with the U.S. attorney general asking a Bureau of Prisons member to sit on the Advisory Board of the U.S. Office of Education. It was, Alexander averred, positively "heartwarming."[8]

Thus it was that outside the Old South, which remained largely steeped in the brutal, agrarian prison practices of the nineteenth century, throughout the first two-thirds of the twentieth century the country was creating the core of a professionalized system based around centralized state correctional departments paying at least lip service to modern, even experimental, correctional theories. While some charismatic prison wardens, such as Joe Ragen of Illinois's Joliet penitentiary, continued to operate their own unaccountable mini-fiefdoms well into the 1960s,[9] state prisons were overall being tamed by the creation of comprehensive codes of conduct; professional training; minimum levels of education and experience for prison employees; accountability structures; and outside oversight mechanisms.

It was a change in keeping with alterations throughout American governance. As the United States moved into great-power and then superpower mode during the twentieth century, with all of the corresponding emphasis on a smoothly functioning state apparatus, massive state and federal bureaucracies sprang up to regulate all aspects of life. Bureaucracy is a critical component of the modern state, and more specifically of the successful, expansionist modern state. Similarly complex bureaucracies and regulatory agencies had been created in Victorian England, as the British Empire sought to spread its form of governance across the globe; in Napoleonic France; in Germany; in Soviet Russia, and in every other nation-state seeking to rein in its populace and make its domain more predictable while simultaneously expanding its power outward.

———•———

Professionalization was in full stride by the early 1960s. It was the age of technocratic liberalism, epitomized by President John Kennedy's determination that science combined with willpower could take men to the moon, and by Lyndon Johnson's perhaps more utopian belief that science combined with willpower could eradicate poverty and deprivation in the United States. Yet as the decade unfolded, it also became the age of pushing the political boundaries, of imagining ever more radical definitions of citizenship and of constitutional rights. As the language and political underpinnings of the civil rights movement began touching layer after layer of American life, a growing number of activists, reformers, and later, self-styled revolutionaries began crafting a philosophy of prisoners' rights. In essence, they started to refer to prisoners as a distinct political class with its own set of grievances and demands, and, increasingly, with the same constitutional protections and rights afforded other vulnerable individuals and groups. "We want freedom for all black men held in federal, state, county and city prisons and jails," read point eight of the Black Panther Party's ten-point platform, published in October 1966. "We believe that all black people should be released from the many jails and prisons because they have not received a fair and impartial trial."

Presented against a backdrop of startlingly swift social and legal change— one that had swept away the legal infrastructure of Jim Crow in the decade between *Brown v. Board of Education* and the passage of the Voting Rights Act, and had placed the rights of women, African Americans, Native Americans, Latinos, and gays at the heart of public-policy debate—the demands of the prisoners'-rights movement, in tandem with the professionalization process, spectacularly altered the United States' penal infrastructure.

In court ruling after court ruling from the early 1970s through the 1990s, despite Martinson's conclusions that rehabilitation was largely a waste of time and dollars, judges found that prisoners could not be treated simply as the state's chattel; that they were entitled to certain standards of health care and education; that they must be granted minimum amounts of privacy and adequate living space; that they had a right to a certain amount of programming designed to help rehabilitate them; that they could not be randomly assaulted by guards; that they could not be left to the mercies of armed prisoner-trustees; and that mentally ill prisoners were entitled to professional treatment. In a stinging mid-1970s ruling by federal judge Frank Johnson, Alabama's entire system was deemed cruel and unusual; Texas's use of an elite group of armed inmates to guard and discipline other prisoners was ruled unconstitutional; and so on. By 1987, estimated Al Bronstein of the ACLU, twenty-eight state correctional systems were under federal court orders to improve conditions. "You had this legal thrust for developing more programs," Bronstein explained. "There was no explicit right to rehab, but [there was] the reverse: a right not to be made worse. Not to be *de*habilitated."

If prisons were, as so many correctional officials believed, a reflection of society's broader values and tensions, it must have appeared to many in the late 1960s and early 1970s—if any confirmation were needed amid the chaos and upheaval of civil rights, the Vietnam War, and the counterculture—that American society was being convulsed by truly extraordinary changes. Once largely invisible to the broader public, prisoners had leapfrogged into the popular consciousness. Once an embarrassing but necessary social accoutrement, penitentiaries were now being denounced as Bastilles, housing, according to this radical critique, not so much garden-variety criminals as political prisoners. And prisoners themselves, from Attica in New York to Soledad in California, were organizing into something not unlike insurgent forces in a guerilla war. Once places of punishment, prisons were apparently on the way to becoming therapeutic communities—and under the orders of the judges themselves, notwithstanding Martinson's warnings and the hostility of large sections of the population and their elected representatives.

———

In the late 1970s, amid this maelstrom, Robert Martinson began to have his own Road to Damascus awakening. Despite a scrappy, and at times vitriolic, exchange with critics of his writings in the years following his *60 Minutes* interview, he was essentially an honest man. As more and more criticisms of his research began percolating out through articles in generally obscure journals, Martinson started to reexamine his original data, and also to investigate new rehabilitation programs. In 1979, beset by troubles in both his personal and professional life, he published an extraordinary mea culpa in the *Hofstra Law Review.* "Contrary to common belief, the rate of recidivism (reprocessing rate) in this country is not high, it is quite low. And, contrary to my previous posi-tion, some treatment programs *do* have an appreciable effect on recidivism." Regarding his "nothing works" finding, Martinson now wrote, "I withdraw this conclusion. I have often said that treatment added to the networks of crim-inal justice is 'impotent,' and I withdraw this characterization as well."[10]

By then, however, the Nothing Works movement had a life of its own. While the 1974 *Public Interest* article had catapulted Martinson into the spot-light, the *Hofstra Law Review* piece was a dud. Nobody in the wider political world paid the slightest bit of attention to it, and no one called Martinson for major TV interviews. In corrections, business went on as usual, which meant that, at the urging of legislators influenced by Martinson's earlier utterances, correctional systems continued to dismantle the infrastructure of inmate pro-grams developed over the previous decades almost as fast as (and later far faster than) the courts ordered more rehabilitation programming imple-mented. In fact, Robert Martinson soon came to realize that the only real im-pact his words had had was within the world of academe: seen as a flip-flopper, his credibility plummeted and he was eventually denied tenure by the City College of New York. He had gone from being the most famous name in cor-rections to being a middle-aged, untenured has-been.

In the winter of 1980, the storied author of "What Works?" opened the window of his ninth-floor Manhattan apartment building and, while his son looked on in horror, jumped to his death. His suicide went largely unnoticed. The media that had lionized him only five years earlier wasted barely any ink in covering his demise.[11]

———•———

Far from slowing down, as Martinson in the last years of his life had hoped it would, the move toward the warehousing model of mass incarceration—put-ting large numbers of people into increasingly bleak prisons for the simple purpose of keeping them away from the broader community—intensified in the years after his suicide.

In the years and decades following Martinson's emergence into the pub-lic spotlight in the mid-1970s, the tough-on-crime movement, in tandem with a growing societal impatience with the increasingly visible layer of misfits, deadbeats, and "undesirables" at the bottom of the social pyramid, provided increasingly conservative responses to core questions about the nature of crime and criminals and the appropriate methods of containment and pun-ishment. Laws such as the 1984 Sentencing Reform Act and the subsequent

Omnibus Drug Control Act largely eliminated judges' discretion in sentencing drug offenders, resulting in large numbers of low-end drug felons being
sent to prison for years and even decades. By the 1990s it had become common
for drug criminals, along with thousands of other repeat offenders in states
with so-called Three Strikes and You're Out laws, to receive longer sentences
than all but a handful of the top Nazis had received for war crimes in the
Nuremberg trials.[12] Albert Speer, one of Hitler's chief confidants, and Baldur
von Schirach, onetime head of the Hitler Youth, were both sentenced to serve
twenty years—a punishment regarded by prosecutors as being second in
severity only to the death penalty or life without parole—but by the early
twenty-first century, according to numbers generated by the Bureau of Justice
Statistics, one-third of all state-prison inmates, or over three hundred thousand Americans, were serving sentences at least that long, tens of thousands
of them for drug convictions or other nonviolent crimes.[13]

In 1997, mainly as a result of the growing number of people being sent to
federal prisons in the wake of these laws, the federal Bureau of Prisons budget
was found to have risen 1,400 percent since 1983.[14] At the same time, the FBI
reported that marijuana arrests had more than doubled between 1990 and
1997.[15] In much the same vein, the 1994 Omnibus Crime Control Act provided
states with financial incentives to eliminate early parole. During that same period, the federal death penalty was expanded to include a host of new crimes.
And in 1996, the Prison Litigation Reform Act made it far harder for prisoners to sue prison systems, far harder for publicly funded law offices to represent them, and far easier for prison systems to shake off federally mandated
oversight, thus encouraging corrections systems to try to evade the changes
mandated by courts over the past three decades.

The result of this spasm of legislative action has been an unprecedented
explosion in the country's prison population—one that seems to bear only
tangential relation to real crime rates and crime trends over time—along with
a cascading series of scandals involving either sadistic guards assaulting inmates or poor living conditions that undermine inmates' health and sanity.
"You're using a sledgehammer to kill a gnat," asserted David Zlotnick, a former federal prosecutor, now a professor at the Roger Williams Law School in
Rhode Island. "Change was needed, but the changes were incredibly excessive
and overly reliant on mandatory minimums. Virtually every judge, there's at
least one case they were involved in where they were appalled by the sentence
they had to give, because they had no discretion." In the 1990s in particular,
the result of the new laws was a fairly comprehensive move away from the re-

habilitation programs that many prison systems had implemented in the 1950s, 1960s, and 1970s, either of their own volition or, in the latter period, under federal court orders.

"We are operating in the mean season of correctional administration," testified Don Cabana, ex-warden at Mississippi's Parchman prison, at the 2005 Tampa hearings of the Commission on Safety and Abuse in America's Prisons. Cabana, a large, bald, tough guy with a folksy manner and a low tolerance for half-truths, had come to believe that the field he'd worked in for most of his adult life was heading in fundamentally wrong directions. "We've sold the public a bill of goods and we've diverted millions, billions of dollars," he told the Tampa audience. "For the first 150 years of American corrections, states built prisons on an as-needed basis, and they were fairly unplentiful. Now we build prisons as an economic engine. If you build the prisons, the prosecutors and the judges will fill them. The public bears as much responsibility as the politicians they've elected—and they need to be told that. In the Mississippi Delta, where it's not uncommon for the heat index to go up to 115 degrees, I'm prohibited from letting inmates have a lousy fan in a cell that is an inferno. That's unconscionable. There's no excuse for that. Good politics doesn't always make good public policy."[16]

In California, Jiru "Jerry" Enomoto, director of the state's correctional system for much of the 1970s, watched in wonder as the prison network over which he had presided mushroomed after his departure. "Even as one who was in the middle of all that, I find myself shocked at the rate of increase," he said decades later, sitting in his suburban tract house in northern Sacramento. Now a casual man in his late seventies, he wore a white V-neck T-shirt and soft-cloth jeans, his feet clad in brown suede slippers and his house cluttered with Buddha statues, Japanese paintings, heavy wooden furniture, and plants. "When I left we had twelve prisons; now we have in the upper thirties. One of the things that happens when a system grows at that rate, the growth is so fast you're not able to prepare enough staff. You place people in positions they're not ready for. You don't have enough people ready to assume responsibilities they get thrust into—and that has a lot to do with the management problems of recent years." Politically, Enomoto believed that the state, which had abolished the research wing of its corrections department and embraced a rather simplistic tougher-is-better philosophy, had taken serious wrong turns when it came to crime and punishment. "Stuff like three strikes is just another reflection of the 'Get tough on crime' attitude. The thing is overly encompassing and includes nonviolent offenders getting a lot of time they don't deserve.

The whole attitude behind it—building more maximum-security prisons— I have mixed feelings about all of that. You have to have facilities for managing some people. But the idea that most people need to be treated in that manner, that creates pessimism. The whole business is hard to be optimistic about, let's put it that way."

"The prison population was booming," Al Bronstein explained to me in 2005. "Which meant more money was needed for building prisons and locking people up and hiring more guards. Security always wins. We have 70 percent fewer educational programs in prisons today than we did fifteen years ago. We've cut back dramatically on the amount of money we spend on programs in prisons, at the same time as overall prison spending has risen."

From Colorado, a female inmate wrote of having to wait several weeks for medical evaluations after she fell and broke her ankle. "I am devastated and can't believe they let me be in pain w/o crutches or a wheelchair. Especially when the chow hall is in a separate building quite a distance away." From Virginia, a man who admitted to sexually abusing his daughter wrote that he could get only ten weeks of mental-health therapy despite being sentenced to twenty-nine years in prison. A female inmate in Troy, Virginia, recounted that "the officers will use force to strap the mentally ill down in 4 points in segreagation unit for them acting out due to there illnesses, and the woman don't understand why, when the force is used the officers will physically abuse the inmate then get the vido camera after. The officer will nag, pick, yell, call names anything to upsit the mentally ill inmates.... They treaten to use the tasers on us for every little thing. The broke a girl's nose last week for not standing for count." From the supermax prison in Tamms, Illinois, a seriously mentally ill inmate wrote of being held in segregation and "maybe every 30 days, if your lucky, does someone come around and talk to you. I saw them leave people in there cells for days who had feces smeared on there bodyes.... I get so mad sometimes I lose all control. Because of this behavior I now have 29 years of segration time."

In Nebraska, a Human Rights Watch report documented findings from 1996 suggesting that at least 11 percent of inmates had been raped while in prison, and perhaps double that number had been in some way pressured to have "sexual contact" against their will—an endemic crisis that could only have continued with the connivance of correctional officers, many of whom apparently turn a blind eye to prisoner-on-prisoner rape, using the fear it inspires as a way to control their institutions.[17] In Wyoming, the Western Prison Project reported in 2005, three correctional officers were fired and six more resigned after an abuse scandal at Rawlins penitentiary involving what outside investigators deemed to be "premeditated assaults" by guards on inmates.[18] At a private prison in Colorado, five guards were charged with having sex with female prisoners shipped in from Hawaii and other states. In the high-security prison of Phillips, Georgia, a 2001 class-action lawsuit alleged that guards routinely beat up prisoners with serious mental illnesses, kicking them, bashing their heads against concrete floors, and forcibly injecting them with the antipsychotic drug Haldol.[19] In Utah, a mentally ill inmate died in 1997 after being strapped nude into a restraining chair for sixteen hours.[20] And in Arkansas, at the end of 2005, the *Arkansas Democrat Gazette* reported that violent cell extractions of inmates, many of them mentally ill, had risen more than threefold between 2001 and 2005. In addition, the paper noted, officers had used pepper spray more than 750 times in the previous year, on an inmate population of 13,500.[21]

———•———

Somewhere along the way, American politics ceased to be shaped by the ideologies and bread-and-butter issues that had dominated U.S.—and indeed world—politics throughout most of the twentieth century. After the Soviet Union disintegrated and the United States' triumphant post–Cold War ascendancy began, the political economist Francis Fukuyama wrote a celebrated essay in which he trumpeted what he called "the end of history."[22] Fukuyama's assumption was that laissez-faire capitalism had so obviously won out, had so comprehensively routed alternative methods for organizing complex modern economies and cultures, that it had become an über-ideology, the uncriticized, almost unnoticed backdrop against which everything else, including politics, took place. It had, he seemed to suggest, almost become a constituent part of the human condition.

Denuded of the phrases and interpretive frameworks of more ideologically competitive eras, the United States' political debate in the 1990s degenerated into a series of "hard" versus "soft" propositions. Were those seeking public office hard on crime or soft? Were they hard on drugs and drug abusers or soft? Were they hard on welfare recipients and scroungers suckling at the public teat, or were they squidgy and soft? In such nonideological terrain—where difficult questions such as "Why are so many people left economically destitute and thus likely to commit a raft of economic crimes, and what social policies might alter this equation?" or "What deep-rooted societal problem is fueling the usage of addictive drugs?" simply have no place—the "hard" faction has huge structural advantages. After all, who wants to be soft and flabby when they can be hard and muscular? The simplistic world of the sound bite, the landscape carved by the rushing torrents of rant radio, is an inherently conservative terrain, impatient with long, complicated answers and technocratic policies, desirous of instant emotional gratification and no-nonsense headline solutions to large-scale problems. And it is as a part of this conservative terrain, creviced by decades of bitter declamations, that today's brutal incarceration megalith must be understood.[23]

CHAPTER 4

VICTIMS, FUNDAMENTALISTS, AND RANT-RADIO HACKS

For seventy-two-year-old Miriam Shehane, trapped in a web of heartbreak spun decades earlier when three young men in Birmingham, Alabama, kidnapped and murdered her daughter Gwynette, the harshness of modern prison conditions is nothing more or less than criminals' just deserts. One of Gwynette's murderers was executed in July 1990; as of 2005 the two others were still in prison.

"I would like to know that the two serving time in prison for killing my daughter have to think they're not in a place that is a place to reside with the comforts of home," Shehane said softly, the years of pain and suffering apparent in her eyes. "Are they able to touch [visitors]? I would hope not. I would like to know they had to pay for their housing. They should have to grow their own food." Generally speaking, the elderly lady asserted when we spoke in 2005, able-bodied prisoners should be sent out to work on the chain gang.

In a state with the worst guard–prisoner ratios in the country and a starting salary for guards not far above minimum wage; with prisons so dilapidated that raw sewage wells up into their yards after a rainstorm; with a ban on "perks" such as milk for adult prisoners; and with a thirty-year history of on-again-off-again federal court intervention against conditions repeatedly deemed cruel and inhumane—from rampant inmate-on-inmate murders to almost nonexistent medical care and extreme overcrowding—this wasn't an entirely unrealistic vision.

Drug treatment advocate Ralph Hendrix, sitting in an inner-city Birmingham office almost unfathomably cluttered with bric-a-brac—a battered horse saddle perched on an old computer, a stuffed peacock with a tie around its neck, a mannequin's head topped with a black cowboy hat, a poster from India, another from China—attributed the harshness of Alabama prison life in large part to the state's hardscrabble rural living conditions. In a city, Hendrix explained, pet owners, bound by the more delicate mores of urban living, generally take their sick animals to the vet to be "put to sleep." By contrast, "out in the country they'll just fucking shoot it in the head. It's such an easy transition to human beings, especially if they're black and poor and marginal. It's brutal. It's tooth and claw. It's very elemental. Those forces pull together and you come up with a very dark way of treating people." While prison policy is generally made in offices in state capitals, prisons themselves are usually located in rural areas, Hendrix argued; and in these areas, whatever the intentions of policymakers might be, in practice the less-sentimental culture of the countryside tended to hold sway.

Shehane lives in the austere state capital, Montgomery, about an hour's drive south from the city where her daughter had died. In the years following the December 1976 murder, she stopped working as a loan officer in a bank in the one-traffic-light hamlet of Clio, and became a full-time campaigner for what came to be known as "victims' rights." She founded an organization called Victims of Crime and Leniency (VOCAL), plastered its office walls with photos of murder victims—young and old, black and white, male and female—and devoted her waking hours to pushing the needs and rights of victims onto center stage.

In many ways, Miriam Shehane is an extraordinary woman. Instead of letting the murder of her twenty-one-year-old daughter destroy her, drag her off into a netherworld from which there could be no return, she had somehow found the emotional strength to use the lessons from her tragedy to help other victims, especially victims of violent crimes. When the legal machinery seemed indifferent to the needs of people who were hurting, or when bureaucracies failed to project simple human warmth to vulnerable individuals in need of sympathy and kindness, Miriam and her volunteers were there to fill the void. When courts dismissed cases on technicalities because a defendant's rights had been violated, VOCAL was there to protest on behalf of the victims. They proffered, in effect, shoulders to lean on for people whose lives and certainties had been shattered. "We never advocated taking one right away from the defendants," argues Miriam. "All we advocated was, by golly give us the same rights. We're trying to be there for the victim, let them know what their rights are, hold their hands and help them go through the system—because it isn't easy if you don't know anything about the judicial process."

Across the country, from the mid-1970s, as the backlash against the political liberalism of the 1960s intensified and the number of prisoners'-rights lawsuits increased, groups such as VOCAL began springing up. In 1975 Philadelphia's district attorney organized the country's first Victims' Rights Week to push for a stronger presence of victims' voices in the judicial process. In 1981

President Reagan proclaimed a national Victims' Rights Week. In 1983 a federal Office for Victims of Crime was established. And in 1986 the National Organization for Victim Assistance began pushing for state constitutional amendments to enshrine victims' rights in law. By the mid-1990s, a majority of states had passed these amendments.[1]

Had groups such as VOCAL restricted their activities to counseling victims, pushing for compensation funds, and working with prosecutors and court officials to humanize often-Kafkaesque judicial bureaucracies, their impact would have been unambiguously positive. Unfortunately, however, they did not limit themselves in this way. Over the decades, VOCAL became a key player in Alabama's increasingly conservative policy discussion around crime and punishment. Once district attorneys, politicians, and parole boards started turning to its members when shaping responses to crime and criminals, the organization was endowed with such a potent aura of righteousness that politicians could ignore it only at their peril. While injecting a level of emotion into the discussion that had long been lacking, VOCAL undermined in the process the ability to analyze data carefully and dispassionately, and displaced the reforms mandated by federal courts in the 1970s after a series of lawsuits had highlighted the massive shortcomings in Alabama's prison system. Shehane wasn't a bad person, but she was not a policy expert or criminologist, either. Yet, in the political climate of the 1980s and 1990s, voices such as hers trumped those of technocrats and court-appointed overseers who had spent decades researching the best ways to blend punishment and rehabilitation and shape a long-term response to crime that went beyond merely warehousing ever-larger numbers of criminals in ever-larger numbers of prisons in ever-harsher penal environments.

"It should be a shameful thing to be incarcerated—and it's not anymore. Crime has gotten so rampant that nobody thinks anything of it anymore—until they have been victimized. And then it's pretty serious when *you* become the victim. People are getting pretty tired of becoming the victim, and we're becoming more and more victimized," Shehane explained in the summer of 2005. Shehane believed that more prisoners, including rapists as well as killers, should be executed for their crimes, and younger criminals should be eligible for execution. "Alabama had an age limit of fourteen or fifteen and then a lot were taken off death row because of the Supreme Court ruling [that prisoners had to have been at least eighteen when they committed their crimes in order to qualify for the death penalty].[2] My position is if they do an adult crime, a fifteen-year-old knows what they're doing." In Shehane's mind, even a twelve-year-old who killed another person should receive, at the minimum, a life sentence without the possibility of parole. Should an eight-year-old get life without parole? "I don't know. I couldn't answer that question. A twelve-year-old, certainly. An eight-year-old, possibly not."

Like many in the victims'-rights world—people who spend their time surrounded by other victims, talking about victimhood, their outrage fueled by anecdote piled on anecdote—Shehane dismissed data from around the country indicating continual drops in crime rates, and violent crime in particular, over the previous decade. Indeed, she seemed almost to view such numbers as a conspiracy to deprive victims of their legitimate status. "I keep hearing that [crime rates are falling]. But I can't see it. We're in the courtroom all the time. I dare say there're not less people stealing from department stores. I question whether the crime rate is falling or not. I question whether it's all reported, because every town likes the crime rate to go down to attract business."

Shehane's attitude is not unique. During the time that crime rates were falling, other groups in other states likewise transformed themselves from essentially much-needed counselors of traumatized victims or family members into frontline policy warriors working to toughen the criminal-justice system. In 1978, Parents of Murdered Children was founded, as was the Crime Victims' Legal Advocacy Institute. In 1980, Mothers against Drunk Driving entered the scene, and, around the same time, Protect the Innocent was born. Most of the victims'-rights groups were founded by family members of murder victims and their core goals were good goals, supported by all sides of the political spectrum. Much of the work they did was extremely important—bringing relief to victims, humanizing bureaucratic responses to criminal activity, and finding ways to crack down on crime, particularly acts of violence. Yet too often their members ultimately came to play a political role that they simply didn't have the expertise to handle, and in so doing, they pushed the national discussion on criminal justice in a more conservative direction.

Not surprisingly, as the victims'-rights movement cohered into a potent political lobbying force, so the size of the prison population grew. Victims' groups pushed for longer sentences for convicted criminals and made it harder for prisoners to get early parole.

"Why is the prison population swelling? I think it is because of the victims'-rights movement," Shehane declared with satisfaction. "We've been so effective at the parole board that we have prison overcrowding now. It has a very positive effect for crime victims. It reduces the number of paroles." Over the decades, Shehane and VOCAL successfully lobbied for the creation of a statewide crime victims' compensation fund; the notification of crime victims and their families before a violent prisoner went up before the parole board; the right for the victims to testify before the parole board; changes to the laws regarding restitution of victims by their attackers; changes in the jury-selection process; the creation of habitual-offender laws; and a slew of other bits of legislation cumulatively intended to make the state appear tough on crime and punishment.

Miriam Shehane herself claimed to distinguish between violent and non-violent criminals; she was open to the notion that some drug offenders should be guided into treatment rather than incarcerated. Yet she was unambiguously proud that her movement had played a role in the massive expansion of Alabama's prison population—despite the fact that much of this expansion was due to relatively low-level, nonviolent offenders being sentenced to long prison terms under mandatory-sentencing and habitual-offender laws passed in large part as sops to the victims'-rights movement. In 1980 Alabama incarcerated 149 out of every 100,000 residents. By the end of 2003, according to researchers from Justice Strategies, a nonprofit criminal-justice organization based in New York, it was imprisoning 635 per 100,000, with much of the change due to an increased emphasis on locking up drug offenders. Between 1994 and 2003 alone, despite a 9 percent drop in crime, the state's prison population rose by over 40 percent, resulting in an overcrowding crisis so severe that local jails ended up having to house convicts for whom the prisons could find no room.[3]

———•———

When CNN's Bernard Shaw, moderating a debate between the presidential contenders in 1988, famously asked Massachusetts governor Michael Dukakis, the Democratic challenger, whether he would want a perpetrator who raped and killed his wife to be executed, it was, of course, a set-up question.[4] In such a setting, the only appropriate answer to such a hypothetical question is something to the effect of "I'd want to rip the bastard's guts out and drape them over his head before finishing him off with a blast from a shotgun." Making matters worse for the Democrat, the debate was held at a time when the George H. W. Bush team was running ads accusing Dukakis of being weak on crime, featuring a black man named Willie Horton who had been released from a Massachusetts prison on furlough and gone on to rape a white woman in her suburban home. But it is precisely because questions like these tend to generate such extraordinarily emotional responses, often antithetical to good public policy, that the architects of modern criminal-justice systems around the world sought to depersonalize the processes of law and order—to insert the courts and the prisons as impersonal arbiters of justice. Revenge is the purview of private emotion; justice, argued thinkers such as Benjamin Rush, the Declaration signer, psychiatrist, and penal reformer, is another beast altogether.

This is not to say that serious crimes don't merit very serious responses. On the contrary; for social order to prevail, punishment of violent crimes in particular must be robust. However, there's a difference between a robust punishment, its exact parameters determined by democratic debate, and a simply vengeful one. Putting someone in prison for decades may well make good policy sense in these circumstances, ensuring that a dangerous criminal is off the streets, in a secure setting where he cannot hurt others. In contrast, dismembering the murderer in public and then desecrating his body, while perhaps appealing to certain base instincts, is likely only to brutalize the broader society, making violence more, rather than less, acceptable and commonplace. Privilege these instincts over the more detached responses of a criminal-justice system, and punishment all too rapidly becomes the purview of the mob. In such circumstances, the punishers themselves start acting criminally and the meted-out punishments become new crimes.

Yet in the world of the sound bite and the emotional arena built by the victims'-rights movement, a conflation of vengeance and punishment has occurred. In this context, Dukakis, a lifelong opponent of capital punishment, came across in his reply as weak, almost emasculated. With no space to distinguish between what he, as a mourning husband, would personally want and what he, as a responsible politician, would promote as good public policy, the Democrat fell into Bush's trap (aided in this case by the moderator), appearing irremediably "weak" or "soft" on crime.

Virtually everyone agrees that a killer should be severely punished; disputes largely center on whether the death penalty or a long prison sentence is most appropriate. However, as the so-called war on crime pushed ever more coercive responses to increasingly low-level crimes, especially those related to drugs, in the 1980s and 1990s the United States ought to have witnessed a vigorous public debate. After all, it costs upward of twenty thousand dollars a year to house a low-end inmate in a state prison. Putting a local screwup or habitual nuisance behind bars for years at a stretch might feel good to righteous, law-abiding citizens, but it comes with a hefty price tag. Multiply that decision a millionfold (there are over a million nonviolent prisoners currently behind bars in the United States)[5] and the hefty price tag becomes astronom-ical. In essence, the feel-good approach to punishment and the impulse to make public policy simply according to what is popular has led to an absurd-ist level of imprisonment that is literally destroying the basis of public finance in many states.

In Alabama, Judge Pete Johnson, the head of Birmingham's drug court, told me in disgust, drug addicts unlucky enough to be tried in rural areas lack-ing drug courts and nearby drug-treatment facilities are routinely locked away for extraordinary periods of time. "We have people in prison for possession of Valium without a prescription. If they're an old druggie, they may get fifteen years. In Alabama, we've got *real* tough drug laws." Under the state's habitual-offender law, Johnson continued, if a person has two prior felonies and is then convicted of any amount of drug possession—even a single joint's worth of marijuana—he is automatically sentenced to ten years to life; if he has three prior felonies the sentence is fifteen years to life. Or, since so much of the criminal-justice system comes down to a crapshoot, these are the mandated sentences *unless* the offenders are lucky enough to live in a county that runs a drug court. These courts run on a parallel track to regular criminal courts, and generally serve to divert nonviolent drug offenders into community treatment programs rather than jails and prisons. Hence, many repeat drug offenders in Birmingham now end up in treatment, while those charged with similar crimes in rural counties that lack the money for drug courts end up sentenced to years, even decades, behind bars.

"It costs a lot of money," Johnson says. "It makes them worse if you give 'em a long period of time. If you leave 'em in prison a long period of time they become institutionalized, dependent on the system—and it becomes a vicious, revolving cycle. We have at least twice as many people in prison as we should. At least. We've got twenty-seven thousand in prison. We should have maybe eight to ten thousand. But politicians in this state get elected by being 'tough on crime.'"

———·———

Mass incarceration is a uniquely American form of hedonism, a carceral out-growth of the pleasure-me movements of the 1960s. If, at a gut level, it feels good to lock people away for vast stretches of time, the rant-radio shills and the school of fundamentalist preachers who proclaim eternal damnation es-sentially argue, why shouldn't we indulge ourselves? With our historic impa-tience with limits, our contempt for barriers to fulfilling our dreams and our desires, we are, in fact, a society ripe for mass incarceration. So long as the majority demands increasingly coercive policies toward the numerical minority, like as not those coercive policies will strut center stage at some point. Similarly, if it satisfies some political itch or another to dismantle welfare programs that provide safety nets to the most destitute among us, why not go ahead and indulge?

"We don't have any poor people. They're invisible," says Jim Estelle, a weather-beaten, hard-bitten former director of the Texas Department of Criminal Justice, sarcastically as he sits in his garden in 2005, shortly before leaving on an annual fishing expedition with his son. Estelle is a staunch conservative on most issues, yet in his critique of conservative approaches to punishment and incarceration, he almost sounds like a radical. " 'Everybody can get medical care. Everybody can get a free education.' But you and I know it's bullshit. The prevalence of bullshit. We've deluded ourselves as a community into believing we provide a free education for everyone, equal opportunity for everyone who wants to apply. And there are people in the community who believe that to such a degree they ignore who's in prison. It's crazy. We're absolutely upside down. Prisons really are a microcosm of the community that produces the prison population. If you're white, Anglo-Saxon Protestant and rich, you *ain't* going to prison. We do stupid things, and it's politically driven, clear and simple."

The instant-gratification message of the 1960s counterculture, twisted and mangled and filtered of all progressive content by radio shock jocks and others in the 1980s and 1990s, produced a truly unique spectacle. What emerged in the United States during these decades was a dynamic, impatient, even radical form of conservatism—a hurricane of demagoguery, indignation, rage, and longing for a romanticized past that swamped functional social policies developed over decades and even centuries.

As America swung rightward, the demagoguery intensified. The Republican Party, having made profound inroads in the South since the civil rights era, used its newfound support to craft powerful national coalitions, binding together economic conservatives from the North and West with social conservatives and Bible Belt fundamentalists from the South. Ronald Reagan liked to bandy about the notion that "welfare queens" were living high on the hog off state largesse. Christian conservative and Republican Party stalwart Pat Robertson, founder of the influential 700 Club, wrote in his book *The New World Order*, "How can there be peace when drunkards, drug dealers, communists, atheists, New Age worshipers of Satan, secular humanists, oppressive dictators, greedy money changers, revolutionary assassins, adulterers, and homosexuals are on top?"[6] From his pulpit in Lynchburg, Virginia, Jerry Falwell, Robertson's closest competitor for leadership of the political wing of the Protestant fundamentalist audience, repeatedly urged that state schools be dismantled and education be taken over by churches. He chastised children's TV shows for their hidden homosexual messages; and, after the terrorist attacks of September 11, 2001, blamed "pagans, and the abortionists, and the feminists, and the gays and the lesbians who are actively trying to make that an alternative lifestyle, the ACLU, People for the American Way—all of them who have tried to secularize America—I point the finger in their face and say 'you helped this happen.'"[7]

Republicans in the post–civil rights era don't overtly talk about race, but they increasingly *do* promote a quintessentially social Darwinist economic vision, one that, historically, has had a particular potency in the states of the Old South. This has involved pushing a cutthroat economic model of low taxes, low wages for working-class employees, anti–trade union rules, deregulation, and underinvestment in public infrastructure, all of which has had the effect of locking into place a desperately poor, often black underclass. As icing on the cake, Republicans increasingly have used the moralistic framework of conservative Christianity to blame the poor for the conditions in which they live, rather than seeking structural explanations and solutions to their problems. That the poor in question tend to be black while their audience tends to be white hasn't always hurt the Republicans' political prospects, for while the South is far from monolithic, illiberal racial sentiments still find their way into cultural and political debates in the region, especially in rural areas.

This demagoguery, in turn, by promoting the idea that the society was besieged by moochers and cultural vandals, further fueled the national move rightward. "What is really at stake is whether or not America will allow the cultural high ground in this nation to sink slowly into an abyss of slime to placate people who clearly seek or are willing to destroy the Judaic-Christian foundations of this republic," North Carolina senator Jesse Helms fulminated in 1990, during one of his tirades against continued federal funding for the supposedly liberal National Endowment for the Arts. Something approximating a self-sustaining mechanism was set in place, in which conservative cultural sentiments generated conservative economic and social policies that, in turn, helped to generate the conditions of economic malaise, social crisis, and rage that provided fodder for more conservative sentiments; which then helped—in an epoch in which progressive political groupings were hopelessly adrift and seemed unable to hit home electorally—to nudge the center of policy debates still further to the right.

Arguably, in no arena was this more apparent than in the racially, emotionally, and increasingly religiously charged realm of crime and punishment.

"I think punishment is biblical," Shehane, a lifelong Baptist, explained to me in Montgomery, after a morning meeting of the three-person Crime Victims' Compensation Commission, which hears from victims of violent crime and their survivors and allocates to them limited financial compensation. Shehane firmly believed in an eye for an eye—believed, in fact, that pushing the strongest possible punishments for criminals was practically a religious obligation. "I always analyze when Jesus was hanging on the cross. And he said there was redemption but he also wouldn't tell the thief that he shouldn't pay for his crime. I also hope the three who killed my daughter ask God for forgiveness and do not spend an eternity in hell. Because that would be the ultimate punishment. I know everybody can get forgiveness from God. But if they do, they should know they have to pay for what they did. And, regardless of whether they do or not, there should be punishment. There are some crimes where the rehabilitation cannot override the punishment. And I take offense to those who call that revenge."

———————

In ages of angst, those who talk the shrillest talk too often become pied pipers, luring their followers into a political trap. In the 1930s, Louisiana governor Huey Long garnered a huge following with his populist tirades and simplistic promises of quick fixes for the country's economic woes. So too did the fascist radio broadcaster Father Coughlin. In the 1950s, as fear of Communism grew, demagogues like Senator Joe McCarthy seized the political spotlight with a bilious brew of half-truths, slanders, and endless insinuations about fellow travelers and treasonous bureaucrats. In the 1980s and 1990s, as globalization and deindustrialization ripped at the economic fabric of America's industrial heartland, it fell to the radio shock jocks and conservative TV talk-show hosts, as well as a plethora of highly politicized fundamentalist preachers, to harvest the rage and direct the fury outward.

In the late twentieth and early twenty-first centuries, no matter who was president, no matter who controlled Congress, no matter how conservative the country got, the litany of problems was always the same for these frenzied orators: too many liberal politicians; too many liberal courts; too many liberal so-called "experts" standing in the way of commonsense solutions to grave social crises; too many taxes funding too many government programs for an array of social leeches; too many secularists undermining traditional religious and cultural values; too many dope peddlers and criminals corrupting children and making Main Street America unlivable. Before a highly publicized scandal revealed that Rush Limbaugh had maintained an expensive painkiller habit for the better part of a decade, the scion of conservative talk radio routinely argued that drug addicts should be incarcerated wholesale, arguably even killed. When critics pointed out that the drug laws disproportionately impacted black Americans, Rush told his audience that this just meant "too many whites are getting away with drug use." Former education secretary and then drug czar Bill Bennett—who, years later, had to publicly admit to a gambling problem—made a name for himself by penning jeremiads about the country's perilous moral decline. During a TV interview, Bennett argued that there was nothing wrong in principle with a caller's suggestion that drug dealers should be beheaded.[8]

———•———

Too often, these grotesque excesses of the rant-radio brigade and their counterparts in the world of television are dismissed as the culture simply letting off steam, as humorous tirades that aren't meant to be taken entirely seriously. Yet every week an estimated 14 million Americans tune in to Limbaugh, 12 million more listen to Sean Hannity, and 8 million turn the dial to "Dr. Laura" Schlesinger. Millions more listen to G. Gordon Liddy and the host of other Rush wannabes. In many parts of the country, right-wing rant radio provides virtually the only window on world events. On any given day, 8 million people watch Rupert Murdoch's Fox News, on which Hannity and the pit-bull conservative Bill O'Reilly hammer away at their pet themes.[9] Day in and day out, these listeners and viewers are fed a diet of vitriol that would put some paranoid schizophrenics to shame.

For over a quarter of a century, commentators have made names for themselves with flamboyant proposals that, while impractical and often unconstitutional, sound good in fifteen-second sound bites. Some have called for the wholesale internment of addicts in camps in the western deserts. Others have advocated mandatory "one strike and you're out" life sentences for violent offenders. They urge wholesale expansions of the death penalty, corporal punishment, and chain gangs, castration for rapists, and an end to all visitation rights for prisoners. Criminals, in this universe, without differentiation are scum, they are subhuman, they are animals, they are monsters. Listeners who lack personal acquaintance with felons, and who might not see a difference between a burglar, for example, and a killer, might well take these diatribes at face value.

Responding to the wishes of voters nurtured on the pearls of wisdom thrown up by Limbaugh and his peers, serious politicians have, over the last few decades, stampeded away from rehabilitation-based correctional theories nurtured to maturity from the birth of the Enlightenment onward. In the 1980s and 1990s state and federal legislators repeatedly stepped in to usurp the discretion of judges in drug cases; to mandate long sentences; to eradicate early parole for prisoners who showed evidence of having reformed themselves behind bars; to take away "perks" such as education, drug-rehabilitation programming, and visitation rights (despite evidence that these are precisely the things most likely to lower prisoners' recidivism); to banish ex-offenders from many kinds of employment; to declare people convicted of drug felonies ineligible for most forms of welfare, government-funded student loans, and public housing. They voted for massive expansions in the budgets of prison systems, even as state funds for higher education, food stamps, subsidized housing, and other public services wilted.

In 1980 Texas had 28,543 prisoners; a quarter century later it had more than 165,000 inmates. California's incarcerated population rose from 21,000 in 1978 to 165,000 in the early twenty-first century. Similar trends held in other big states, such as New York and Florida. So, too, were the smaller states caught up in this societal tsunami. Oklahoma's incarcerated population in 1980 was 1,746. By the early 2000s, it was well over 20,000 and a total of more than 57,000 Oklahomans were either behind bars or on parole or probation. Alaska's prison population rose by more than 60 percent between 1993 and 2002 alone. Even tiny North Dakota, a state with one of the lowest incarceration rates in the country, saw its prison population double between 1994 and 2002. At the federal level, the change was still more stark, with the Bureau of Prisons population rising from 24,252 in 1980 to over 188,000 twenty-five years later.[10]

At the same time, as the number of prisoners was skyrocketing, from the local level up to the presidential, America's political leaders increasingly defined the function of prisons as punishing social miscreants rather than attempting to rehabilitate them and prepare them for a successful, law-abiding transition back into society. In his 1996 book *Between Hope and History*, President Bill Clinton boasted of having successfully prodded Congress to pass federal "three strikes" laws and of requiring federal prisoners to serve 85 percent of their sentences before being eligible for parole.[11] Republican senator Phil Gramm told an audience at a campaign stop in Iowa that same year that he wanted "to stop building prisons like Holiday Inns. I want to take out the color TVs and weight rooms. I want to turn our prisons into industrial parks."[12]

"Prisons are not crowded," announced a state senatorial candidate in Hawaii that same election season. "This is a shibai [sic] created by criminal-coddling judges who care more about the comfort of criminals than community safety. The solution is to impeach the judges who twist the meaning of cruel and unusual punishment."[13]

———•———

Miriam Shehane herself hadn't put anyone in prison for the rest of his or her life; but indirectly, and arguably unintentionally, her grief and the grief of countless thousands of other victims and relatives of victims had opened the door to political changes that ultimately resulted in the prolonged, often life-long incarceration of hundreds of thousands of individuals. Some of these men and women *were* extremely violent, but many others were not, being instead neighborhood nuisances, addicts, and low-end but habitual offenders—repeatedly arrested for drug crimes, welfare fraud, property offenses committed to fund untreated addictions, and other selfish but not deadly activities—against whom the waves of the victims'-rights movement were now relentlessly crashing.

For Shehane, the sense of victimization would never, *could never* stop. Through the victims'-rights movement, she had created a monument to her murdered daughter. To stop working on the issue would be, in the profoundest way possible, to cease tending to her daughter's memory. "I think, how much longer can I go on? And should I devote more time to my grandchildren and my living children and my husband? And yet I still see so many crime victims that justice does not prevail. I started a one-woman crusade in Gwynette's memory," recalled Miriam. "Because her killing made no sense. I guess I do it to try to make some sense out of it—because my first reaction to her death is, 'There's got to be a reason.' And I guess this is the only reason I can come up with."

In this realm of emotion and catharsis, the criminal-justice system can never truly focus on rehabilitation; it can only ever really be about punishment. When victims, amply backed up by the rant-radio shills, become an identity group with the distinct demands and needs of any other identity group, and when enough people define themselves politically as *victims,* elected officials will always have much to gain and little to lose by portraying themselves as surpassingly tough and unsentimental when it comes to crime and punishment. The long-term economic and societal costs of punitive policies such as "three strikes and you're out" are simply not of interest in this context. "The victims'-rights movement created pretty much a storm in the eighties," explained Shehane. "It's taken a long, hard road to gain that recognition and that respect."

CHAPTER 5

REDUCTIO AD ABSURDUM

At 7:35 a.m., after eating their breakfast rations—inedible-looking low-grade salami, bologna, ham, and turkey sandwiches, a cracker, some milk, and a small piece of fruit—the fifteen women of the Maricopa County Jail chain gang shuffle off the bus, tethered in groups of five. It's a routine they're used to: the bus, emblazoned with the words "Sheriff's Chain Gang," presumably so that drivers on the interstate know exactly what their sheriff is spending their money on, brings them the twenty miles west on I-10 from the main jail in Phoenix several times a month. Slowly, they head toward the blue portable toilet at the edge of the county's unromantically named White Tanks cemetery for paupers.

One at a time, the women step into the plastic room, the chain trailing off their ankle and through the door, keeping it from fully closing. The rest of the crew stand clustered a couple feet back; every bodily noise emanating from the chamber is audible. "If we start thinking they're taking too long," explains Officer J. C. Hale, the ever jovial supervisor of the female chain gang, who spent the breakfast hour telling his charges about his recent trip to Mexico, "we say, 'Come on! Hurry up!' "

Inside, someone has etched into the plastic toilet-paper holder a lone cry of protest: "Fuck off." There doesn't seem to be much else to say.

———•———

Fifteen minutes after the crapping-and-pissing expedition began, the prisoners are lined up in three columns of five, and begin their slow march around the chain-link fence perimeter of the cemetery's arid expanse. At 8:07 they arrive at the far corner to greet the contents of the green minivan, driven by a large African American mortician, and another hearse, which has just pulled up. Inside the vehicles are stacked, like boxes of produce, four shapeless blue chipboard coffins. The women stand still, facing a row of open graves cut into the dry, orange-brown Arizona earth. Behind them are four huge concrete slabs, to be placed atop the coffins after they have been lowered into the earth, presumably to ensure that the dead remain exactly where these women have buried them.

The women wait silently, in heat that is fast heading toward one hundred degrees, until 8:30, at which time the for-hire chaplain and the ancient nun with the holy water arrive in the chaplain's old white Pontiac Sunbird to utter a few perfunctory words read from a red Bible with a gold cross on its cover, and to sprinkle the earth with blessed liquid, while the prisoners painfully, painstakingly, lower the large coffins into the ground. Each team takes a turn, then steps back while their colleagues tackle the next coffin. In their black-and-white-striped uniforms, the back of their coarse shirts embossed with the huge logo "Sheriff's Inmate," the sweating, unkempt women—white, Hispanic, Native American, but on this month's roster no African Americans—look like characters in an early-twentieth-century movie about life in the Old South.

As they work, manually lowering the coffins onto pulley systems and then winching the coffins six feet down, pairs of fighter jets, F-16s and F-18s, from the nearby Luke Air Force Base, soar into the desert-blue sky overhead, their wings almost touching, the noise deafening. Some of the women cry as they bury these anonymous, unwanted dead. Others just look blank.

Chaplain Chapman, an old man wearing a short-sleeved brown shirt, dark pants, and gray shoes, is perfunctory in his duties. "Good morning," he drones monotonically as the first burial gets under way, the name of the dead man inked in pen on the side of the coffin. "This is the day the Lord has made. Let us be glad. This gentleman's name is Edward Shinkle. He was born on September 18, 1944. Let us pray." He quickly, formulaically recites the Lord's Prayer, after which the wrinkled old nun with the flip-up sunshades aggressively sprinkles holy water on Shinkle's coffin. Between the second and third burials, as the chained prisoners stand and sweat, Chapman turns to them and quickly blesses them for doing the Lord's work.

The hypocrisy is so raw it literally takes my breath away.

———•———

The day I visited, the chain gang had risen from their beds inside the Estrella Jail—unlike some of their peers, who sleep in tents, these women were housed in proper cells—before 5:00 a.m. At 5:21, Officer Hale had ordered them to "fall out" into a military-type formation in the hallway outside their cells. After their uniforms had been inspected, they marched down the staircase into the common area on the ground floor, along which other inmate-workers had lined the three chains. In groups of five, the women stepped forward, put their left ankles out, and stood still while the chain was looped around their black boots and fastened by an inmate-trustee with a large padlock. It was all done without any violence, any force, almost like an impersonal medical procedure.

Then, in formation, the women had shuffle-marched outside to the waiting bus, chanting in unison, "Left, left. Left, right, right, left" as they went. "We see it as a chance for the girls, the ladies, to actually complete something for themselves," Hale explained to me as they prepared to drive away from the jail, the early-morning sun just starting to rise over the low-lying buildings.

Surprisingly, at least in the presence of their guards, many of the women seemed to agree with Hale's analysis.

"It's the structure," said one shackled inmate.

"I needed something different," offered another.

"Teaches you responsibility," muttered a third.

Gradually, though, the comments became more hostile.

"Sometimes it's a little embarrassing. People drive by, laugh, and take photos. Every day, at least one or two people. You learn humility on the chain gang. It's very humiliating, makes you not want to come back." And then, a heavy-set young woman with mouse-brown hair tied up in a black scrunchie, her face pitted with acne, spat out that the whole thing made her feel "like an idiot. Like a piece of garbage. It's humiliating. We hate it all the time. I don't believe in it. I wouldn't put my dog on a chain gang. How can you look a person in the eye and put a chain on them?"

Later that morning, after burying the dead, the sweating, exhausted women march back around the cemetery, along a convoluted route that eventually returns them to their bus.

"Mark time. You got your mark, put your hand out, get that spring. Once you start marching, look forward at the back of the head [of the woman in front of you]," shouts Officer Hale. Then his tone changes to one of jovial, cloying familiarity. "Here we go. March time, march. Forward march!" And the women, their black army-surplus boots worn at the heels, many with full-scale holes, shuffle forward under the hundred-plus-degree sun, several of them stumbling most unmilitarily over their chains. They march past decades of anonymous paupers' graves, some with little brass-circle markers etched with a name and a date, most just marked by an anonymous white plastic rod. Hale ramps up the bonhomie.

"Mind the chains. You don't want to fall," he says earnestly as the women clank across the desert. "Your turns are looking really good," he exclaims, as they execute a right-angle turn without falling over their shackles.

I'm not sure which is a more lonely fate: to be condemned to bury strangers while chained at the ankle and guarded by gun-wielding, offensively stupid officers, or to die alone and unmissed—perhaps after years of cycling in and out of the criminal-justice system—and spend eternity buried in this miserable excuse for a cemetery, your rest continually violated by the sonic booms of fighter jets catapulting through the sound barrier above.

———·———

The members of Maricopa County's chain gang are all ostensibly "volunteers," having chosen the work detail in lieu of being sent into Administrative Segregation, known as "the Hole," as a punishment for minor rule infractions such as smoking in the jail yard, wearing nonregulation clothing, spitting. Sheriff Joe Arpaio, the self-proclaimed "toughest sheriff in America," is good at manufacturing "volunteers" for his chain gangs, the key component of his endless self-promotion efforts. A gruff former federal narcotics agent, first elected by the citizens of metropolitan Phoenix in 1992, Arpaio, who was seventy-three in 2005, distinguishes himself by making the rules more petty than those in other jails, making it all but inevitable that inmates will break them. He then offers them the alternatives of isolation or the chain. In a way, it's simply a parallel process to the broader expansion of the United States' use of incarceration in recent decades—ever more trivial offenses are categorized as imprisonable crimes, resulting in a ballooning incarceration rate despite roughly constant crime and addiction rates. It's a dog-and-pony show intended solely to magnify Arpaio's macho image for his electorate—and it works.

Over the years, as a result of the chain gang and various other actions guaranteed to raise the hackles of groups—*liberal* groups—such as the American Civil Liberties Union, no lawman in America has received more press, more sensational publicity than Joe Arpaio. And as he knows all too well, virtually no publicity is bad publicity. Arouse the wrath of civil liberties organizations, get the city and the county, the state, and the feds to open investigations into your practices, and as long as the message is "Arpaio's getting tough with the criminals," chances are the electorate will lap it up. The uncomfortable truth, however, is that the convicted inmates in the jail are generally little more than local screwups and misfits, people arrested on misdemeanor charges such as vagrancy, drug possession, shoplifting, petty theft, and stealing from cars; and the not-yet-convicted, while they might be accused of far more serious crimes, are, in the eyes of the law, not yet guilty and therefore not yet actually serving time. In fact, in a conservative climate, in which rant-radio hacks and right-wing rabble-rousers hold increasing sway, getting berated by the ACLU is a badge of honor. So, too, apparently, is being investigated by the local U.S. attorney's office, the Justice Department, and the Internal Affairs bureau, all of which have looked into allegations of wrongdoings by the sheriff's department since Arpaio took charge in the early 1990s.[1]

The chain gang was initially reserved for male inmates. Then Arpaio created the female version, and he has even considered creating a chain gang for juveniles. In one notorious incident, he paraded his male inmates around in fluorescent pink underwear while moving them into a new housing unit. Then there are the Korean War army-surplus canopied tents, their sides open to the elements, in which he houses thousands of prisoners on row after row of double-bunked cots, there to bake in the summer and freeze in the winter. If the female inmates in Tent City, as Arpaio christened the place, need to use the toilet at night, they have to traipse across the yard and into the main building. The men's area is dotted with portable toilets.

The food in the Maricopa County jail system is almost inedible. Arpaio boasts that each inmate meal costs his jail only twelve cents; much of it is donated, and some appears, according to those who have eaten it, unfit for human consumption. "It costs more to feed our dogs and cats," he states happily. And even if the inmates wanted to eat it, there's not much to eat: Arpaio provides his inmates with only two meals a day. Salt, pepper, coffee, and smoking are all banned. There's the prohibition on inmates having radios and the ban on inmates writing letters to people on the outside. (Instead they can send postcards with a picture of the chain gang on the front.) At one point there was a much-trumpeted decision to end face-to-face visits between inmates and their friends and family; the glass barriers that had previously separated visitors were replaced with rusty metal plates, and nowadays the visits are carried out over old telephones.[2] Today, inmates who are parents aren't even allowed to touch their babies when the children are brought to visit.

"Mom and Dad were putting drugs into the diapers, and the babies were muling the drugs in," declares the officer taking me on a tour of the jail. There's an aggressive, almost jubilant undertone to her voice, as if the babies themselves were the enemy.

In large part because of these ongoing creative stunts, Arpaio has become an electoral powerhouse, a maker and breaker in Maricopa County politics. In 1996, four years after his first election, potential opponents looked at his

85 percent approval ratings and shied off from campaigning against him; he won reelection unopposed. In 2000 he won handily again, and in 2004, even after reformers successfully spotlighted his dubious practices and ran a bare-knuckles campaign against him, he still beat his opponent, Dan Saban, by a comfortable 14 percent. Admittedly, turnout was low—in a county with close to 3 million residents, Arpaio got 106,269 votes to Saban's 80,938—but a clear majority of those who *were* motivated to vote wanted more of the same from their tough-man sheriff.[3]

On the nineteenth floor of the Wells Fargo building, in the heart of ultra-modern downtown Phoenix, Sheriff Arpaio holds court. Unlike most sheriffs, whose offices are in the county jail complex, Arpaio operates like the CEO of a major corporation. The waiting area of his office is paneled with expensive wood, and on the wall of the receptionist's room hangs a huge blowup of a magazine cover photo of Arpaio, emblazoned with the tag line "Crime Never Pays." On a table are four trophies, three for sports contests the sheriff's team has won, and the fourth, festooned with the Stars and Stripes, etched with the words, "Champion for Decency: Sheriff Joe Arpaio."

Arpaio himself sits in a vast office, behind the sort of desk a millionaire financier might occupy. He is a fat man in a short-sleeved blue shirt, a red patterned tie with a silver pistol tiepin, and dark slacks. "We have the only female chain gang in the history of the world," he blusters, the inanity of the claim almost being canceled out by the force with which he utters it. "Nobody in the history of the world has had women hooked together in chain gangs. We've done it eight years. No problem. They love it."

And why do it?

"Common sense, number one. Number two, when I grew up, which is many years ago, if I did something wrong they took away my radio—so I could not hear *The Green Hornet*. If you did something wrong, you took away privileges and were punished. So I can't understand why nobody wants to use the word 'punish' when people are in jail. If you do something wrong, you should be punished. I understand the criminal mind. When you go to jail, you should never live better than in the Ritz-Carlton hotel. Very simple philosophy." Like the Victorian tough-on-crime brigade, Arpaio is preoccupied with the notion of less eligibility. "There are many people that love to give up their liberty," he warns darkly. "Because they can get good food, live free."

What makes this somewhat oafish character interesting to me isn't his tough posturing per se; it's the fact that the electorate laps up the posturing. Arpaio has become a master of mass psychology, pandering to a collective desire for spectacular punishment, and in so doing, becoming a massive political force in the Phoenix area. Only Los Angeles County and Illinois's Cook County have sheriff-controlled jail systems larger than that over which the Maricopa County sheriff holds sway. Arpaio's humiliation rituals and "make the bastards work" philosophy taps into a well of public anger, an anger the media and politicians have fueled over the past few decades with the increasing, albeit largely misleading, emphasis on rising crime rates and a rampaging criminal underclass. And there *is* something deeply, viscerally seductive about Arpaio's methods. After all, why shouldn't the bastards be put to work on a chain gang, why shouldn't the bastards shiver a little at night, why shouldn't the bastards fight waves of nausea when presented with disgusting food, and why shouldn't they be left to crave even the brief touch of a baby's hand on their cheeks? It is, Arpaio repeats, almost as a mantra, just good old-fashioned common sense, the self-evident principle of less eligibility in action.

"The reality is stark," wrote the sheriff in 1996, in his autobiography–cum– political screed *America's Toughest Sheriff: How We Can Win the War against Crime.* "Either the good guys will prevail and restore some sense of decency and honor and respect to our society, or the bad guys will come out on top and destroy everything we hold dear.... Win or lose. Right or wrong. Good guys versus bad guys. Sometimes life is that straightforward."[4] He is, he argues, simply reinjecting salt-of-the-earth intuitions into a criminal-justice arena hijacked during the liberal 1960s and their aftermath by technocrats, radicals, and intellectuals. "I'm elected. I *only* report to the 3.5 million people who live in the county," he explains to me. "So I can't be fired except by the voters. If I wanted to put inmates in pink underwear, which I did six years ago, if I'd had to report to a mayor that pink underwear would have taken five years to set up. I did it in an hour. I will take that chain gang and put it on Market Street in San Francisco, I'll put it anywhere and I will survive. That's how confident I am in these programs. Voters like it everywhere. I'm on thousands of talk shows. I never get a negative. I get letters from all over the world—and I answer every one. They say, "Come up here and be our sheriff.""

For over a decade, voters and conservative cheerleaders have eagerly absorbed this self-promotional nonsense. Commentators who know nothing about the myriad sociological theories of crime and punishment sit down with the sheriff, roll up their sleeves, and, safe from the feminizing influences of liberalism, get down to real man-to-man talk. After their conversations, when they write up Arpaio and his jail—over the years, the sheriff, one of America's truly great media whores, claims to have been the subject of more than fifteen hundred profiles, many of them little more than hagiographies —they send forth breathy stories about how the Wild West and the crime-fighting posse still live. In a candid moment, Arpaio acknowledges the political dimension of all his work. "I may be the greatest politician there is," he declares, "because everybody feels I'm *not* a politician."

Dora Schirro, the reform-minded director of the Arizona Department of Corrections, put it slightly differently. "I have great affection for Arpaio," she averred when we met in her office late one evening in 2005. A recent transplant from Missouri, the workaholic fifty-five-year-old was settling in for another long night of reading paperwork and trying to bring the notion of rehabilitation back into her state's burgeoning prison system. "Almost as much as he has for himself. He does any number of great deeds. But he works very hard at keeping them quiet. Maybe the difference is I don't have to get elected. Joe is an art form. I don't know that anyone else will be that extreme. When you look up close at 'commonsense' beliefs, you discover, more often than not, that they're nonsense." Schirro's views put her so far outside the correctional mainstream that she called her package of changes—centered on mandatory education, job training, and intensive programming for those soon to be released back into the community—a "parallel universe."

The body of the prisoner, in the words of Michel Foucault, controlled down to the minutest detail, becomes subject to a state "power that explores it, breaks it down, and rearranges it."[5] Foucault believed that, in the modern era, the intricate operations of the prison had largely replaced the public spectacle of punishment. Yet in large parts of contemporary America, the two have become increasingly intertwined. The antics of the Maricopa County sheriff and his staff, as they pursue public approval, essentially give free rein to the age-old desire for punitive exhibition, for rituals that personalize punishment and involve the public and the offender in a pas de deux, a theatrical production in which emotions need not take a back seat to cold rationality. The chain gang, the pink underwear, and the dyed-green sandwich meats are watered-down, sanitized, modernized versions of the pillory and the stocks, of the practice of tarring and feathering criminals and parading them through town, of shaming rituals that ranged from branding to the lopping off of ears and noses.[6]

Arpaio's fiefdom is, in short, the reductio ad absurdum. It is the logical endpoint of the political and cultural currents that have been swirling around crime and punishment in the United States since the early 1970s, since the technocrats and the policy wonks were replaced, in the shaping of criminal-justice systems and practices, by something akin to the mob unleashed. "To behold suffering," wrote Friedrich Nietzsche in his *Genealogy of Morals,* "gives pleasure. But to cause another to suffer affords even greater pleasure. Pleasure in cruelty is not really extinct today; only, given our greater delicacy, that pleasure has had to undergo a certain sublimation."[7]

While I was in Phoenix, a middle-aged, impeccably dressed, posh-accented journalist from the ultraconservative English newspaper the *Daily Mail* was also in town, tooling around the desert in a luxury rental car, working on a commentary that would run as part of the ongoing debate in Britain about how to shame young offenders into breaking their criminal habits. The day I observed the female chain gang, he observed the male one. As I was leaving Arpaio's office after our interview, my British counterpart was coming in. On my last day in town, a large, foul-mouthed female officer took us on a joint tour of the jail. Halfway through our tour of Tent City, she caught a female inmate in possession of an unauthorized extra pair of underwear. "What's your name?" the officer screamed. "What do you have that is mine? Where do you live? You have fifteen minutes to deposit what's not yours. I'll check up on you! Believe you me!" Then, calming down, she turned to another officer to deliver up her victim. "She can be your YB for the day."

What did "YB" stand for? "Yard Bitch," the officer admitted, and she laughed a guilty laugh.

Afterward, the *Daily Mail* man and I chatted for a few minutes. I expressed amazement at the conditions inside this jail, explaining that I had visited hundreds of correctional institutions around the United States, almost all of them run by unsentimental, tough-as-nails administrators, and this was clearly one of the worst. We talked about the harshness of the conditions and went our separate ways. When he got back to London he wrote for the *Mail,* "In the week when a Labour minister provoked fury by saying young offenders should be made to wear uniforms, meet the U.S. sheriff who makes his convicts do hard labour in pink underpants. And guess what? Even the prisoners say his tough justice works."[8] The sheriff, my companion wrote, urging the British government to adopt similarly muscular policies, had "a robust approach to crime and punishment," and creations such as the chain gang allowed "the good people of Arizona [to] daily see justice and punishment in action in their community." None of that squishy, soft, woolly-headed liberalism for this well-paid columnist. No, he was a man of the people, just like Sheriff Joe.

There are two big problems with all of this romanticization of toughness. First, Arpaio repeatedly claims that his inmates are "killers," "the worst of the worst," and so on. That's simply not true: some of those awaiting trial might be accused of horrendous crimes, but in the American legal system the principle of innocent until proven guilty means that such inmates cannot be treated as felons until they are tried, convicted, and sentenced. Once they have been found guilty, serious criminals do not stay in their local jails; instead they are moved to one of Arizona's maximum-security prisons. Indeed, anyone sentenced to over a year behind bars is automatically placed under the jurisdiction of the state rather than the county. Those who remain, after conviction, in Arpaio's jail are by definition low-level offenders who have been sentenced to less than one year in prison for crimes such as drug possession, relatively minor fraud, forgery, and possibly theft and assault. Many are in for parole or probation violations. They are, in short, the kind of people who might annoy the community, disgust the community, even enrage the community with their selfish and stupid behavior; but rarely are they the sort of people who would *terrify* the community. And since pretrial detainees, including those accused of more serious offenses, are presumed innocent and cannot be sent out onto the chain gang, it is the lower-end convicts, rather than the "worst of the worst," who end up as poster children for Sheriff Arpaio's toughness.

Most of the women on the chain gang were in jail for violating the terms of their probation, their original charges ranging from drug sales to forgery to theft to assault. Their sentences ranged in length from three months to one year. But acknowledging this would not serve Arpaio's political ends. After all, while making killers and armed robbers work in 120-degree heat while shackled at the ankles might make old grannies feel warm and happy inside, assigning the same duty to those grannies' wayward, drug-addicted granddaughters, in jail for cocaine possession, probably wouldn't produce such a comfortable sensation. Hence the elaborate performance by Arpaio and his team, the strenuous efforts to continuously portray themselves as the thin blue line between safety and destruction.

The second problem is one of data. For Arpaio to claim that his practices work, he would have to show, using more than just anecdote, that they measurably lower recidivism—the rate at which ex-inmates return to crime and, ultimately, cycle back into the correctional system—and that is well-nigh impossible to do. Arpaio's fans quote numbers purporting to show that only about 16 percent of his inmates return to crime; but those numbers have not been backed up by independent experts, nor have they been compared, by skilled statisticians, with recidivism rates in comparably sized jail systems in jurisdictions that are not run like that of the Maricopa County system. Moreover, even if true, given that jails house those not yet convicted as well as those soon to be sent to prison for years, if not decades, the numbers alone say nothing. It's perfectly possible that many of those in jail are subsequently found not guilty, meaning they weren't criminally minded in the first place—a not unreasonable proposition given the extraordinary growth in jail-admission numbers in recent years; given that others are short-term residents in to sleep off a drunken tear; given that Arpaio's sheriffs, under his no-nonsense mandate, sweep numerous low-level arrestees into jail and include them in their numbers when calculating recidivism rates; and given that still others have, since Arpaio became sheriff, spent time in jail and been sentenced to long prison terms under the war on drugs, and, still in prison, they have not yet had a chance to return to crime. The old adage that there are lies, damn lies, and statistics holds particularly true here, given Arpaio's propensity for self-promotion.

What's more, even if the bulk of those who graduate from the jail *do not* return to jail in Maricopa County, that's a far cry from knowing they have been truly rehabilitated. They may still be taking drugs and living lives of crime in other jurisdictions, untracked by Arpaio's propaganda machine. They may be just as educationally and economically destitute as they were before, just as far outside the mainstream. Arpaio's institution may simply scare people into other counties and states, rather than scaring them straight.

————

In recent years, practitioners working to promote rehabilitation have come to believe that the approach most likely to change inmates' behavior fundamentally, over the long term, is almost diametrically opposed to Arpaio's fear-based methods. "How do you create an environment that supports deep human change?" the executive director of the Fortune Society, JoAnne Page, asked rhetorically in 2004 while showing off a new and widely applauded residential program the society runs for addicted ex-prisoners in upper Manhattan. First, says Page, a lawyer by training, you have to accept the idea that "change isn't linear, that people work in spirals, that you don't get silver bullets for long-term, deep-seated stuff. A lot of the clients here either have burnt their bridges or don't have any bridges [to burn]." In other words, success is neither instantaneous nor measurable in absolutes. It's about changing lives and shifting attitudes slowly over time—not least by convincing people that those charged with housing them actually care about their lives, a situation clearly lacking in the tent cities of Maricopa County.

Page has the rare ability to create prodigious goodwill and optimism among the down-at-heel clients she works with. Part of this has to do with her extraordinary tenacity and her mastery, cultivated over decades, of the complex art of generating funding for nonprofit ventures, but part of it is her way of making residents feel respected, important, meaningful on the human stage. When new clients come to be interviewed, no matter how ratty they look, no matter how down-and-out their manner, Page heartily welcomes them, looks them in the eye, asks if they have any questions, and at the end of the interview, holds out her hand to give them a handshake. The body language is clear: *you're valuable; you're among equals here.*

"That kind of easy warmth, you just feel," Page says. "And it colors the place. And it's also the base from which you can do real work with people. This is all about seed-planting. We won't judge you by your past. We care about who you are when you walk in and what you want. If you treat people a certain way, they live up to it. This is basic stuff. It's what every religion teaches. Most people really respond to being valued and trusted and in a place they feel safe."[9]

—————

Yet despite the work of people like JoAnne Page and organizations such as the Fortune Society, the dominant national language for discussion of prisons and prisoners remains that of coercion, distrust, and fear. While Arpaio takes this ethos to an almost comical extreme, many other sheriffs and political figures have gone down similar, if somewhat less dramatic, routes over the last few decades. For a few years in the late 1990s, the state of Alabama reinstituted its chain gang for felons. In Lexington, North Carolina, according to Reuters journalist Alan Elsner, Sheriff Gerald Hege painted the inside of his jail bright pink in order to make inmates feel like "sissies"; routinely referred to criminals, to their face and in conversations with constituents, as "scumbags"; and, like Arpaio, took away "perks" such as coffee and exercise facilities.[10] In Iowa, cooks in prison kitchens were ordered to cut back on the amount of meat they put in their goulash and replace it with macaroni. And in Texas, the daily calorie allotment for inmates was scaled back from 2,700 to 2,500.[11] In 1990, rising political star Newt Gingrich cosponsored a bill with Texas senator Phil Gramm, the National Drug and Crime Emergency Act, calling for the declaration of a five-year national emergency during which extraordinary measures would be taken to "win the war on drugs and violent crime." The bill, which ultimately failed to pass, would have provided for wholesale incarceration of drug addicts, "zero tolerance" for anybody caught with any drugs, and a national mobilization on par with that of World War II and the Cold War.[12] Six years later, in 1996, at the height of the war on crime, presidential hopeful Gramm released a campaign brochure asserting that existing policies were too lax. His policies, he said, would grab violent criminals "by the throat": "If I have to string barbed wire on every military base in America," he wrote, "I'm going to put those people in jail and keep them there."[13] That same year, Congress passed the Prison Litigation Reform Act, making it far harder for inmates to sue correctional systems, and restricting the ability of publicly funded legal offices to take on prisoners' cases. In California, Governor Pete Wilson and his successor Gray Davis—one a Republican, the other a Democrat—both rose to power through a ruthless "out-toughing" of their political opponents on anticrime rhetoric.

Meanwhile, across the country, several New Hampshire legislators proposed a law that would have allowed teenagers convicted on graffiti-vandalism charges to be spanked on their bare bottoms by local sheriffs. They, along with legislators in other states, had apparently been inspired by the public caning of a young American in Singapore two years earlier to try to bring corporal punishment back into the American criminal-justice system. And at a 1998 Summit on Corrections, Massachusetts governor William Weld declared that prisons should be "akin to a walk through hell."[14]

Within the logic of less eligibility, Weld's statement made perfect sense: by the end of the twentieth century, conditions for America's poorest and most educationally underserved communities were so hopeless that they could almost be considered a kind of free-world purgatory. Every major city had a large substratum of homeless people living in its edge zones; drug addiction, despite decades of "war," remained endemic in many neighborhoods; hundreds of thousands of mentally ill men and women, unable to access underfunded community mental-health services, careened between the streets and local jails or state prisons; a collapsing public education system was locking increasing numbers of young men and women into a state of near illiteracy; and the growing practice of offshoring manufacturing jobs to third world countries had created dead zones out of swaths of land previously home to stable working-class communities.[15]

In the first years of the twenty-first century, this situation got even worse. From 2002 to 2003 alone, according to a study by the U.S. Conference of

Mayors on hunger in the United States, requests for emergency food assistance rose an average of 17 percent in cities across the country. In Boston, the food bank reported a 50 percent rise in requests for milk, cereals, and a variety of other child-related "nutrition foods." In Detroit, as the auto companies shed jobs, the numbers of people relying on food pantries to put meals on their tables sharply rose. In Louisville, Kentucky, food pantries had to give out 20 percent more baby formula in 2003 than they had the previous year.[16] And it wasn't just the unemployed, lumpen underclasses who were hungry; officials estimated that almost four in ten of the adults requesting emergency food assistance actually had jobs. The jobs just weren't paying enough to cover basic expenses.[17] How else, therefore, to ensure that people didn't commit crimes simply so that, as Arpaio feared, they could qualify to be housed, fed, and provided with rudimentary medical attention behind bars? The prisons must be made worse than purgatory—must be made, in Weld's fruity language, truly a "walk through hell."

In the increasingly divided, nonempathetic, muscular, and martial culture of contemporary America, preachers, politicians, and law-and-order pundits line up to denounce the idle, reckless poor. Legislators cut off welfare funds and restrict food stamps; voters demand draconian punishments in endless wars against criminals; and showmen such as Joe Arpaio wow the crowds with spectacular humiliation escapades and an endless patter of tough-on-crime, tough-on-criminals platitudes.

In most places and most times, men like Arpaio would be footnotes, almost absurd in their crudity. But in a context in which the culture and politics of the moment promotes the actions of such men and women as paradigms of virtue, imbues their actions with an almost messianic sense of purpose, and creates bureaucracies and institutions that justify cruelty in the name of a greater historical mission, they leap from the end pages into the centerfolds of history. That is what is ultimately so dangerous about the modern American incarceration machine: it creates conditions that render cruelty, neglect, humiliation, and dehumanization unavoidable, and then rewards the practitioners of the cruelty by hyping them as public heroes in a fight to the death between Good and Bad visions of society. That sense of mission explains why Arpaio has been such a potent force in Phoenix for over a decade, and also explains, at least in part, why America slid so easily and disastrously into accepting torture as part of the country's national security strategy in the wake of the 9/11 terror attacks.

———•———

Back in Phoenix, Detention Officer Ennis—a short but powerfully built African American woman wearing wraparound shades along with her khaki uniform, tells me that she asked to work supervising the Maricopa County chain gang. Ennis, who was stationed in Germany while serving in the army, and holds her shotgun over the gang with what seems like relish, says she enjoys the social interaction and the outdoor nature of the job. "We've had people as old as fifty-two on the chain. It's their choice. It's voluntary. You put in a tank order and you're on the chain for thirty days. It's like the thirties and forties when they had chain gangs. Same kind of thing. The majority of the inmates love it. It's their opportunity to get out, see the community."

"Does the work make these women free?" I finally ask her, the Nazi's concentration camp slogan *Arbeit macht frei* practically ringing in my ears. "Yes," Ennis replies, without hesitation and clearly without knowledge of the monstrous original use of this phrase. "It gives them the opportunity to get out, tear up a field, clean up a road. It gives them the opportunity to return to the community. It helps them learn discipline, remain calm. I think it's a great program. There are citizens that are all for it. The average person likes it. It's getting the inmates out doing general work they'd have to pay county workers to do otherwise."

PART TWO

POPULATING BEDLAM

CHAPTER 6

OPEN FOR BUSINESS

Surrounded by harsh scrub-ridden desert and enormous saguaro cacti, along with a smattering of cotton fields and pecan farms, Florence, Arizona, is a raw town whose men and women drink hard, at old saloons such as Gibby's Bar, and talk a talk that more delicately constituted city dwellers might shy away from in horror.

These days, as in so many other depressed Main Street communities, there's no shortage of correctional officers. They come from the vast and constantly growing state prison that's been in Florence for as long as Arizona has been a state; they come from the county jail; they come from the two private prisons (one for low-end felons from Arizona, the other mainly for out-of-state inmates from Alaska and Hawaii); and they come from the sprawling federal holding facilities in the dirt-poor neighboring town of Eloy (some run by the government, others under private contracts) that hold Immigration and Customs Enforcement and U.S. Marshals Service detainees. Many of the guards commute from job-starved communities across southern and central Arizona. Some of them used to be copper miners, with union jobs working the local red-rock mountains. In the 1990s and 2000s, in this state that mines more nonfuel minerals than any other, many of these jobs were downsized as companies sought to maximize productivity. In the single year from 1991 to 1992, Arizona shed nearly a sixth of its mineral-mining jobs, reducing the workforce from 14,900 to 12,600.[1] The incarceration industry is taking up the slack.

"Our town supposedly has 17,500 people in it," mused Don Penson, an iron-jawed retired major from the state prison, whose son-in-law was warden of the privately run Correctional Services Corporation (CSC) Florence West facility, in 2004. "[But] only 3,500 are free-world people." The rest, he explained, were prisoners. In 1978, when Penson began working in corrections, Arizona had about 3,200 inmates; by 2004 that number had risen to over 31,000 and was still growing.[2] The original push for this growth was the tough-on-crime movement, the same cultural groundswell that had picked up Joe Arpaio and landed him in a swank skyscraper office in downtown Phoenix; had led Congress to pass tough mandatory-minimum sentences for drug crimes; had led New York, Michigan, and so many other states to ramp up their drug-sentencing laws; had inspired California's three-strikes laws; and had resulted in explosive growth in incarceration in even traditionally low-tax rural states such as Wyoming, Colorado, Kansas, Nebraska, and South Dakota.[3] But Arizona's penal growth was far in excess of the national average, fueled at least in part by a powerful private-prison lobby that, in the first years of the twenty-first century, succeeded in getting the industry exempted from most state taxes. Excessive incarceration trends also appeared in New Mexico and Oklahoma during these years, two other states with potent private-prison industries and with legislators who either received large political contributions from these companies or were paid consultants to them. With a vested interest in securing prisoners for private prisons, these lawmakers were particularly likely to pass punitive legislation likely to result in more people being sentenced to prison terms by state courts. At the same time, many of the legislators were adamantly against raising state taxes to pay for the additional prisons, making these states fertile stomping grounds for private prison companies.

The depth of the inroads made by the national private-prison lobby came to light in a somewhat unexpected manner. After the toppling of Saddam Hussein in 2003, President Bush sent an $87-billion supplemental appropriations request to Congress, of which $400 million was devoted to building two supermax prisons in Iraq and another $10 million was set aside to hire one hundred prison consultants for six months, an average of $100,000 per consultant.[4] Soon afterward, Gibby's Bar was full of talk about how Terry Stewart, onetime head of Arizona's Department of Corrections—he left to found a private security and prison consulting firm, Advanced Correctional Management—had gone to Iraq, along with his old DOC deputy, Chuck Ryan, and many of their former colleagues from the prison system, to advise on "prison reconstruction." They were joined by former Utah Department of Corrections director Lane McCotter, now director of business development for corrections at Management and Training Corporation (MTC), based in Centerville, Utah. Until the Abu Ghraib revelations and the deteriorating security situation scared them off, MTC was considering a bid, in conjunction with another private U.S. prison company, to manage one of Iraq's new prisons.[5]

"In importing democracy in America to Iraq," said Brett Huggins, a public defender, vice president of Arizona Attorneys for Criminal Justice, and somewhat cynical, beer-swilling Gibby's regular, "we've decided they needed a private prison system. It's another Bush giveaway to corporate America."

———•———

In the 1990s, private prison companies in Arizona began luring state-employed guards onto their payrolls by offering better salaries and short-term bonuses. They did not emphasize the fact that, unlike the unionized state guards, whose union, the American Federation of State, County and Municipal Employees (AFSCME), had negotiated a generous and guaranteed pension package over the years, private guards received a benefits package that was virtually worthless in the long term. For a few thousand dollars in ready cash, new guards were giving up the possibility of a lifelong guaranteed retirement income.

"Ten grand was the going rate last year," said David Mendoza, longtime legislative director for AFSCME, over breakfast in downtown Phoenix in mid-2004. "Five thousand dollars up front; five thousand if they stick with it for a couple years. That buys a pickup truck. The young ones, not thinking about retirement, they're easy prey."[6]

After the terrorist attacks of September 11, 2001, the exodus intensified as private prisons aggressively expanded their reach at both the state and federal levels, particularly in the burgeoning business of immigration detention. As of 2005, Florida Police Benevolent Association (PBA) lobbyist Ken Kopczynski, who has spent years tracking the expansion of the private-prison sector, had identified close to three hundred state and federal prisons, jails, juvenile-detention facilities, and holding centers for illegal immigrants operated by the private sector, housing somewhere in the region of 132,000 people nationwide. Many of these have opened since 9/11 and many more are in the pipeline, with proponents allegedly telling locals at public meetings in prospective prison towns that building detention facilities is practically a patriotic duty.[7] The PBA opposes these institutions on the grounds that, because they pay guards poorly, cut corners on training, and have a poor track record on security, they put public safety at risk.

The Florida PBA is by no means alone in its opposition to private prisons, with many state politicians and local community groups having fought such institutions in recent years. In Arizona, activists managed to put the kibosh on a planned thirty-two-hundred-bed private "superprison" for women, an institution that would have been the world's largest women's prison.[8] In Santa

Fe, New Mexico, where Lane McCotter's MTC ran the county jail—which a state audit found to lack adequate classification processes for inmates, grievance procedures, record keeping, and programming—opponents prevented the siting of a private immigration holding facility.[9] In Maryland, proposals for a vast, privately operated federal facility were defeated after both of the state's U.S. senators attached their names to the "No" campaign. "We are," senators Barbara Mikulski and Paul Sarbanes wrote in a letter to then–attorney general John Ashcroft, "adamantly opposed to placing a privately run maximum security detention center in any Maryland community that does not want it. . . . In addition, we oppose the Office of the Federal Detention Trustee's plans to turn a maximum security detention center over to a private contractor. Previously, such arrangements have often signaled a sweetheart deal that comes at the expense of the community and taxpayer."[10] State officials in Pennsylvania also stepped in to block construction of a private facility to house one thousand inmates shipped in from the nation's capital.

But while opponents have successfully applied the brakes against a handful of proposed facilities, private prison companies in the post-9/11 years have nonetheless positioned themselves as central participants in the incarceration business. "They say, 'Here's economic development. This business wants to come in and give you jobs,'" Edwin Bender of the Institute on Money and State Politics told me in 2004. "They don't tell the communities the companies make a profit on the margins, and that profit relies on low wages and poor job training."

Throughout the border states of the Southwest, across the Southeast, and in the Midwest, ribbons of privately operated federal facilities began springing up in the early years of the new century, with Texas having by far the largest number. In 2004, Kopczynski estimated that seventy-three of the country's close to three hundred private detention centers were in the Lone Star State. A few months earlier, private companies had begun bidding for the privilege of running a twenty-eight-hundred-bed facility warehousing U.S. Marshals Service detainees waiting to be deported. Eight companies put in bids, and the border town of Laredo soon became the front-runner for the institution's likely location. As of early 2006, the Marshals Service had not yet decided which company to award the contract to; but all indications were that the $100 million project would soon get under way.[11] Fifty more facilities, according to Kopczynski's estimations, were divvied up between Arizona, California, and New Mexico.

———•———

In the mid-1980s, the early days of the prison boom, a handful of private companies, most with broad expertise in the security industry, saw an opportunity to cash in on the spending spree. Offering cash-strapped states low-cost, bulk-rate prison beds in facilities staffed by low-wage guards, they were, in a way, trying to do for prisons what Wal-Mart would do to the retail industry in the 1990s, and for several years their business model appeared unstoppable. Corrections Corporation of America (CCA), Wackenhut, CSC, and others made enough headway to take their enterprises public, and both stock prices and profits rapidly headed north. By 1990, CCA was reporting annual revenues of $55 million, and by 1994, when the company moved onto the New York Stock Exchange, its revenues were $120 million. Wackenhut also went public in 1994, after years of heady growth, with annual revenues of $84 million.[12]

By the early 1990s, as states scrambled to find beds to house war on drugs prisoners, three strikers, and others on the wrong end of the tough-on-crime stick—by this point, close to one hundred thousand prisoners were being added to the nation's total each year—private prisons, built at speed to cookie-cutter designs, were seen almost as angels of salvation. Often the companies did not even bill the states for their building costs, preferring instead to re-coup their money at the back end—which meant that everyone involved had a stake in keeping a steady stream of new prisoners flowing into the system. Private prisons claimed to be able to operate at a lower cost per inmate per day than state prisons could; they often incorporated newer technologies and architectural innovations; and they stirred up competition in a field that had long been the purview of largely unaccountable state bureaucrats.

One after another, state legislatures, many of whose members had accepted campaign contributions from private prison companies, opened their corrections systems to these companies and lavished tax breaks on them. Many of the bills they passed on this issue were drafted by the industry-friendly American Legislative Exchange Council (ALEC), a coordinating body set up in the 1970s for conservative state politicians and business interests. ALEC has also been instrumental in crafting legislation that limits access to welfare programs and food stamps, cuts taxes (especially corporate taxes), and rolls back environmental and workplace-safety regulations.[13]

Soon, more than 4 percent of all prisoners—and a far higher proportion of the inmates sent to prison in the recent past—were being held in private facilities, and many analysts were predicting that the infant industry would grow exponentially as the millennium approached. Some hoped to take over the management of entire state prison systems; as far back as the 1980s, CCA had approached Tennessee (ultimately unsuccessfully) with a proposition to do just that. Others took a stealthier, more incremental approach. In New Mexico, a state that went further than any other in its zest for privatization, by the year 2000 fully 40 percent of state inmates were living in private prisons. Not coincidentally, in the late 1990s, New Mexico's house majority leader, senate president, and other senior political figures were paid consultants of the private-prison industry.[14]

"People want to see wrongdoers go to prison, but at the same time they don't want to pay for it," explained Geoffrey Segal, director of government reform policy at the pro-privatization Reason and Public Policy Institute, in 2004. Private-prison enthusiasts pointed to a Vanderbilt University study and the work of Charles Thomas, then a professor of criminology at the University of Florida, indicating that private prisons had delivered more bang for the buck than their state and federal counterparts over the past two decades. They didn't mention the fact that both the Vanderbilt study and Thomas's project were funded by the private-prison industry. (Thomas was subsequently fined tens of thousands of dollars and forced to resign his position after Ken Kopczynski, the Florida Police Benevolent Association lobbyist, filed charges against him with the Florida Ethics Commission.)[15]

In the second half of the 1990s, however, private prison companies began taking some serious knocks. Independent studies called into question their ability to cut costs, and a number of high-profile abuse and escape cases dented confidence in their facilities. Several states, including North Carolina, Arkansas, and Montana, placed strict limits on the operations of private prisons within their jurisdictions, corroding the value of their stock, and a series of lawsuits by disgruntled investors further ate away at credibility and profits. Perhaps most devastating of all, CCA and other companies found that private firms had built too many prisons entirely on spec, so when the prison population stopped growing so dramatically (rising by a mere few percentage points each year, as opposed to the more than 5 percent increases recorded during the heyday of growth), the companies found themselves with expensive prisons and no prisoners to fill them. At the same time, more attention was paid to their dubious employment practices and their treatment of inmates.

Back at Gibby's Bar, a guard who used to work at a private facility in Florence made a series of allegations against the facility: staff were ordered to arbitrarily gas inmates; prisoners were locked up in isolation units without correct administrative procedures; senior officers were hired who had been fired from state prisons for having sex with inmates and smuggling contraband; and, on one occasion, a man who had previously served time as a U.S. Marshals Service detainee was hired as a guard in the same facility where he had previously been held. The guard also alleged that he was ordered to report to work despite having a serious blood blister that had temporarily blinded him in one eye. When I visited the facility while writing an article for *The Nation*, CCA declined to let me into their Arizona facilities or to interview staff, rendering it impossible to determine whether conditions have subsequently improved.

Inside other prisons, such as the medium-security CCA facility in Youngstown, Ohio, staff abuse of inmates, as well as inmate-on-inmate violence, was so extreme that state agencies ultimately yanked their contracts and left the prison empty. A study by the Washington, D.C.–based Sentencing Project found that the Youngstown site, which housed maximum-security inmates in a general population with lower-level offenders, had in a fourteen-month period seen thirteen stabbings, two murders, and six successful escapes.[16] Ironically, several years later, the facility reopened as a private prison for federal detainees.

Meanwhile, the U.S. Department of Justice took legal action against the Wackenhut-run Jena Juvenile Justice Center in Jena, Louisiana, after its investigators concluded that guards were routinely beating, gassing, and verbally abusing their wards.[17] Private facilities in Texas, from which serious sex offenders had escaped, were tainted by allegations that the escapes were due to lax security, while at other institutions guards were sexually assaulting inmates. And in one Texas prison, in 1997, officers made a training video showing themselves "beating, stun-gunning, and unleashing dogs on naked prisoners from Missouri; injured inmates were dragged face down back to their cells."[18]

Private prisons, many observers concluded, had promised far more than they could safely deliver. In so doing, they had unleashed a race to the bottom, in which state and private facilities vied with each other to house the greatest number of inmates and create the cheapest possible "product." Once the provision of prison beds had become a competitive, market-driven industry, few correctional systems felt confident enough to maintain high levels of expensive programming for inmates, the kind originally designed to lower recidivism rates. Thus in the 1980s, and more particularly the 1990s, even the administrators of the most progressive U.S. prison systems—in states such as Minnesota and Maine—were forced, out of necessity, to run their penitentiaries as little more than warehouses for their human inventories. Constrained by the quality of programming they could offer inmates, and by the sheer number of new inmates coming into the system, these state agencies were further constrained by the ever-present background threat that if they didn't operate on bargain-basement principles, legislators would eventually step in and hand over their systems to private, for-profit corporations.

In 1973 Minnesota had passed a Community Corrections Act, intended to subsidize local programs so that less-serious offenders could be monitored in the community rather than sent to prison. From this was created Project New-gate—which put nonviolent youthful offenders into residential programs while funding them to attend university courses part-time—and about thirty other residential programs in the Twin Cities area. The commissioner of corrections went so far as to announce that if this experiment were successful, the state would be able to close one of its prisons due to a declining inmate population. Similar programs were instituted in Kansas and Maryland. "*Utopian's* the right word," Pat McManus, onetime deputy director of Minnesota's Department of Corrections, recalled with nostalgia in 2005. "It was hopelessly naive and romantic. But it was very real, very genuine. It worked for some people, didn't work for others. It was successful, didn't create community stirs." But then the state's prison population started to mushroom, rising from around two thousand up to nearly twelve thousand over a quarter century of continual growth. Even after private prisons came under increased scrutiny, this new model—high incarceration rates at a wholesale cost—remained locked in place.

———•———

In the post-9/11 world, however—a world in which state budgets have taken years of hits while the demand for incarceration has remained high, and in which the federal government is looking for more short-term holding facilities for immigrant-detainees—much of the scrutiny has simply evaporated. The 1990s scandals surrounding the country's large private-prison companies are largely considered water under the bridge by legislators responsible for crafting incarceration policies. In the early years of the twenty-first century, CCA hired new managers; paid out $120 million to settle lawsuits brought by disgruntled investors; and launched an aggressive public-relations campaign to convince legislators that it was ready for business again.[19] At the same time, Wackenhut's prison holdings were successfully spun off into the independently run GEO Group.

Following these changes, cash-strapped state and federal agencies once again turned to CCA, GEO Group, and other companies as a way to maintain their prison complexes without having to raise taxes or seek voter approval for the issuance of billions of dollars of general-revenue prison bonds. Referring specifically to federal agencies responsible for detaining illegal immigrants and those charged with federal crimes, Geoffrey Segal explained, "It'll be very hard for any of these agencies to build a new facility without strongly considering it being private, simply because they don't have the money."

Many small states have chosen to export large numbers of their prisoners to out-of-state private facilities rather than bear the cost of building their own new prisons—and a handful of legislators in western states have (so far unsuccessfully) suggested building private prisons in Mexico to house noncitizen state prisoners who would otherwise serve time in the United States and be deported upon release. In December 2003, in New Hampshire, the Governor's Efficiency Commission—specifically software entrepreneur John Babiarz, who had never previously worked in corrections, and one other commission member—recommended privatizing the entire Department of Corrections.[20] "New Hampshire needs the money elsewhere," Babiarz explained in 2004. "States have to have prisons and people need to be incarcerated. The question is how do we do it cheaper? We can't do it alone as a government agency. Maybe just the *idea* of privatization has some people thinking they need to operate more efficiently."

At the same time, many impoverished counties have essentially converted themselves into for-profit prison speculators, often in conjunction with private companies, their lobbyists, and an array of somewhat shady middlemen. In a manner not dissimilar to that of the prisoner-leasing companies of nineteenth-century Dixie, these small counties have issued bonds to build prisons and immigrant detention centers and have then approached federal agencies, trying to woo prisoner contracts by offering the lowest possible per diem prices. Often the prison's annual operating cost is many times higher than the total county budget.

Elsewhere, communities have gone out of their way to attract state-run prisons, offering free land and infrastructure development as incentives. In 2001, U.S. Department of Agriculture researchers estimated that 350 counties across the country had built new prisons since 1980.[21] Their rationale? The construction money generated by state-backed bonds, or by existing correctional budgets; the flow of revenue into the regions through the prisons' operating expenses; and the jobs created. In these relative backwaters, prisons were seen as lifeboats in savage economic seas. Since New York State began its prison-building boom in 1982, all thirty-eight new prisons have been opened upstate, mainly in rural counties—hundreds of miles from New York City, where most of the prisoners come from.[22]

———•———

In the sweltering heat of mid-August 2005, thousands of beneficiaries of this booming industry gathered inside Baltimore's sparkling glass convention center for the annual conference of the American Correctional Association. It was a chance for meet-and-greet, for the suppliers of prison produce to meet the buyers: the wardens, the correctional administrators, the guards' union representatives. Some of the exhibitors in the enormous basement exhibition area were similar to those whose high-tech wares, applicable in both military and civilian contexts, I had seen in West Virginia several months earlier— explosives-scanning machines, data-mining software, perimeter security equipment. Many of the others, though, were far more mundane. There were phone companies with glossy brochures explaining, in soothing terms, their prison business model, which is essentially a kickback deal with the state: they get a monopoly on collect calls from prisons, charge vastly inflated prices to their literally captive market, and share the profits with the correctional system. There was Office Depot, its brochure advertising Post-its with the tag line "Stick Practically Anywhere" and a picture of a guard with his hand outstretched on a cellblock, a Post-it saying "Hold on" stuck to his palm. There were companies selling clear plastic toothbrushes, their transparency a selling point for administrators fearful of any and every device being used to hide drugs and weapons. There were educational-video producers, health-care companies, and prison-clothing manufacturers. There were also an array of architectural firms that, in recent years, had spawned entire divisions devoted to designing and building ever more secure prisons at practically breakneck speed.

In the 1970s, few of these companies would have thought it worth their while to attend a gathering of correctional professionals. Today, in an era that Tony Cameron, head of the Scottish Prison Service, wryly labeled "the Age of Imprisonment, for better or worse" during a workshop presentation at the Baltimore conference, the business of prisons is simply too lucrative to ignore.

———•———

Close to six hundred miles southeast of Florence, Arizona, the dying oil town of Pecos, in the remote West Texas county of Reeves, was praying that GEO Group could bring to town eight hundred state prisoners from Arizona—and fast.

Pecos—bona fide cowboy territory, home of the world's first rodeo in 1883, boomed in the 1950s, its farmers' pockets flush with cotton dollars. It declined somewhat in the 1960s, and in the 1970s it boomed again, floating on the West Texas oil rush. In the 1980s, when the local oil industry bottomed out, the city once more lost its bearings. Its population of thirteen thousand started dwindling, then collapsing toward its present level of nine thousand. Young people started leaving, cinderblock and wood houses were left to decay, and the dry, dusty desert began to reclaim abandoned lots. Ugly and aimless, Pecos began casting around for a third boom. With prisons, Reeves County officials thought that they had found the answer.

In the late 1980s, the county issued revenue bonds to build a one-thousand-bed prison, which it then leased out to the Federal Bureau of Prisons. In the mid-1990s, a newly elected judge, Jimmy Galindo, and the four county commissioners arranged for another bond issue to construct a second one-thousand-bed prison. Again, the feds stepped in with a nice contract, lured by the low per diem fees charged by Reeves County.

Outside the prison system, however, things were going from bad to worse. A decade-long drought crippled local farming; a local frozen-food company closed down, taking more than five hundred jobs with it; and a salt mine shut, taking eight hundred more jobs. Prisons—as well as the ubiquitous edge-of-town Wal-Mart—were, it seemed, the only source of income.

Against this backdrop, Galindo and the commissioners got greedy. As in several other impoverished, politically disempowered Texas counties in recent years, in Reeves County the political leadership adopted a prison-building scheme that, in practice if not in theory, put the county at huge financial risk, enriched a few contractors and prison companies, and left a wealth of bad feeling and mistrust in their wake. With no indication that the Bureau of Prisons was interested in a third Pecos facility, Galindo and the commissioners authorized the issuance of bonds for yet another addition to the prison, taking the total value of the bonds issued for prisons since the late 1980s to approximately $90 million—a vast sum in a county with an annual budget of only $5 million. Costing tens of millions of dollars and built entirely on spec, the prison, a prefab shard on a windswept desert plateau, opened for business in the fall of 2003.[23]

"Judge Galindo really thought he could make Pecos the prison capital of the United States," declared county treasurer Linda Clark, who vehemently opposed building the third prison, not because she didn't like the idea of making money off prisoners, but because she thought it was an unsound business proposition. There was, as Clark had feared, only one problem with Galindo's plan: the federal government had decided it didn't want to send any more prisoners down to Pecos. Some disgruntled officials believed this might have been because so many locals were failing the background check for employment at the existing two facilities due to criminal convictions in their own pasts. With no prisoners and no incoming money, Reeves County found itself having to service a bond debt that came to close to five hundred thousand dollars a month. The alternative was to let the debt go unserviced and forfeit both ownership of the prison and the county's ability to issue bonds for other projects in the future. What little surplus the county had been making on its contracts with the Bureau of Prisons for the first two facilities (money that had gone to cushion the general fund slightly) now went back into servicing a debt for the empty third prison. Galindo abruptly left his office in the county courthouse and set up shop in a small building within the sprawling prison complex a mile southwest of town. There, carefully guarding the paperwork relating to the deal from the prying eyes of his county treasurer and auditor—as well as a handful of ineffective, somewhat conspiratorial residents who had sworn to bring him to his knees—he began, according to other county officials, desperately wooing the private-prison sector, hoping it would come in and bail out the county.

At the end of 2003, GEO Group agreed to step in and take over the three facilities on a ten-year contract, and to use its out-of-state contacts to bring in prisoners to fill the empty, dollar-eating third site. Since the prison was already built and the county had to service the debt, it was essentially a risk-free proposition for the corporation. Moreover, according to county auditor Lynn Owens, as soon as the total prison population for the three facilities rose above 2,200, GEO's monthly fee from the county would rise from $62,500 to $330,000, whether that population was 2,201 or 3,000.[24]

Since the two existing prisons had a combined population of more than two thousand, and since the county still had to pay the guards' salaries, prisoners' medical expenses, programming costs, food expenses, and utilities, Owens believed this contract, negotiated by Galindo, was something of a sweetheart deal for the private company. So why pay GEO so much money? "We've spent almost a year now trying to attract inmates to RCDC [Reeves County Detention Center] 3," Owens explained resignedly. "We haven't attracted inmates. Through GEO's expertise they can generate us inmates."

Using that expertise, GEO immediately began wooing Arizona, a state that imported thousands of prisoners from Alaska and Hawaii to do time in its private facilities, while, in a weird manifestation of the logic of the global marketplace, simultaneously exporting its own state prisoners to private sites in Texas and Oklahoma. For Alaska and Hawaii, it was cheaper to send their inmates to private prisons in Arizona rather than building their own new prisons. Meanwhile, Arizona, which had an abundance of prisons, found it could get a better per diem rate to house excess prisoners in private prisons in Texan counties than in its own facilities. "We're going to have to pay all the bills," complained Clark bitterly. "The county is responsible for everything—except GEO is going to manage the facility. It's a sweet deal for GEO. They manage the prison and try to get us on our feet, get us some inmates in here. Hopefully we'll sign a contract with Arizona. They're the only ones who will send us any inmates."

Three of the four Reeves County commissioners didn't return phone calls asking for comment on the GEO deal when I visited Pecos in the spring of 2004. The fourth, Felipe Arredondo, arranged to meet me at the courthouse at eight o'clock one morning. He showed up in theatrical style, wearing knock-off Ray-Ban sunglasses, a ten-gallon hat, a baseball jacket, khakis, and cowboy boots, but he stayed only long enough to say that the other commissioners and the judge had forbade him to talk, and then he dashed out to his green pickup truck—which he had, with a further flair for the dramatic, left running outside.

Galindo himself ignored repeated phone messages and visits to his courthouse office. I finally managed to corner him in his prison office early one morning. The judge was a large man with salt-and-pepper hair and an ingratiating smile that rapidly turned sour when asked questions about the prisons. He stated that he *wanted* to provide information but was legally prevented from doing so by a clause in the existing contract with the Bureau of Prisons. When I pointed out that there was no contract with the bureau to fill prison number three, Galindo insisted that there soon would be. Would he show me that contract and that provision? Sure, he answered, all smiles, but only if I hired a lawyer and filed a formal public-information request.

The important thing for me to understand, the judge insisted, was that he was only interested in providing jobs to his constituents. "It's unfortunate that so many people are incarcerated," he said, a slight frown of empathy on his face. "But given the laws with regards to drug trafficking and other illegal activities, that trend more than likely is not going to slow down. I believe we provide a vital service to our customers—and we live in a part of this country where it's very difficult to create and sustain jobs in a global market. [Prisons] become a very clean industry for us to provide employment to citizens. I look at it as a community-development project. When I came in, it was a 6-million-dollar operation. As we speak, it's a 36-million-dollar operation. I hope you look at it from our perspective, as a community-development project."

———•———

Amazingly, when it came to county prison construction and private-prison corporate brazenness, Pecos didn't top out the scale. A slew of even poorer, even less populated counties had been effectively hijacked by extraordinarily aggressive prison companies that had convinced the commissioners to build prisons and holding facilities on spec, paid for by bonds issued through shell companies known as "public facility corporations" (whose board members were the county commissioners and judges), and to sign contracts that brought the private companies in to manage whatever prisons ended up opening. In each instance, the private company essentially built in the right to walk away from the project, at no cost to itself, should the prisoners and the money not start flowing in within a specified, and quick, time frame. Feasibility studies of these deals by opponents of the industry cast doubt on whether the counties would ever be able to break even on their prisons; yet even before the first prisoners arrived, the private companies and their middle men routinely made huge profits on the money raised from gullible private investors by the bond issues.

In the tiny hamlet of Sierra Blanca, the county seat of Hudspeth County, Texas, just east of El Paso, junk bonds claiming to pay an astonishing 12 percent interest (close to double the interest paid on the Pecos prison bonds, and a far higher rate of return than that offered by the stock market at the time), were funding a 24-million-dollar facility, to be operated by the Louisiana-based Emerald company—the same company that had, a couple years earlier, convinced La Salle County, in South Texas, to issue an even larger junk bond for an equally shaky prison project. As in La Salle, the company vowed that the prison would lure either immigration prisoners or U.S. Marshals Service detainees, and in so doing, generate a domino effect of huge economic advances. Yet in both cases, the huge prisons were effectively going to tap the arid counties' existing reserves of water—meaning, in effect, that no new businesses could subsequently come in without the county having to outlay huge amounts of cash to upgrade their water infrastructure.

When I walked into county judge Becky Dean Walker's office on the second floor of the sprawling Hudspeth County courthouse to ask her about the decision to get into the incarceration business, the first question she asked was,

"Are you sure you're not with Billy Addington?" At the end of the interview, she repeated the question, at which time I asked who Billy Addington was. "He's the only one in town against the prison," the judge answered. Walker's husband, who had just walked in, added bitterly, "He's always against *everything* in this town."

Addington, it turned out, was indeed against the prison. A thin middle-aged man with long, straggly hair and the threadbare clothes of someone with not a lick of spare cash, Addington lived in a stone house on an unpaved road, surrounded by hulks of old rusting cars. His phone number was unlisted—because of death threats issued against him over the years, he claimed—and his property was protected by snapping dogs. Addington's grandfather had moved to Sierra Blanca close to a hundred years earlier, and Bill regarded this hostile corner of West Texas as his heritage, preserving its integrity his obligation. He had alienated the town's political elite by waging a decades-long, ultimately victorious legal campaign to stop the government from opening a huge radioactive waste dump in the county; and he had cemented his reputation as a crazy radical by waging a public-relations war against the county's decision to open a toxic-sewage sludge dump. Every day, for nearly a decade, between two hundred and four hundred tons of New York State sewage—waste deemed too toxic for dumping in the Empire State—was unloaded from rail cars and emptied onto seventy-nine thousand acres on the other side of the low-rise mesa from Sierra Blanca. In 2004 Addington found himself the most vocal opponent of the new concrete prison being constructed a mere stone's throw from his property. "It's built on a house of cards," Addington said fiercely. "It is a risky thing."

Risky or not, Sierra Blanca's new facility was rapidly rising from its foundations, another rolled-barbed-wire, concrete-surrounded scar on the West Texas scrub—and another symbol of the new priorities and new economic realities shaping an increasingly hollowed-out America. There was, said Judge Walker, no reason *not* to build the prison. If it went well, she reasoned, it might bring the depressed county a handful of jobs. If it didn't, "The county could suffer if we wanted to bond something again. It'd be harder to get bonds. But Hudspeth County is poor enough that it doesn't *do* bonds. I'm not sure exactly how it works. I don't know. What the county hoped, the commissioners was hoping to accomplish, is jobs."

CHAPTER 7

TILL THE END OF TIME

Over the last thirty years, an increasing number of states have gone down the route that Miriam Shehane and her political allies helped chart for Alabama, imposing extraordinarily long sentences—longer, it is worth repeating, than many of the top Nazi war criminals, including Hitler's confidant Albert Speer, received at the Nuremberg trials after World War II—not just on murderers and rapists, but also on perpetrators of relatively minor crimes. Even before the national prison population exploded during the 1980s and 1990s, many parts of the South had already made the life sentence (or finite sentences that were all but life terms) routine parts of the criminal-justice arsenal. This practice has helped to sustain the growth in America's archipelago of penal institutions, and in turn that very growth—the availability of a seemingly endless supply of cells in which to house prisoners—has fueled the continual movement to ramp up the lengths of criminals' sentences.

To get to Louisiana's eighteen-thousand-acre Angola prison, known colloquially as "the Farm," one drives twenty miles off the highway an hour north of Baton Rouge, past a sign to Solitude, past a landscape of old plantations, trailers, and broken-down wooden shacks, deep into the verdant, swampy Mississippi Delta. The prison holds more than five thousand prisoners, about three-quarters of whom are African American.[1]

About 90 percent of the inmates in Angola are there for life, or for sentences that will last almost that long.[2] Sentenced to hard labor, most of them serve out their days in the fields along the Mississippi River. They grow corn, potatoes, squash, and soybeans—4 million pounds a year in all, harvested to feed prisoners across Louisiana, as well as state employees in a variety of government agencies. The prisoner-laborers earn between four and twenty cents an hour and are guarded from dawn to dusk by horseback-riding, gun-toting officers.

Deep inside the prison's perimeter lies Lake Killarney, a muddy expanse of water disturbed by the protruding stumps of dying trees. A short distance away, along bumpy lanes that wrinkle the flat landscape, two cemeteries are surrounded by white picket fences. Point Lookout One, the older cemetery, is entirely full. Its grass is lined with simple white concrete crosses. Next to it is Point Lookout Two. The newly opened burial ground is nearly empty now, but over the years it will fill up with the bodies of those who have lived and died as prisoners of Angola.

"We all live with the hope of getting out of here," said Tommy Floyd, a man whose somewhat skinny, almost collegiate appearance belied the fact that he was a convicted murderer. When I met Floyd at the end of 2003, he was twenty-nine and had been at Angola for seven years, and a parish jail for five years prior to that. He had been sentenced at age seventeen for killing a man while trying to rob him out on a levee. The week before he received his sentence, his father died. Slated to spend the rest of his life on the inside, Floyd spent much of his time hoping to return one day to the outside world. "*If* is one of our main words: *if* we get out. Since I've been here, one skill I've become a master at is evading reality." If Floyd did somehow get out, he wanted to work, he said, with children at St. Jude's Hospital, putting to good use the skills he had learned as a volunteer in the hospice at Angola. Beyond work, he wanted to eat "a big old pot of deer rolls, and chicken and dumplings"—anything but the potatoes and rice served up in the prison cafeteria. Given the seriousness of his crime, however, Floyd was not likely to taste those dumplings anytime soon.

In the early 1970s, the U.S. Supreme Court upheld the constitutionality of the life-without-parole sentence (LWOP). The case, known as *Schick v. Reed*, involved a soldier, Maurice Schick, stationed in Japan, who had been sentenced to death in 1954 for killing an eight-year-old girl and had his sentence commuted in 1960, by President Eisenhower, to life without any possibility of parole.[3] Schick had appealed the "without parole" provision, but the Supreme Court held that Eisenhower had had the right to impose such a restriction. Until the mid-1990s, however, most states shied away from imposing such sentences; Louisiana was one of only a handful to give jurors or judges the option of imposing the punishment, also known as "natural life."

Then, as fear of social disorder peaked, LWOP suddenly gained adherents. In an era when the public demanded increasingly tough sentence codes, conservative law-and-order types liked the inherent harshness of such a sentence, and the victims'-rights movement supported it. Politicians liked the ease with which they could tout "life without parole" within the few seconds of a sound bite. At the same time, from the other end of the spectrum, many liberals embraced it as a politically viable alternative to the death penalty in heinous murder cases. "I don't know if it's a good policy," Richard Dieter, executive director of the Death Penalty Information Center, based in Washington, D.C., remarked to me in 2003. "But it's a practical alternative to the death penalty that the public may be willing to accept. Having a stated alternative that sounds tough makes a big difference."

In addition to the cold, rational arguments in favor of LWOP, a life sentence with no possibility of release has innate emotional appeal as a means of retribution. Indeed, since the eighteenth century, permanent incarceration has had support from death-penalty abolitionists, according to Hugo Bedau, professor emeritus of philosophy at Tufts University and an expert on natural-life sentencing. The eighteenth-century Italian philosopher Cesare Beccaria and, a generation later, the British political theorist Jeremy Bentham, in particular, argued that a select few criminals should be permanently segregated from the broader society. As they grow old behind bars, the very infirmity of multiple murderers, war criminals, or sensational thrill-killers such as Charles Manson makes evil seem banal, its practitioners pathetic. The image of Rudolf Hess, Hitler's onetime deputy, as a nonagenarian pottering around in Spandau Castle in the 1980s comes to mind; such scenes symbolize the power of the criminal-justice system, at its best, to bring the tyrannical and the feared to their knees.

In 1993, America's LWOP movement gained momentum after a murder case in South Carolina in which a man named Jonathan Simmons, who had sexually assaulted two elderly ladies and beaten to death a third, was sentenced to death after the judge neglected to tell jurors that, if convicted and given a life sentence, he would be ineligible for parole. The state's supreme court upheld the sentence, but on appeal, the U.S. Supreme Court found that the judge should have explained the life-without-parole provision to the jury.[4] From that point on, judges were required to tell jurors in capital cases when a natural-life sentence was available as an alternative to execution. As a result, by the late 1990s, in many places jurors in capital cases were given only two choices for those they found guilty: execution—a punishment carried out roughly once every ten days in the United States since the resumption of executions in 1976, mostly in a handful of southern states, with Texas dispatching far and away the largest number of people—or permanent imprisonment. By the early twenty-first century, thirty-five of the thirty-eight states that had the death penalty also had LWOP, as did eleven of the twelve states that didn't. The sentence was also an option in the District of Columbia and under federal law.[5]

Unfortunately, throughout the 1990s, the expansion of LWOP and other sentences that have the effect of putting people behind bars for the rest of their lives was not restricted to capital cases. Instead, in a process uncannily parallel to the expansion of the list of crimes for which defendants could be executed or transported abroad in eighteenth- and early-nineteenth century Britain, a growing number of states applied natural life to a list of crimes far longer than capital murder, including drug crimes and petty crimes by habitual offenders. As in imperial Britain, many who bore the brunt of this ratcheting up of the sentencing laws were inebriates, addicts, and low-grade hoodlums rather than true sociopaths.

This wasn't surprising. After all, once LWOP became an option in Louisiana, it rapidly became an almost routine punishment for a host of different crimes. In 1970, 143 prisoners were serving life without parole in the state;[6] by 2003, when I visited Angola, well over 3,000 were. Thousands more were also sentenced to exceedingly long terms, such as ninety-nine years, that make them technically eligible for parole, but in practice function as life sentences because the state's Board of Pardons and Parole hardly ever grants release to such inmates. By 2006, Angola was housing about 800 inmates who had been in prison for more than twenty-five years. While many of Angola's lifers, like Tommy Floyd, were convicted killers, hundreds of others were not. Astonishingly, about 150 of Louisiana's natural-lifers were serving life after being convicted of dealing heroin, and most of these were low-level dealers, not kingpins; rather than selling to get rich, they were men who sold to sustain their own addictions.[7]

"Almost twenty-seven years for one bag of heroin," fifty-four-year-old Roy Sawyer said bitterly, referring to the crime that brought him to Angola in 1976. Sawyer, an African American, was in poor health, with failing eyes, high blood pressure, and hepatitis C. He was originally sentenced to life without parole, with the sentence suspended for a five-year probationary period, and sent to a local drug-treatment center called Odyssey House. At some point, Sawyer left the facility and was picked up by the police, at which time his probation was revoked. Amazingly, because he had violated the terms of his probation by absconding from Odyssey House, he was sent to prison for life, to serve the term that had been originally deferred.

"It's horrible," said Sawyer, whose mother had died two years earlier and who hadn't had a visit or a letter from anyone on the outside since then. Sawyer had a daughter, but the last time he saw her she was only one year old. "I don't believe I can stay here for the rest of my life. I'm going to fight to the finish."

As in Louisiana, so Michigan's mandatory sentences, approved in 1978, also consigned many lower- to mid-level drug dealers (anyone convicted of delivering over 650 grams of heroin or cocaine) to life terms, and many others to scores of years behind bars. When a reform campaign led to the repeal of the so-called "650-lifer" statutes in December 2002, twelve hundred men and women became eligible for parole.[8] Before they were partially rolled back in December 2004 and August 2005, New York's Rockefeller laws, passed in 1973 at the urging of then governor Nelson Rockefeller, imposed a series of graduated penalties for drug offenses that often operated as life sentences.

Many of these penalties were handed down to young women who had served as drug couriers for their boyfriends. They could not bargain for lower sentences by giving information about the drug trade, because they did not have any. Even after the law changed, New York retained the ability to put away small-time dealers for extremely long periods of time. Oklahoma still occasionally puts low-level marijuana offenders behind bars for life.[9] In California, the Three Strikes And You're Out law has effectively given life terms to thousands of people with two previous "serious" felonies who have been convicted of nonviolent, relatively minor third felonies such as shoplifting, drug possession, or burglary. The same is true in Alabama, where more than fifteen hundred of the state's twenty-seven-thousand-plus prisoners were serving LWOP in the early twenty-first century, many under the state's habitual-offender statute. Several of these inmates were middle-aged men first convicted of crimes years earlier, during their youths, who had, in midlife, been trapped by local police officers in marijuana-sales sting operations.[10] Florida, under a policy known as "tough love," has a "10–20–LIFE" law for defendants who use guns to commit their crimes, which has put hundreds of criminals in prison for the rest of their lives.

Meanwhile, in Texas, impoverished defendants with lackadaisical court-appointed defense attorneys frequently end up with sentences so inane they would be the stuff of comedy if they weren't so tragic. In 1999, in the tiny panhandle town of Tulia, almost 10 percent of the African American population —about fifty people out of approximately five hundred—were arrested in a series of drug sweeps and accused of being drug dealers. The evidence against them was absurdly flimsy: there were no confiscated drugs, virtually no drug paraphernalia, not even taped conversations suggesting drug deals were taking place. Instead, the men and women of Tulia—most of whom lived in shacks and trailers in a neighborhood known, until the recent past, as "nigger town"—were convicted solely on the word of an undercover narcotics officer. The officer, Tom Coleman, was a freelance agent who roamed from one jurisdiction to the next, hiring out his entrapment services to local sheriffs' departments: befriending local addicts and dropouts, smoking drugs with them, and jotting their names down, in ink, on his arms and legs. Then, not bothering to place into evidence the drugs he had supposedly bought, he would provide law-enforcement officials with lists of individuals he claimed had sold him narcotics.

Despite the paucity of hard evidence, juries in Tulia handed out sentences that sometimes came to more than one hundred years behind bars. Until a media-generated outcry prompted reluctant state officials to launch an investigation—which ultimately found that Coleman's evidence was untrustworthy and his word equally shaky, exonerated the Tulia inmates, and led to their release—many of these men and women spent years living in maximum-security institutions in various parts of the Lone Star State.[11]

Many other states now also impose life sentences for noncapital offenses, either drug-related crimes or nonfatal crimes of violence. The proportion of lifers in the prison population has remained roughly constant since the early 1980s, at somewhere between 9 and 11 percent;[12] but as the number of people behind bars has risen several hundred percent, so has the absolute number who will never live anywhere else.

At the end of 2001, about eighty-six thousand prisoners in the United States were serving life terms, compared to half that number fifteen years earlier. By 2006 that number had, according to best-guess estimates, risen to well over one hundred thousand.[13] Statisticians at the federal Bureau of Justice Statistics estimated that 40 percent of lifers, or somewhere in the region of fifty thousand people, were serving their sentences for crimes other than murder. Of these, 11 percent, or more than six thousand, were serving life on drug charges, several thousand for possession of illegal narcotics. The Bureau of Justice Statistics doesn't track how many of the lifers aren't eligible for parole, but given the number of states that have adopted the LWOP sentence, the number of lifers in states that have abolished parole for those sentenced to life —and the numbers serving life sentences under an array of three-strikes and habitual-offender laws—it is clear that a significant percentage will never be released.

———

Two hundred miles north of Angola, in the Forcht-Wade correctional facility, fifty-six-year-old Floyd Williams was serving a life sentence for a crime he committed in 1962, at the age of fifteen. In the cotton fields of pre–civil rights Louisiana, Williams raped a woman who was over the age of eighty. He was black and his victim was white, and given the time and place, he was lucky not to have been lynched, said warden Anthony Batson, crudely but matter-of-factly.

When he was sentenced, Floyd Williams's parents hadn't even come to watch the court proceedings. The only person with him was his court-appointed attorney. It was a particularly lonely way for a defendant not much older than a child to be sent away forever. "The judge said, 'Natural life. Hard labor.' Back then, I didn't really know what it meant to me."

"When I was young I didn't know what I had," he said, referring to those few teenage years before he went to prison. "Being wild. Ripping and running. [Inside prison] an old man sat me down and said, 'How much time have you got?' I said, 'I got a life sentence.' He sat me down and said, 'Do you know what that means?' 'No.' 'Well, you've got a lot of time to play with.' I made it through with people helping me to grow up." With help and encouragement from older inmates, Williams joined prison churches and various in-prison associations.

Forty years later, Williams was trusted with grooming and caring for Forcht-Wade's bloodhounds and weapon-sniffing dogs. Each of the eight large animals he tended cost more money to purchase, train, and maintain than their keeper could hope to make in his prison lifetime. Looking at Williams and his dogs, I almost felt that this prematurely old man preferred the company of the animals to that of other human beings. Out on the edge of the prison, Williams seemed practically at peace.

Floyd Williams had been in prison so long—since before he was old enough to shave—that he had to struggle to remember the details of life out-side. He sat on a wooden bench, looked at the nearby trees, and pondered the question of his memories. (Watching him, Warden Batson muttered, with a somewhat disconcerting southern joviality, that Williams reminded him in appearance "of that gorilla in the movie *Mighty Joe Young*.") Eventually, Williams said, "I remember a little. Picking cotton. My people had me in the fields. I had to work. I had a flat-top hairstyle with a little conk [chemical straightener] to make the hair slick back a little bit. Wore Levis. My bebop cap; two-tone color. Red and white and some stripes on it. Cowboy hat, too. But mostly I growed up in Angola and DeQuincey [prisons.]" The onetime teen rapist had been out of prison only for family funerals, most recently his brother's in 1998. Occasionally he spoke on the phone with a church lady who had befriended him several years earlier; he was no longer able to phone his mother, as her phone had, he said, been cut off. He hadn't had a visitor in years. "My mom, she live in Shreveport now," he explained. "My mom be round about sixty-nine or seventy. I'm fifty-six. I got one sister. No sir, I haven't seen her since 1972. My last visit was my sister-in-law. I had two brothers dead and two locked up."

Over the years, over the decades, over the better part of half a century, Williams had had plenty of time to dwell on how his life had turned out. "I've growed up to be a man now," Williams said softly, one eye bloodshot, his large body resting on a wooden chair near the dog kennels, mosquitoes buzzing his head. Talking about the rape he carried out forty-one years ago, he said, "I realize things. What a fool I've been."

Williams had applied for a commutation of his sentence from four governors. Each had refused to sign, probably wary of the risks of a public backlash in releasing a man with such an appalling crime in his past. Whether Williams was "rehabilitated" (whatever that means, exactly) was impossible to know for sure. He seemed a calm, somewhat pensive old man; his guards trusted him to roam the prison and tend to attack dogs. "I don't think he'd hurt anybody again," Warden Batson said. But even if Williams could somehow get another chance on the outside, it was not clear to the warden that, in his heart of hearts, he really desired one.

"I don't think he wants to go home," Batson quietly said of his institutionalized charge. "He's just as well off here as he would be at home." After all, what does an old man who has been in prison since the age of fifteen—an old man who has spent a lifetime being judged for the insane actions of a deeply disturbed boy—have to go home to? What chances does he have of getting a job, of starting a family, of navigating the complexities of twenty-first-century life?

———•———

While the contours of the tough-on-crime movement emerged from the particular mixture of fundamentalist religion, conservative politics, and racial tensions in the states of the South, once released into the atmosphere, the virus of extremely conservative punishment politics didn't remain geographically isolated. By the early 1990s, extraordinarily harsh, expensive, and socially destructive crime-and-punishment laws were being passed across the country. And outside the South, perhaps nowhere was this more the case than in California, the anything-goes Eden at the end of America's rainbow.

"On November second, everything just went to hell," Christy Johnson, a long-haired, pretty but exhausted-looking San Juan Capistrano, California, woman told me in late 2004. In her nowhere-to-turn rage, Johnson practically jumped out of her seat in the little Mexican restaurant by the railway tracks where we were having dinner. "And you've got to get up and go to work and put a smile on your face and pretend like it doesn't bother you."

Johnson had been certain that, ten years after California's voters had locked the state's notoriously harsh three-strikes law into place, voters on Election Day 2004 would pass a reform that would strictly limit the kinds of crimes that would qualify a person for a three-strikes sentence, and allow those already in prison on a nonviolent third-strike offense to apply to be resentenced. Right up until the final result was declared late that evening, she knew in her bones that Proposition 66 would win majority support, which meant that her husband Dan, a lanky, mustached man serving a three-strikes sentence on a two-bit drug charge in R. J. Donovan prison—a drab-looking medium-security facility surrounded by scrubland about twenty miles from San Diego, barely a stone's throw north of the Mexican border—would be swiftly resentenced. Under the terms of the new law, he would already have served more than enough time, and would therefore be coming home to Christy for the holidays. Any other outcome made no sense to her.

Dan Johnson was a trained sheet-metal worker and a longtime cocaine addict. In the 1970s and 1980s, he had been arrested numerous times on relatively minor drug charges; in the late 1980s, he had been convicted for several gas-station robberies, committed to fund his out-of-control drug use. Ironically, he'd spent only a couple years in prison for the robberies, a spree that could easily have spiraled into violence meted out by the robber, and that only ended when one of the gas-station attendants shot Dan through the neck. Yet years later, when he was arrested with a small quantity of cocaine and paraphernalia that suggested he intended to sell the drugs, it was the minor drug charge that proved the catalyst for a three-strikes sentence. In 1994 Dan was one of the first Orange County residents convicted under the Three Strikes and You're Out law. He was found guilty on three separate drug charges and sentenced to seventy-five years to life (a sentence later reduced to twenty-eight years to life). The day of the sentencing, Christy and Dan cemented their relationship by getting married at the local jail. Dan was then transported to prison to begin serving out the rest of his life behind bars.

It was hard to see how Dan Johnson's sentence could survive passage of Prop 66. When he came home, Christy's life would begin to get back to normal: there would be two income-earners in the house, so she'd no longer have to skimp on food and clothes to make the mortgage payments. She'd be able to show her dying father that she'd be taken care of after he was gone. She'd be able to announce to the world that she had a man about the house who could look after her.

Late on the night of November 2, when it became clear that Proposition 66 had failed and the realization hit her that Dan wouldn't be leaving prison anytime soon, something snapped inside Christy. "I've never felt so much anger. I need to break something, hit something. I've never felt like that before. It's like ripping your heart out day after day after day. I feel stuck, because this thing isn't handled, this thing isn't resolved. I'm stuck. It's a horrible feeling." For Dan and a slew of other three strikers at R. J. Donovan, the sense of disappointment was magnified by a prison guard's address to the prisoners over the PA system: "The governor has spoken," Dan later recalled the guard saying, apparently referring to the fact that Governor Schwarzenegger had poured millions of dollars of his own money into the campaign to defeat Proposition 66. "Now quit your whining and do your time." So angry did this make the prisoners that a riot almost ensued.

Statewide, 53.2 percent of voters had come out against the reform. In Orange County, where Johnson had been prosecuted under Three Strikes, the "no" vote was far more definitive, with 64.1 percent of voters opposing the reform. "The worst part [of Proposition 66] was the retroactivity of it," explained Orange County DA Tony Rackauckas, sitting in his Santa Ana office in December 2004, his strong chin, suntan, and slicked-back black hair, gray at the temples, giving him a more than passing resemblance to Charlton Heston in his younger years. "Redefining strikes and letting people out who were violent felons. It would guarantee new crimes and new victims."

In the mid-1990s, Rackauckas, a judge at the time, had run for the office of district attorney, promising to undo the excesses of then-DA Mike Capizzi, who had used Three Strikes to the maximum extent possible. Banishing discretion, Capizzi had ordered his team of prosecutors to prosecute "wobblies" —crimes that could be tried as high-level misdemeanors or low-level felonies —as felonies so as to qualify defendants for Three Strikes sentences. Rauckackas acknowledged that Three Strikes had at times been used inappropriately. In perhaps the most egregious instance, a fifty-two-year-old businessman, who had been in trouble when he was eighteen and then stayed clean, suddenly faced a life sentence when he got into a row with his wife. Police were called to the house and discovered that the man owned a gun, which, as a felon, he wasn't allowed to do. In that particular case, the judge had refused to allow the

Three Strikes prosecution, sentencing the man to attend anger-management classes instead. Of course, in many other instances the defendants were not so lucky. "I felt there were injustices under the policy," Rackauckas explained. "It was creating an atmosphere not good for the whole criminal-justice system."

Years later, however, Rackauckas argued that the DA's office no longer acted cavalierly, that the kinks in the original Three Strikes mechanism had been ironed out, that those being prosecuted under Three Strikes were over-whelmingly unrepentant serial criminals, and that systemic reform, such as that proposed by the language of Prop 66, would do more harm than good. If there were injustices, he said, people should bring them to him to consider rather than throw the baby out with the bathwater by passing a sweeping legal change. He would personally, he averred, be open to looking at any habeas case filed by a three striker who felt his conviction was unjust. "I'm certainly willing to review cases that people bring to me under that category," Rackauckas asserted. "I would always do that. And I've done that, on occasion. I certainly have no interest in keeping someone unjustly locked up for the rest of their lives. But I think those cases have pretty much gone to court and been reviewed."

Orange County had prosecuted about thirty-five hundred individuals under the second- and third-strike provisions of the original law since its passage in 1994, and it still had somewhere in the region of four hundred residents serving at least twenty-five years to life as a result of the law.[14] Rackauckas, an elected official in a conservative county, was in no hurry to have all of these cases reopened. Moreover, his office believed Three Strikes was a useful tool of coercion, a Damoclean sword that could be dangled over defendants to force them to accept plea bargains. Under his leadership, Orange County's prosecutors were filing about four hundred Three Strikes cases each year, the great majority of which were then plea-bargained down in exchange for lesser sentences. So strongly did Rackauckas feel about this that he had released one of his deputies, Brian Gurwitz, from his prosecutorial duties for several months so he could work full-time on the "No on 66" campaign.

Men like Dan Johnson, the DA's office felt, had shown an ongoing lack of remorse over the years, had failed to curb their addictions, and could not be trusted to act within the bounds of the law if released under the proposed resentencing system. "Mr. Johnson," said Rackauckas, "possessed narcotics with the intent to sell knowing he was a third-striker. When he was out on bail for this third-strike felony case, he possessed narcotics with the intent to sell. Mr. Johnson is a slow learner and he refused to rehabilitate."

So Dan Johnson continued to live his life in prison, and Christy Johnson continued to get up at 5:00 a.m. every Saturday, doll herself up to look her best, and drive two hours south to the prison in her beat-up green Volkswagen Jetta to visit her forty-six-year-old husband, in his prison-issue light-blue shirt and dark blue pants. She would buy them both overpriced fast food in the prison cafeteria, peeling off dollar bills (the only kind allowed inside the visiting room) from the wad of notes she brought down each week; and she would cobble together scarce dollars to pay the prison photographer to snap a couple photos of her and Dan in the yard attached to the visiting room. As visiting time drew to a close, the two would perform a little ritual. Dan, putting on a manly air, would try to shoo her away quickly; Christy, going goo-goo girly, would start to pout and call Dan mean. Then they would kiss several times and hug each other. Finally, she'd walk ever so slowly out the doors, and watch Dan through the glass as he headed back to the prisoners' exit and waited for the guards to come, take him into another room, and strip-search him before escorting him back to his cell.

————•————

Yet while laws developed over three decades of "toughness" continue to impose disproportionate punishments on criminals such as Johnson, by the turn of the twenty-first century an increasing number of states were starting to reject the old approach, especially when it came to drug crimes. And surprisingly many of those doing the challenging were from the conservative wing of America's political spectrum.

At the philosophical core of the war on drugs, as fought by the likes of President George H. W. Bush's drug czar Bill Bennett, were two ideas: drug use was morally wrong in itself, and drug use made people more likely to commit a host of other crimes, from prostitution to burglary to murder. To fight drugs, the drug warriors insisted, it wasn't enough to go after the narco-kingpins; government agencies and courts must also disrupt the drug market's supply-and-demand structures by prosecuting, and imprisoning, low-level street dealers, even users themselves. It is largely because of this intellectual maneuver that the United States' prison population grew so dramatically, and in such stark contrast to the situation in other industrial democracies, in the 1980s and 1990s.

In 1986, 38,541 people were sent to prison for drug crimes; ten years later, the number had skyrocketed to 148,092.[15] By the early twenty-first century, more than 1 million people were serving time in the country's prisons and jails for nonviolent offenses; almost half of these, 458,131, were incarcerated for drug offenses.[16] In 2000, the Center on Juvenile and Criminal Justice estimated that the price tag to localities, states, and the federal government for keeping these men and women behind bars was approximately $9.4 billion a year, with many billions more spent by state and federal agencies on drug interdiction, drug-related law enforcement, and drug-related prosecutions.[17] Faced with this and other studies (such as a 1995 report by the D.C.-based Sentencing Project indicating that nearly one in three black men in their twenties was in prison, on parole, or on probation, many for drug-related activities), an increasing number of political figures were willing to declare the war on drugs a failure. "We need a rational sentencing policy," said John Conyers, an outspoken Democratic congressman from Michigan, in 2005, "that encompasses such measures as fair and equitable sentencing, treatment instead of incarceration, drug courts, reentry programs, and restored judicial discretion."[18]

But the new thinking wasn't just coming from politicians on the left. By the 2000s, opponents ranged from public-health activists to libertarians such as former secretary of state George Schultz, who served under President Ronald Reagan. On the one hand, a diverse crowd of critics argued, despite huge increases in imprisonment, war on drugs policies had failed to make progress toward a drug-free America. On the other hand, with the federal government and many states heading deep into the red, the war was simply too expensive to sustain.

Harsh laws that required lengthy minimum sentences for the possession of even small amounts of drugs had created a boom not just in the imprisonment of addicted men—particularly those with black and brown skin—but also in the incarceration of women, tearing mothers away from their children and placing a huge burden on already stretched foster-care systems.[19] Moreover, in addition to the domestic strains generated by the drug wars, many of the country's costly overseas commitments—especially in the Caribbean and Latin America, where U.S. forces had been deployed in shadowy operations in remote parts of Colombia, Peru, and several other countries—were now determined by the logic of a militarized response to narcotics.

And yet drug use had, according to a number of studies, actually soared, with the number of teenagers saying they had used illegal drugs doubling from 1992 to 2000.[20] Even though it is notoriously hard to get accurate numbers on illegal drug use, the sheer volume of studies reporting higher use at the very least blunted the edge of the arguments espoused by drug war advocates. While the crack and heroin epidemics were coming slowly under control, new epidemics were taking center stage by the early twenty-first century. So-called party drugs such as ecstasy were a staple for huge numbers of teenagers and young adults; an underground market in prescription drugs, such as the pain-killer OxyContin—to which talk-radio celebrity Rush Limbaugh became addicted—was flourishing; and, especially in rural America, the manufacture and use of methamphetamine, accompanied by a wave of violent crimes, pros-titution, and family breakdown, was becoming as serious a problem as crack had been in the late 1980s.

In 2002 Asa Hutchinson, administrator of the Drug Enforcement Admin-istration, told the Senate Caucus on International Narcotics Control that "manufacturers of methamphetamine increasingly use national forests as lab-oratory sites." On other fronts, he warned that "cocaine and 'crack' cocaine remain readily available throughout much of the United States," and that heroin trafficking, much of it originating in Colombia and Mexico, had spread along with heroin use to "suburbs, smaller cities, and towns." As for Oxy-Contin, its "abuse is a growing problem throughout the nation . . . with phar-macies targeted nationwide for robberies of this drug."[21] The war on drugs had become, in many ways, a textbook policy failure, siphoning off huge resources in an attempt to deal with drug use as a matter of law enforcement rather than public health, with decidedly unsatisfying returns. Now, after a quarter of a century of attrition, a number of state politicians were willing to try new ap-proaches to the problem.

———————

In the late winter of 2003, New Mexico's former governor Gary Johnson was tending to a broken leg in preparation for an expedition to climb Mount Everest. His daredevil athleticism was, fans and foes both acknowledged, a marker of the same temperament that had allowed Johnson—a millionaire Republican devoted to fiscal conservatism and fond of "I pulled myself up by my bootstraps" rhetoric—to become the only governor ever to support drug legalization while in office. "Johnson was a huge advocate," recalled Jerry Montoya, in charge of one of the state's county needle-exchange programs, "ahead of federal policy in terms of thinking, in terms of philosophy."

During his tenure, Johnson had angered liberals through his hostility to tax-and-spend policies, his fondness for privatizing government functions—including prisons—and his frequent vetoing of new government programs. But he made enemies of traditional conservatives as well, primarily over his outspoken views on drug policy. He combatively declared the war on drugs "a miserable failure" and ambitiously pursued alternatives, including studying the possibility of legalization. In 2002, the last year of Johnson's tenure, state legislators, nudged on by the governor, voted to limit the ability of state police to seize the assets of those accused of drug-related crimes; to return a degree of case-by-case discretion to judges trying nonviolent drug cases; and to waive the federal ban on welfare benefits for former drug offenders who had completed their sentences and been released.

Although in his middle age he abstained from alcohol, caffeine, and even sugar, Johnson admitted that in his younger days he had dabbled with drugs. "I didn't hide it," he explained when we met in 2003 in his chalet-like house on the edge of the ski-mecca town of Taos, in northern New Mexico. "Growing up [in the 1960s], I smoked marijuana regularly in college and a little bit after college. And I experimented with other drugs." Combined with a strong libertarian streak, this experience made him a somewhat iconoclastic thinker on drug policy. "If we legalized all drugs tomorrow, we'd be better than we are now regarding death, disease and crime reduction," he argued forcefully. "There'd be more money into education; and more money into treatment for those who want or need treatment. At present rates, I'm going to see, in my life, 80 million Americans arrested for illegal drugs. The human cost of what we're doing is untold." After thinking for many years about the problem of drug addiction, Johnson concluded that policies such as distributing clean needles and providing heroin addicts just enough of the drug medically to satisfy their cravings would do more to manage addiction than simply sending the police out to round up addicts. Echoing the arguments made by opponents of Prohibition in the 1920s and early 1930s, he also came to believe that legalizing some categories of drugs and carefully regulating their sale would remove a huge pool of money from organized crime cartels, boost government tax revenues, and free up large amounts of money for drug-education programs and health centers.

Retired judge Woody Smith, who served on the bench in Albuquerque in the 1980s and 1990s before joining a Johnson task force on drug-law reforms, said of Johnson, "He believes our approach [to the war on drugs] was wrong, from a personal liberty standpoint and a pragmatic standpoint." Smith had also concluded that the country's approach to drugs needed to be drastically overhauled. "Legalization and regulation are the only answer," he argued. "It's not a perfect solution, but it's a hell of a lot better than what we're doing now."

On the back streets of the poorest barrios of Albuquerque, teams of workers with Youth Development Inc. (YDI) take their vans from one client-addict to another. Late into the night, they visit shooting galleries, private homes, and the cardboard shelters built in alleyways by some of the city's homeless. At each site, they reclaim dirty needles, fill in forms identifying the number of needles returned, give out an equivalent number of clean needles, provide bottles of needle-cleaning solution, and offer HIV tests. This was once a fairly underground operation, but in the wake of Johnson's reforms, grants from the New Mexico Department of Health and money from the federal Centers for Disease Control and Prevention (CDC) began supporting several groups like YDI. As of 2003 YDI and other groups were distributing hundreds of thousands of clean needles per month to approximately seven thousand card-carrying clients—and in exchange retrieving hundreds of thousands of dirty needles, thus dramatically reducing the likelihood that diseases such as HIV would be transmitted among the drug-using population.[22]

New Mexico's harm-reduction approach is widely acknowledged as a public-health triumph. Health experts saw a brief window of opportunity in which to create workable needle-exchange programs that could prevent HIV from spreading as hepatitis C already had, and the programs worked: in a state with one of the largest per capita IV-drug-using populations in the country (New Mexico recorded 11.6 heroin deaths per 100,000 between 1993 and 1995, compared to a national average of 5.4),[23] the needle-exchange program kept HIV to a bare minimum within the close-knit community of users. A study in 1997 found that, while the majority of the state's intravenous (IV) drug users had been exposed to hepatitis C—suggesting that considerable needle-sharing was taking place—less than 1 percent of IV users tested positive for HIV.[24] Six years later, Department of Health experts estimated that the HIV number was still below 3 percent, a fraction of the 27 percent reported by the CDC for cities such as Boston, Miami, and Washington, D.C.[25]

"My whole attitude about drug use and drug users has changed," asserted Rosie Clifford, a nurse who worked in a public health center in the hard-scrabble community of Los Lunas, twenty miles south of Albuquerque. "I used to be very conservative, very law and order. But even if you're really conservative, and you look at needle exchange, you ought to see it as a good way to stop the further spread of HIV and hepatitis and any blood-borne disease."

Danny, a twentysomething heroin addict when the needle-exchange volunteers introduced me to him in 2003, had been a client of YDI since 1999 and spoke with gratitude about the group's services. "I don't have to worry about used needles, about diseases," he said simply. "There was a time if I needed a new syringe I'd have to buy it for five bucks and you don't know if it's new or not." YDI also provided Danny with health-education pamphlets, and he knew that, if he needed one, the group would arrange for a doctor to visit him at home. Elsewhere in the state, in Rio Arriba County, near the nuclear laboratories of Los Alamos, public health workers were distributing not only needles but Narcan, an injected medication that can reverse the effects of a heroin overdose. They believed they had saved about a dozen lives by training addicts in its use.

Many of the communities in this beautiful mountainous region are desperately poor. Many of the roads are dusty and unpaved, dotted with impromptu altars set up in memory of those killed in car accidents—or murdered in battles over drugs and drug money. Heroin and methamphetamine addiction is so widespread here that in some homes three generations of users share their drugs. Yet while police in many parts of the United States routinely arrest users—and even level paraphernalia charges against addicts bringing dirty needles to exchange programs—when I visited Rio Arriba county the police chief, Richard Guillen, was allowing harm-reduction coordinators into his jail and encouraged his officers to coax addicts to seek treatment. Guillen believed that the old approach to drug addiction had failed: "All we're doing is interdiction at the federal level," he said, "and we haven't been successful in reducing demand." By contrast, he claimed, his local police recognized that "an addiction to drugs is just like any other illness. Let's try to get them treatment, counseling. Without treatment, all we have is a revolving door."

———

While no other state went quite so far as New Mexico in rethinking its approach to illegal drug usage, voters in states across the country, along with a growing number of state and local elected officials, shifted their support away from incarceration-based antidrug strategies and forced significant policy changes in the early 2000s. From conservative states such as Louisiana to more traditionally progressive states like Michigan, from heartland states such as Arizona, Colorado, and Kansas to coastal states such as California, all the big questions came up for debate: Should marijuana be decriminalized, at least for those with pressing medical needs? Should mandatory-minimum sentences for low-level drug offenders be abandoned? Should prison terms for nonviolent crimes, such as theft, resulting from a person's addiction to drugs be replaced by mandatory treatment? Should governments fund needle exchanges and other harm-reduction programs for IV-drug users as a way of controlling epidemics?

At the local level, the answers to these questions were increasingly yes, yes, yes, and yes. In 1996 voters in Arizona passed Proposition 200, transferring thousands of drug offenders into treatment programs. In California, a similar initiative passed in 2000, Proposition 36, channeled tens of thousands of addicts into treatment, and within two years reduced the number of inmates imprisoned on drug-possession charges from more than twenty thousand at the time of the law's passage to just over fifteen thousand in June 2002.[26] A similar law was passed by legislators in Hawaii.

A survey conducted by the Pew Research Center in 2001 found that fully 73 percent of Americans favored allowing marijuana for medical use; 47 percent favored rolling back mandatory-minimum sentences for nonviolent drug offenders; and 52 percent believed that drug use should be treated as a disease rather than a crime.[27] The following year, a CNN/*Time* poll found that 80 percent favored allowing marijuana to be used as a medicine.

In 1998 Michigan repealed the state's notorious "650-lifer" laws that mandated a life sentence for those caught in possession of more than 650 grams of certain narcotics. Then, on Christmas Day of 2002, Governor John Engler signed legislation that further rolled back the state's tough mandatory-minimum drug sentences and its equally tough "lifetime probation," which had been imposed on many drug offenders following their release from prison. The following year North Dakota repealed its one-year mandatory-minimum sentence for those convicted on a first-time drug-possession charge, in the wake of a similar change enacted a few months earlier in Connecticut. Indiana and Louisiana also repealed some of their statutory sentences, and Louisiana—the state with the highest incarceration rate in the nation—restored parole and probation options for inmates convicted of a host of nonviolent offenses. In Kansas, a sentencing commission proposed major reforms of the state's mandatory sentencing codes coupled with an expansion of treatment provisions. Despite opposition from conservative legislators, these recommendations were accepted in late March 2003.

"It's definitely a change of philosophy regarding how you deal with drug offenders," Barbara Tombs, executive director of the Kansas Sentencing Commission, stated when we spoke shortly afterward. "With the state budget cuts and [many] drug treatment programs in prisons being eliminated, there is an urgent need to look at alternatives to incarceration for drug prisoners." Even Mississippi, traditionally one of the least-merciful states in the country when it came to punishing criminals, repealed the strictest of its sentencing provisions, making it possible for nonviolent offenders to apply for parole after serving a quarter of their sentences rather than the previous minimum of 85 percent.

At the same time, a clutch of states—Alaska, California, Hawaii, Maine, Montana, Nevada, Oregon, Vermont, and Washington, as well as the District of Columbia—adopted medical-marijuana legislation, legalizing the drug's use for specific medical conditions such as AIDS wasting. A similar measure in Colorado, passed by a citizens' initiative, was invalidated only by a technicality; a few years later, in November 2005, voters in Denver passed a symbolic initiative decriminalizing personal possession of up to an ounce of marijuana. Unenforceable because it clashed with state law, the initiative was, nevertheless, seen as a sign of the Denver electorate's strong dissatisfaction with the war on drugs.

———————

Taken as a whole, these reforms and political movements represented the biggest change to state drug policies in over a generation. But they weren't enough to end the national war on drugs. Legislators in many states continued to reject reforms; a divided statehouse in North Carolina, for example, narrowly voted against changes to the mandatory-minimum sentencing requirements several years in a row. Instead, lawmakers opted to build four more one-thousand-bed prisons. Nor were the reforms enough to stanch the growth in the overall U.S. prison population, with much of the rise still due to drug sentencing. Indeed, by 2002 fully one-third of all sentences handed down by state courts were for drug offenses, 20 percent for dealing, and 12 percent for possession.[28] In 2004, a decade after the long decline in crime began, Minnesota and Idaho's prisoner populations both grew by over 11 percent in a single year, and Georgia's system grew by more than 8 percent.[29]

In addition, the regional pullouts from aspects of the drug war weren't enough to stop increasing numbers of people in many locales from being arrested and charged with pot-related misdemeanors. In New York, plummeting crime rates and a drop in the number of people arrested, convicted, and imprisoned for felonies were partially offset by rapidly rising marijuana arrests. As the city's police force strove to implement so-called quality-of-life policing strategies during Rudy Giuliani's mayoral term, they arrested ever more people for smoking marijuana on building stoops or in city parks, and cycled them into jail for short stays.

Perhaps most important, while state legislatures had finally opened up financial and moral debates over drug policy in their jurisdictions, the federal government refused to climb on board. Bureau of Justice Statistics data show that the number of people charged with drug offenses in federal courts more than doubled between 1984 (11,854) and 1999 (29,306). During that fifteen-year period, the amount of time a federal drug prisoner could expect to serve in prison also more than doubled, from thirty months to sixty-six months. By 2003, the bureau was reporting that 37 percent of all charges filed in federal courts related to drug offenses. The time these people could expect to spend in prison had also increased significantly, even since 1999; average sentences were now nearly seven years. It became almost impossible for convicted drug offenders in the federal system to avoid prison time. In 1988, 79 percent of those convicted were sent to prison. By 2003, the number had risen to 92 percent.[30] In 2004 alone, the Bureau of Prisons, the system of prisons for housing federal inmates, grew in size by over seven thousand prisoners, expanding the total number by over 4 percent and leading to chronic overcrowding within the federal system.[31]

On many issues, from gun ownership to environmental regulation, George W. Bush's administration blindly backed the conservative cause of states' rights, rolling back federal controls and giving state systems a degree of discretion on critical social and economic policies that they hadn't experienced in half a century. But when it came to narcotics, the same administration blocked even mild attempts at state drug-law reform. The Justice Department fought medical-marijuana laws in court and launched a massive public-relations campaign against pot use. It even encouraged federal prosecution of those who legally distributed medical marijuana under state laws, looking to redirect tens of millions of dollars in drug-war funds to prosecute both medical-marijuana users and those who provided them with the drug. "[Then–attorney general John] Ashcroft is willing to push even the smallest cases," asserted David Fetello, director of the Campaign for a New Drug Policy, when I interviewed him in 2003. "We're seeing a new level of pettiness and aggression."

During Bill Clinton's presidency, the country's drug czar, General Barry McAffrey, was criticized by drug-policy reform advocates for his refusal to discuss legalization initiatives and his zeal for militarizing the drug wars overseas, in particular committing U.S. troops to coca-eradication campaigns in Latin America. But at least toward the end of his reign, McAffrey talked somewhat critically about the uncontrolled growth of the American prison system.

In the years following his departure, John Walters, appointed by President Bush to succeed McAffrey, pursued the hardest of hard-line drug policies. Under Walters, the Office of National Drug Control Policy (ONDCP) encouraged state prosecutors to go after medical-marijuana providers, especially in California, and drove underground virtually every medical-marijuana buyers' club in the country. It held press conferences opposing citizens' reform initiatives, and, in the wake of the 2001 attacks on America, it sponsored extravagant newspaper and TV advertising campaigns costing tens of millions of dollars that explicitly linked teen drug use to terrorism, using the argument that some terrorist organizations were apparently generating funds by distributing heroin and, to a lesser extent, cocaine.

Walters also put pressure on state legislators, declaring that many drug-law reforms would contravene federal laws. Before the 2002 elections, he traversed the country, stopping in Arizona, Michigan, Nevada, and Ohio, campaigning against medical marijuana and meeting with newspaper editors to push his case. When Congress debated reauthorization bills for the ONDCP in 2003, House Republicans, at the urging of the White House, inserted amendments that would have allowed the office to spend almost $1 billion in public money on ads attacking state and local ballot measures that promoted drug-law reform, as well as to redirect $60 million in federal funds for the prosecution of medical-marijuana users. Ultimately, the entire reauthorization package died in committee, and ONDCP funds kept flowing only on a temporary and emergency basis. At the time of this writing, however, the White House was still pushing for Congress to pass a longer-term reauthorization bill.

As a result of federal intransigence, despite the wind having been taken out of many states' drug-war sails by economic crisis and voter dissatisfaction, the prison population continued to expand nationally, albeit at a slower rate than it did during the breakneck growth years of the 1980s and 1990s. Throughout the United States, hundreds of thousands of drug offenders were serving years behind bars, and tens of thousands of prisoners—many convicted of heinous crimes such as murder, but thousands of others convicted of repeat low-end felonies such as fraud and drug possession and sentenced under habitual-offender statutes—were serving decades-long, and in many cases life, sentences. Such were the hard realities wrought by three decades of "wars" on crime and drugs.

CHAPTER 8

STOREHOUSES OF THE LIVING DEAD

For prison reformers, the problem wasn't just that the incarcerated population kept ballooning, or that more and more counties in the United States' increasingly dilapidated hinterlands were seeking correctional facilities to house this population. An equally pressing issue was the types of prisons that were sprouting up, and the ultrasecure modifications being designed for existing sites.

As the number of prisoners and the number of prisons grew in the 1980s and 1990s, belief in the rehabilitative function of incarceration declined. "Rehabilitation" suggested softness in an age when the political climate cried out for hardness. It implied a social-work function for prison guards and correctional personnel at a time when politicians and their voters seemed to want only punishment. "In the nineties," stated American Correctional Association president Gwen Chunn, who cut her teeth as a correctional reformer in the 1970s, "the notion of 'Get tough' came from the very top and permeated the entire system."

Not surprisingly, as more prisoners were manufactured by posturing tough-on-crime legislators, and more towns and villages turned themselves into hubs for the burgeoning incarceration industry, conditions within many prisons headed south. Sometimes, through overcrowding and penny-pinching, the conditions seemed simply to drift that way, almost without being guided. "When you have a system that is terribly overcrowded and when you have cutbacks in the economy, you automatically set up a situation that predicts a lot of things," Chunn averred. At other times, the move into harsher incarceration terrain was very much a calculated result, a deliberate attempt to "toughen up" the conditions of confinement, to create supermax prisons and control units within which increasingly large numbers of inmates would be confined. Euphemistically termed "adjustment centers," they were in a way the brass knuckles of incarceration, instruments designed to mentally break and crush the most dangerous, troublesome prisoners.

In the summer of 2001, over six hundred inmates in the notorious supermax prison of Pelican Bay, in the rainy redwood terrain of northern California near the small, onetime lumber town of Crescent City, refused to eat their prison meals.[1] The food-strikers argued that the prison was literally driving them insane, and they wanted things to change. They lived their lives—more than twenty-three hours of each day—in tiny barren concrete cells the size of walk-in closets, grouped in pods of eight cells radiating out in spokes from control booths. They were fed their meals through mail-type slots in their doors. They were allowed out into the chilly yard to exercise for less than an hour a day; and they were escorted to the showers just a few times a week. Because this was a supermax, the inmates weren't allowed to decorate their walls; they were permitted no televisions; and their commissary rights were limited, as were the number of noncontact visits and phone calls they were granted each month. At least they *were* allowed books. In Texas's supermaxes and Florida's Closed Management Units (until a lawsuit pressured the Department of Corrections to modify its rules), reading, apart from religious texts, was a privilege denied most inmates.[2]

Approximately twenty-five-hundred years ago, Plato described the netherworld of Tartarus as a place where the only-partially-damned would have to watch the eternal torments of the incurables—those individuals whose souls would never be redeemed. In their suffering, the incurables would serve as a warning to others, a post-death deterrent force aimed at preventing only marginally damned souls from further straying in their thoughts and actions. Ancient historians, from Polybius to Livy, talked of the notion of hell as a vital, if fantastic, way of managing the passions of the mob. In the early Christian era, five hundred years after Plato, the Roman writer Plutarch described, in extraordinarily vivid detail, the different punishments awaiting various categories of sinners in the afterlife, as well as the shaming rituals that formed a core part of this vision. Virgil, in the *Aeneid*, and Dante a millennium later, divided their underworlds into landscapes of minutely calibrated, and differentiated, sinners and responses to sin.

In the clinical precision with which different punishments are meted out to various categories of unmanageable prisoners; in the combination of sheer torment, shaming, and deterrent politics employed, today's supermax prisons have become a modern-day netherworld for society's damned—its living dead. In many, albeit more prosaic, ways it is a world as rife with symbolism, a world that speaks as much to the fears and nightmare visions of our age, as Tartarus and hell did to the peoples of Plato and Plutarch's times.

In January 1995, more than six years before the Pelican Bay food strike, inmates had won a class-action lawsuit, *Madrid v. Gomez,* against the California Department of Corrections (CDoC), with Judge Thelton Henderson finding that the staff at Pelican Bay had systematically brutalized prisoners; that the ways in which prison administrators categorized inmates as gang members violated due process; and that seriously mentally ill inmates were becoming far sicker, were, in the lingo, "decompensating" within the confines of the huge, escape-proof complex.[3] In a stinging rebuke to CDoC—a department that, in July 2005, under Governor Schwarzenegger, was somewhat optimistically renamed the California Department of Corrections and Rehabilitation—the judge ordered that a special master be appointed to oversee Pelican Bay. "The physical environment reinforces a sense of isolation and detachment from the outside world, and helps create a palpable distance from ordinary compunctions, inhibitions and community norms," Henderson wrote in describing the severe beatings, the third-degree burns inflicted on one mentally ill inmate, and the use of restraining weapons routinely employed against others. "The Eighth Amendment's restraint on using excessive force has been repeatedly violated at Pelican Bay, leading to a conspicuous pattern of excessive force."[4]

Henderson ordered Pelican Bay to create a special secure wing for its most seriously mentally ill prisoners, within which more resources for treating their symptoms would be concentrated. He also ordered the prison to modify some of the most extreme conditions for its other inmates. What the judge didn't rule, however, was that the supermax model per se was a violation of the Eighth Amendment; so, while the administration of Pelican Bay was overhauled, the basic parameters of the system stayed the same. In the years following, while the violence wasn't as overt and the most explicitly disturbed inmates were removed from the segregation units, the basic conditions of sensory deprivation stayed intact. In California, several years after Henderson's ruling, more than eight thousand inmates continued to be double-bunked in locked-down cells, meaning that two men shared an eight-by-eight-foot cell for close to twenty-four hours a day. A measure of the effect of this double-bunking: in the late 1990s, at least eight Pelican Bay prisoners were murdered by their cellmates.[5]

As summer faded to fall, the food strike at Pelican Bay collapsed, but the issues that prompted it remained. Nationally, according to the U.K.-based penal expert Roy King, writing in an essay published in the journal *Punishment and Society* in 1998, following a spasm of supermax construction throughout the 1990s, some twenty thousand prisoners were incarcerated in supermaxes in the United States, at an average cost to taxpayers of about fifty thousand dollars per inmate per year. Tens of thousands more were imprisoned in long-term secure housing units, essentially miniature versions of the supermaxes within other prisons.[6]

In Arizona, according to a 1997 report by the National Institute of Corrections (a branch of the U.S. Department of Justice) titled *Supermax Housing: A Survey of Current Practice,* 8 percent of prisoners were being housed in supermaxes, and another 28 percent were being kept in segregation units. In Mississippi, as many as 12 percent of the state's inmates were being kept in supermax conditions by century's end, and the state estimated that it needed to house fully 20 percent of its inmates in supermax facilities and another 35 percent in "routine segregation."[7] In Virginia, Colorado, and several other states where tough-on-crime rhetoric had taken particular hold, approximately 5 percent of inmates lived in supermax prisons and many more in secure units. And in Texas, somewhere in the region of ten thousand prisoners lived in these units, with the numbers predicted to increase dramatically as the state opened up more supermax prisons in the years to come.

By the beginning of the year 2000, a partial survey by the *Corrections Yearbook* estimated that over 42,000 U.S. inmates were in some form of segregated housing. In Florida, more than 7,000 segregated inmates were double-bunked. In the Florida Corrections Commission's annual report for 2000,[8] the department urged the state to build another Special Management Unit to house 1,000 more inmates; construction costs were estimated at nearly 50 million dollars. In New York State alone, 1,500 double-bunked supermax cells had been opened since 1997. And by the end of 2000, according to the state's Department of Correctional Services, a total of 5,505 inmates were kept in "disciplinary housing."

"The forceful rushes of this isolational perversion has pulled my essence into a cesspool," wrote one mentally ill segregated correspondent to prison monitor Bonnie Kerness, of the American Friends Service Committee. Accompanying his florid words was a penciled image of a grown man curled up into a fetal position against a brick wall. "This just ain't life, pathologized in a subsumed litany of steel and cement codes preoccupied with the disturbing thrust of death."

"I have over 6 friends who couldn't cope with the confinement and while in solitary confinement begin to become delusional and the mental health staff ignored the signs and as a result they each committed suicide," an inmate from Maryland wrote to me in the summer of 2005. Another scrawled a rambling note from a prison in Arizona: "Mental health treatment here is a joke 100mg of Thorizine and the Doctor comes up to your cell and asks what your problems are and your suppose to tell him in front of the whole run like you want 120 inmates knowing what your problems are. Its rediculas this whole system is rediculas if I want to get any help or attention I have to threaten to kill my self and or smear shit all over my self."

From Washington State came a missive on segregated prisoners "shit-bombing" mentally ill inmates brought into the Hole. "Shitbombs: admixture's of those prisoner's feces and urine that they'll throw or 'shoot' SHU [secure housing unit] prisoners with. They use the disposable ink pens innermost thin hollow plastic tubing in conjunct with syrup packets that are of a rubberized plastic and hold appx. 4 ozs. They manufacture little shitbomb vacuum cleaner-like bags with the pen tubs for use in being pin-point accurate: during indoor 'yard' the thin narrow corridor that runs the length of the tier; said asshole/predators will walk right up to SHU-er's cell fronts and (the tiniest crack/opening is all they need) they will then shoot their shit and piss mixtures all over either the prisoner and/or his papers, linens etc. Is it a wonder that some M.H. prisoner hung himself in W.S.P.'s SEG unit within the past immediate 2 or 3 years?"

Trying to explain what life in lockdown was like, one prisoner, incarcerated since his teen years, wrote from Corcoran, California, on lined yellow paper, "Do me a favor Mr. Abramsky! Go into your closet (you do have a walk-in right?), turn the light on, remove everything, insert a cot, a change of underware (T-shirt, boxers, socks), a few reading materials, writing supplies, and live there a week. Only a week. But imagine for that week that that's where you have lived since you were 17 years old." The prisoner went on, "Imagine that while you're hear, the Police constantly are putting you down. Taking your things. You make a little something nice to make your concrete box more comfortable and they take it. Then berate you. How long before the caged dog bites back?"

———

In October 2001, halfway across the continent from Pelican Bay, U.S. District Court judge Barbara Crabb issued a preliminary ruling in a class-action lawsuit brought by inmates at the supermax prison in Boscobel, Wisconsin, who claimed that the extreme isolation, resulting mental stress, and restrictions on personal property at the prison constituted a violation of their Eighth and Fourteenth Amendment rights.[9] A little over a month earlier, Crabb had heard testimony from fifty-seven-year-old Terry Kupers, a Berkeley psychiatrist and author of the book *Prison Madness*. Four years earlier, Kupers, a member of Physicians for Human Rights, had worked as a researcher for a Human Rights Watch report on supermax prisons in Indiana. The report, *Cold Storage*, had documented high levels of mental illness and brutality within the state's two supermax facilities, and researchers had found several prisoners who had accumulated so many disciplinary infractions that they were slated to spend literally decades in the isolated segregation units.[10]

Now, in Wisconsin, Kupers had gone into court to tell the judge that "there're a lot of crazy people in here and they need to be removed on an emergency basis because it's not safe." He testified that he had interviewed inmates who had been diagnosed with paranoid schizophrenia and continued to hallucinate despite high doses of Thorazine. In his declaration to the court, he wrote of prisoners who had previously been admitted to hospitals for psychotic behavior who were nonetheless kept in the harshest conditions of isolation at the prison.

Judge Crabb's ruling ordered the Department of Corrections to immediately remove five mentally ill inmates from Boscobel and provide an independent mental-health assessment to any inmate with symptoms of mental illness. "The conditions at Supermax are so severe and restrictive," Crabb wrote, "that they exacerbate the symptoms that mentally ill inmates exhibit. Many of the severe conditions serve no legitimate penological interest; they can only be considered punishment for punishment's sake." Subsequently, following a settlement agreement reached in March 2002, the state agreed not to house any seriously mentally ill inmates in Boscobel, and moved thirty-nine men out of the prison. For those prisoners remaining in Boscobel, the state agreed to let them out of their cells for more than an hour a day (the previous norm), to increase the number of phone calls inmates were allowed to make to family members, and to introduce some educational and vocational programs. The state also agreed to improve the prison's medical services and limit the use of restraining devices and stun guns.[11]

For longtime advocates such as attorney Jamie Fellner, of Human Rights Watch, such a blanket judicial statement against the conditions prevalent in supermaxes was the holy grail. Yet it applied only to Boscobel, Wisconsin's only supermax; elsewhere in the country, such prisons continued to flourish, their conditions unchanged by Judge Crabb's ruling. "The moral critique," Fellner told me, "is this: Secure Housing Units have been designed at the best with utter disregard for human misery. At the worst it's a deliberate use of human misery for deterrence and punishment."[12]

"There are few if any forms of imprisonment that produce so many indices of psychological trauma and symptoms of psychopathology in those persons subjected to it," wrote Craig Haney, a professor of psychology at the University of California at Santa Cruz who studied the effects of isolation on prisoners, in 2001. The symptoms, Haney went on to write, included everything from uncontrollable rage to lethargy and helplessness, from panic attacks to emotional breakdowns all the way up to hallucinations, psychosis, self-mutilation, and suicidal impulses. "This kind of confinement creates its own set of psychological pressures that, in some instances, uniquely disable prisoners for free world reintegration."[13]

———•———

Precursors to the supermax model first emerged in the early 1970s, as a response to rising inmate-on-staff violence and the growing menace of powerful prison gangs such as the Black Guerillas. The catalyst was a series of murders carried out by federal prisoners against their guards at Marion penitentiary in Illinois. In the wake of this bloodshed, prison authorities developed procedures to minimize inmate–staff contact, finally "locking down" the entire prison in 1972, feeding the inmates in their cells, and closing down the communal exercise yard. Eventually, they began to explore the idea of making the general prison population safer by creating separate high-tech "supermax" prisons in which the worst of the worst would be imprisoned in permanent lockdown conditions. Their plans eventually led to the construction of the federal supermax at Florence, Colorado, home to such infamous criminals as the Unabomber, convicted 9/11 plotter Zacarias Moussaoui, and, before his execution, Oklahoma City bomber Timothy McVeigh.

In states like California—where eleven prison guards were murdered between 1970 and 1973, and a staggering thirty-two prisoners were killed by other inmates in 1972 alone—prison planners quickly latched on to the potential of this new model. After August 1971, when the black-nationalist prisoner George Jackson and three prison guards died in a shootout at San Quentin, many maximum-security prisons, such as Folsom, Soledad, and San Quentin, were put on "lockdown." At the same time, California's guards, increasingly fearful for their lives as prisoners influenced by the political rhetoric of the Black

Panthers and the less ideological language of Southern California's street gangs rose up in "rebellion," abandoned their old trade union and coalesced into the more assertive California Correctional Peace Officers Association. "There was a great deal of fear," James Park, associate warden at San Quentin during these years, remembered thirty years on. He was now an old man, with a walrus mustache and sparse gray hair, his green shirt tucked into the elastic waistband of his rumpled blue pants, but he still had an almost photographic memory for events and people in California's prison history stretching back until the days just after World War II, when he was first hired into the system. "We had four to five thousand employees carrying guns off duty because they were convinced the Black Panthers were going to come get them. And we had demonstrations outside the prisons—college students, that sort of thing."

Within a few years, as the bulk of California's huge population swung their support behind law-and-order conservatives instead of the political radicals who had sought to make revolutionaries out of prisoners (or, rather, to define prisoners as an oppressed political class), the CCPOA had emerged as the most powerful guards' union in the country. Taking advantage of their newfound political clout (which would increase exponentially in the 1980s and 1990s as the union began heavily funding local and state political figures; the union was the single largest contributor to the campaigns of both Republican governor Pete Wilson and his Democratic successor, Gray Davis),[14] the guards pushed for tighter security policies and greater emphasis on isolation for those prisoners, especially gang members, who were categorized as being particularly dangerous.

In the late 1970s, after prisons such as Folsom had experienced years-long lockdowns, California's prison planners began actively working to create new supermax units. These wouldn't be ordinary cellblocks with extraordinary security precautions; instead, they would be prisons within prisons—an architectural leap back toward the Panopticon system designed by Jeremy Bentham in the late eighteenth century, updated to incorporate late-twentieth-century state-of-the-art electronic surveillance and control technology. Yet, unlike Bentham's hypothetical prison, intended in large part as an act of theater designed to convince the world at large of the futility of crime—and supposedly calibrated, in tune with the most progressive philosophy of the day, to remodel prisoners' behavior in a way that would convert them into law-abiding citizens upon their release—the new supermax units were not intended to "rehabilitate."

How prisoners would behave back in the community after serving years

in such environments was a question entirely outside the orbit of their cre-
ators. Rather, they would serve a similar function to that of the Babylonian
netherworld, mythologized four thousand years ago and described by the historian Alan Bernstein, in his book *The Formation of Hell,* as a "tightly sealed
storehouse of the dead, surrounded like a Bronze Age city by a series of con-
centric walls."[15] They were, quite simply, intended to temporarily entomb the
worst of the worst, to store them for a specified time before dumping them
back onto the streets from whence they'd come.

By the mid-1980s, after the white-supremacist Aryan Brotherhood gang
killed several prison guards, a special California Department of Corrections
task force recommended to then-governor George Deukmejian that the state
go a step further. Instead of being content with supermax units, the state
would now embark on a massive program of building entirely new prisons,
labeled "special housing," for hard-to-control inmates. Corcoran opened in
1988, followed a year later by Pelican Bay. In a system where prisoners were
officially categorized into four levels, the supermaxes added an unofficial fifth
tier: what the San Francisco prison investigator Tom Quinn termed a series of
"Pentagons" designed to concentrate in a few facilities the meanest, baddest
gang lieutenants and sociopaths in the system. These would be the Alcatrazes
of the modern age.

Throughout the 1990s, despite year-by-year declines in crime, one state
after another pumped tens of millions of dollars into building supermax
facilities. And as the tough-on-crime, tough-on-criminals political rhetoric
heated up, more and more prisoners were moved into supermaxes and secure
housing units, sent after a disciplinary review process or an administrative
maneuver that allowed prison authorities to place inmates in "administrative
segregation" without a hearing. In a comprehensive survey carried out in 1997,
the National Institute of Corrections found that thirty-four correctional systems were either already operating supermax units or were planning to open
at least one within two years, with more than fifty such sites in existence
around the country.[16]

Defenders of supermaxes argued that the restrictions provided a way of
establishing control in inherently dangerous environments. "A prison of this
nature is necessary," thirty-two-year-old warden Todd Ishee, who had by then
been in charge of Ohio State Penitentiary for a year and a half, explained to
me in late 2001. "In 1993, our maximum-security prison at Southern Ohio
Correctional Facility was host to a riot. One correctional officer was killed.
A number of inmates were killed and several injured. Following the riot, the

department made a decision that a five-hundred-bed facility of this nature was needed to control the most dangerous inmates." However, while having such restricted facilities as prisons of last resort might make sense for some inmates, critics have argued almost from the get-go that far too many inmates are being removed into these quasi fortresses, victims of a political climate in which legislators and prison administrators tripped over themselves to appear as tough on criminals as the law would permit them to be.

In Ohio, for example, state senator Robert Hagan, appointed to a committee to oversee his state's prisons, concluded that fewer than half of the inmates at Ohio State Penitentiary (OSP) should be considered maximum-security material. His belief seemed to be backed up by Corrections Department data indicating that, of the more than 350 inmates incarcerated at OSP in the late 1990s, only about twenty were ringleaders of the 1993 riot, and another thirty-one had killed either an inmate or a correctional officer while in the general prison population. The rest were convicted, by departmental disciplinary panels, of assaults within the prison system (often no more than a fistfight with another inmate), of having attempted to escape, or of posing a more vaguely defined "security threat" to the workings of the prison machinery. These catchall categories have been used, some monitors argue, to remove jailhouse lawyers—inmates who offer legal advice to fellow prisoners—and other ordinary convicts. In Virginia, independent consultant Jim Austin, hired by the Department of Corrections to examine its inmate classification system, found that the state should be putting more inmates into medium-security prisons. Instead, in the late 1990s Virginia shelled out $150 million to build Red Onion and Wallens Ridge, two supermax facilities with a combined capacity of twenty-four hundred prisoners, both of which rapidly started generating serious allegations of staff-on-inmate violence.

While Canada, to the north, based its penal practices "on research and empirical evidence," postulated Allen Ault, onetime corrections director in Colorado, Georgia, and Mississippi and program director of the National Institute for Corrections from 1996 to 2003, "in America it's strictly run by politics. Research plays little part in state corrections. Crime is back down to the 1970s level, yet the inmate population still rises. So there's no correlation between crime and the inmate population." Ault believed that rising social tensions had played out in a public demand for ever-tougher penal practices, and that what he termed "knee-jerk sentencing laws" had created a dangerously large, and thus hard to control, prison population. "We don't do things by research and facts. We do things by politics."

"We built prisons, carpeted them coast to coast, but there was not money to *do* anything with the people in prison," theorized Allan Breed when I met him in 2005. Breed was a tough-looking octogenarian with a weathered, tan face dominated by extraordinarily bushy eyebrows and intensely focused blue eyes. He had spent much of his career as a special master, someone appointed by federal courts to oversee state prison systems, including that of California, and had seen firsthand the ways in which tough-on-crime rhetoric had affected the United States' penal landscape. "It became a vicious cycle. We lock up more people, don't do anything with them. At the same time, you're getting riots. Parole was the next victim. Inmates had nothing to fight for—good behavior didn't get them anything, because mandatory-minimum sentences were so long. You get a riot in prison and legislators respond by saying, 'We've got to build supermaxes.' As far as prisons are concerned, I could send you to some prisons that are clean, modern, but I really don't know of any that help offenders obtain the skills they need to stay out of trouble when they leave. With a few isolated exceptions, it's not happening anywhere."

Nationally, according to the Florida Corrections Commission, fully one-third of the correctional departments that operate supermax prisons report placing inmates in them not for serious offenses but because there simply isn't enough short-term disciplinary housing in lower-security prisons.[17] And while, in Ohio at least, the data *do* indicate that inmate-on-staff violence has decreased somewhat in the years since the Ohio State Penitentiary opened, they do not support the other claim of such institutions: that they increase the safety of the general prison population by isolating the most violent minority. Indeed, in the year 2000 there were 441 inmate-on-inmate assaults within the Ohio prison system, compared to 394 in 1997, the year before OSP opened. Nationwide, according to *Corrections Yearbook* data, there were 13,379 inmate-on-staff assaults in 1994 and 24,128 inmate-on-inmate attacks. Five years later, after the rash of supermax openings, there were 16,152 inmate attacks on staff and 31,314 inmate-on-inmate incidents. And in 2001, while inmate-on-inmate assaults had declined slightly to 28,827, inmate-on-staff assaults had risen to 16,435. Because the prison population had grown during those years, this *did* represent a slight decline in the rate of incidents per ten thousand prisoners, but only a very slight one. In fact, like so many criminal-justice measures based principally on politics, the policy is a Faustian bargain purchased at a staggering financial and social cost.

Inside these high-tech prisons, the inmates, deemed incorrigible by the correctional system, protected by hardly any outside oversight, are often subjected to particularly brutal treatment. In Texas, in what can only be described as an example of what sociologist Hannah Arendt famously termed the "banality of evil," correctional bureaucrats devised a system that punished segregated inmates who didn't return their food trays by putting them onto a "food loaf" regimen, during which the prisoners were fed loaves of all of the day's ingredients mashed together; and they created paper gowns to be worn by prisoners who tore up their regular prison clothes, and "paper masks" for inmates who spat at correctional officers. All of this is minutely documented by prison regulations, with Texas's administrative-segregation plan, published in 2001, stating that "the initial review date and subsequent review dates of those offenders placed on paper gown or paper mask restriction or the food loaf shall be documented on the Segregation Confinement Record. . . . When an offender is placed on a food loaf, paper gown, paper mask or property restriction, the date, time, reason for restriction, review dates and the signature of the officer must be documented on this form."[18]

In California the lack of outside oversight and the dramatic expansion in the power of correctional guards led to huge increases in staff-on-inmate violence at the top-security prisons. Indeed, said Tom Quinn, in 1987 (a year before Corcoran opened, but well into the permanent-lockdown experiment), guards in California killed two more prisoners than had been killed in the entire previous twelve years combined. A decade later, Corcoran prison's administration was completely overhauled after details emerged, many of them in a hard-hitting series of investigative articles published by the *Los Angeles Times*, that correctional officers had promoted fights between rival gang members and had then shot the pugilists apart, often with lethal consequences. In *The Nation* magazine, journalist Alex Cockburn detailed other stories such as guards setting inmates up to be raped by known sexual predators, and guards beating shackled men, newly arrived at the prison, while reportedly screaming, "Welcome to hell."[19] Despite the documentation of these allegations, local juries, in a town whose economy was almost totally reliant on the prison, refused to convict the handful of guards brought to trial in the wake of the events.

At the sparkling new Red Onion and Wallens Ridge prisons in Virginia, Human Rights Watch and other organizations documented claims by inmates —including those imported from New Mexico and Connecticut—that they were "initiated" into the prisons with a beating by guards, and that guards routinely resorted to stun guns and restraining chairs to control their inmates. One inmate even alleged that guards shoved the open end of a pair of handcuffs into his rectum.

Meanwhile, in the large supermaxes of Texas, self-mutilation was running rampant within a few years of their opening, with inmates slashing at their veins in order to get attention from prison staff. When I visited one supermax facility in the late 1990s, I witnessed guards joking among themselves about the "mutilators." According to a highly critical report by Dr. Thomas Conklin, who evaluated mental-health care within the Estelle Unit in Texas in 1998, "All suicide gestures by inmates are seen as manipulating the correctional system with the conscious intent of secondary gain. In not one case was the inmate's behavior seen as reflecting mental pathology that could be treated."[20] In the first eight months of 2001, there were 250 attempted suicides within the Texas prison system. Ironically enough, Jim Estelle, the departmental director after whom the unit was named, was no fan of the enforced idleness, the lack of vocational training, and the high stress levels that largely defined such places. "The administration of a correctional institution ain't rocket science. It's really pretty simple. If you keep it clean, quiet, safe, then if you feed them well and assign them to productive, constructive work assignments, there's a whole lot of hostility, anger and negative energy dissipated in that process." Arguing for intensive job training for inmates to prepare them for their eventual release—something impossible to implement inside the locked-down environs of the supermax—Estelle said in 2005, "We don't get journeymen cooks, bakers, plumbers, electricians. We don't even get good rodeo men. We get the inept, the stupid, the flotsam and the jetsam, that you in the outside world kicked out and ignored. That's what we get in the prison system."

In Ohio State Penitentiary, seventy inmates were placed on suicide watch during the first year of the prison's existence, and three succeeded in taking their own lives. "They bring you here, separate you, and eliminate all contact, thinking that it will mentally break you down, but in all essence it's creating a person who could possibly become very dangerous to himself or others," wrote one inmate, in response to a 1999 survey on conditions at OSP carried out by the husband-and-wife attorney team Staughton and Alice Lynd.[21] Another wrote, "When you keep beating a dog what's that dog going to do? Bite you. What would that dog do if he had no hope and nothing to do? I will be released from here in November, and you know what, I'm a very bitter man."

Not surprisingly, given their harsh conditions, even the best-run supermax facilities witness huge rates of mental illness among their inmates. A study carried out by the Washington State Department of Corrections on its "internal management units" found that "approximately 30 percent of IMU residents show evidence of serious mental illness. This is substantially higher than the 10–15 percent estimates of prevalence in total inmate populations."[22] In Texas, psychology experts hired by plaintiffs' attorneys in the decades-long *Ruiz* lawsuit, a massive class-action suit alleging wholesale constitutional violations by the Texas Department of Criminal Justice, found that mental-health care in these units was often virtually nonexistent, with officers grievously undertrained in dealing with psychotic prisoners, medications being administered haphazardly, and dangerously high patient–staff ratios.[23] Meanwhile, at the Tamms supermax in the cornfield belt of southern Illinois, a class-action lawsuit was filed against the Department of Corrections in 1999 by a group of mentally ill inmates who alleged that their health was being adversely affected by the prison environment. The suit referred to the inmates beating their heads against the cell walls, seeing demons crawl out of the walls, biting their own shoulders, and slicing their arms, necks, and abdomens. One inmate, in August 1998, allegedly began eating his own flesh in front of a correctional officer.[24]

———

The great chicken-and-egg question is whether healthy inmates go mad under these extreme conditions of confinement, or whether it is mentally unstable, impulsive general-population inmates who commit the sorts of disciplinary infractions that result in them being shipped off to SHUs or supermax prisons in the first place, where they are then more likely to decompensate.

Some psychiatrists, such as Harvard professor Stuart Grassian, have testified in court that sensory deprivation leads otherwise mentally healthy individuals to develop extreme manifestations of psychosis, with symptoms including hallucinations, the hearing of voices, uncontrollable rage, paranoia, and almost catatonic depressions. Grassian and others have also documented examples of extreme self-mutilation, from inmates gouging out their own eyes to cutting off their own genitals. "Maximum security prisons and mental hospitals for the criminally insane [are]," wrote James Gilligan, former director of the Center for the Study of Violence at Harvard Medical School, and author of the influential book *Violence: Reflections on a National Epidemic,* "extreme environments. What I have learned about humans is that the instinct (physiological) of self-preservation does not hold when one approaches the point of being so overwhelmed by shame that one can only preserve one's self by sacrificing one's body (or those of others)." Using the tools of the supermax prison, Gilligan argued, "does not protect the public; it only sends a human time bomb into the community."[25]

Other psychiatrists are more cautious, arguing that while some perfectly healthy people are driven insane by these dehumanizing settings, a more common problem is that mildly mentally ill inmates are often precisely those who find it hardest to control their behavior while in general population. Because they get into trouble with the guards, they are the inmates most likely to wind up in secure housing units, and once in the SHU they are the inmates most likely to decompensate and to end up far more seriously psychotic, and ultimately more dangerous, than they were in the first place. Judge Henderson acknowledged this in his *Madrid v. Gomez* ruling, writing that "as Warden Marshall described in an August 1991 budget request, the high incidence of mentally ill inmates at Pelican Bay is predictable because mentally ill inmates frequently exhibit behavioral problems, and inmates with a history of misconduct are often transferred to Pelican Bay." In a 1999 case involving the use of segregation in Texas (*Ruiz v. Johnson*), the court likewise found that "inmates, obviously in need of medical help, are instead inappropriately managed merely as miscreants...TDCJ [Texas Department of Criminal Justice] has knowingly turned its back on this most needy segment of its population."

In 2003 I researched and coauthored a report for Human Rights Watch, *Ill-Equipped: U.S. Prisons and Offenders with Mental Illness,* documenting the problems faced by the hundreds of thousands of seriously mentally ill men and women who have served time behind bars during the past several decades. In state after state, I found that prisons were acting as magnets for mentally ill people who, had they had better access to community mental-health facilities, might well have been diverted into appropriate treatment before they committed crimes and got ensnared in the criminal-justice system. Within prison systems, supermaxes were further siphoning off the mentally ill after they had failed to abide by the prisons' rules and regulations. In other words, mental illness predisposes people to engage in the kind of erratic, destructive behavior that is likely to land them a disciplinary hearing and a trip to the SHU or a supermax prison; and yet, the Human Rights Watch report concluded, this is precisely the sort of environment most likely to result in already ill people decompensating into psychosis. Prison codes, in short, end up sending to the SHU precisely those inmates who are least able to handle SHU conditions, creating twenty-first-century equivalents of the pre-psychiatric asylums of centuries past. Attorneys for the Prisoners' Rights Project in New York argued that several of their clients had spent many years bouncing back and forth be-tween secure housing units and the state's main forensic psychiatric center. Researchers in Oregon and Washington State found a similar pattern.[26]

This is not an encouraging scenario. With tens of thousands of inmates now cycling through the supermax and SHU systems, and with many states releasing such inmates onto the streets when their sentences are up without first reacclimatizing them to a social environment, there is a real risk that the internal prison-control systems of the 1990s, combined with "tough on crime, tough on criminals" political rhetoric, will lead to large numbers of extremely damaged individuals returning to society over the coming decades. Although no national tracking surveys of ex-SHU inmates have been carried out, there is anecdotal evidence that many are made more violent by their spells in iso-lation. In 1998 I reported for the *Atlantic Monthly* on an individual who had shot a sheriff's deputy dead at point-blank range shortly after being released from Pelican Bay.[27] Prison observers such as Bonnie Kerness, of the American Friends Service Committee, talk about a new generation of cons coming out of supermax prisons with hair-trigger tempers. One ex–Rikers Island jail res-ident, participating in a rehabilitation program run by the Manhattan-based Fortune Society, recalled that inmates routinely referred to the jail's "Bing Monsters," the Bing being the nickname for the Rikers SHU. "The impact on society could be devastating," former correctional officer Steve Rigg, who worked at California's Corcoran prison in the mid-1990s before he blew the whistle on his fellow officers for organizing gladiatorial fights between pris-oners, remarked when I interviewed him in 2001. "There's more recidivism of a SHU inmate. They breed the worst."

———•———

During the heady days of the 1980s and 1990s, "The sky's the limit" seemed the favored response to a host of questions: How much money could states devote to corrections? How many people could be convicted of misdemeanors or felonies and shipped off to jail or prison? How "tough" could laws get? How many prisons and jails could be built to house everyone convicted under these tough laws? How many state employees could be hired to secure all of these facilities? How many programs could be removed from prisons, and how many rights could be taken away from prisoners? Quite simply, there were no limits. The essence of tough-on-crime posture-politics was to write blank checks, and later try to cobble together ways to pay the bills and deal with the nonmonetary social costs of mass incarceration.

So hell-bent were most states on negating the notion that they were in the business of rehabilitating or "correcting" inmates that most actually changed the names of the departments managing their prison, parole, and probation systems. Bureaucracies in charge of keeping people incarcerated, as well as the agencies in charge of managing individuals on probation and parole were, in other words, no longer to emphasize their rehabilitative function. For parole and probation departments in particular, whose employees had long been seen more as social workers than as law-enforcement officers, this was a dramatic shift. In Arkansas, for example, the probation department was renamed the Department of Community Punishment. In Wyoming, the Board of Charities and Reform became the Department of Corrections. In Georgia, the name of the Department of Corrections had been changed in 1972 to Department of Offender Rehabilitation; in 1985, it was changed back. Throughout the 1990s, the word "rehabilitation" was removed from one correctional department after another, until, by the early twenty-first century, only Ohio retained the word in its departmental heading. "They didn't want to hear politically they had anything to do with rehabilitation," explained Allen Ault. "It was all punishment. It's strictly run by politics. Research plays little part in state corrections."

Not until the bursting dot-com bubble combined with the national mania for tax-cutting lowered state revenues, and the terrorist attacks in September 2001 sent the broader economy into a downward spiral, did significant numbers of politicians start to question the blank checks being written for prison systems. Suddenly, in the early years of the Bush presidency, politicians across the political spectrum began looking for ways to get more bang for their bucks when it came to punishing offenders. Studies showing that existing sentencing and prison practices were often facilitating cycles of imprisonment, release, and reincarceration for new crimes or for parole violations—what the journalist Joel Dyer labeled a "perpetual prisoner machine" inexorably pushing up the total prison, parole, and probation population—were dusted off and trotted out by newly cost-conscious officials.[28] Conversely, studies that, in opposition to the "Nothing Works" movement, indicated that there were ways to interact with offenders that reduced the chance that they would return to crime swiftly became de rigueur. Organizations such as the Urban Institute attracted large grants for their work around what came to be called "reentry programming": preparing soon-to-be-released prisoners for a law-abiding life outside. And, albeit in small quantities, the federal government began releasing funds for the states to use in transitioning prisoners back to their communities.

"When we hit 2 million incarcerated and every state had massive budget deficits, something had to give," said reentry specialist Joan Petersilia, of the University of California at Irvine, in 2005, shortly after she had been placed in charge of a large state-funded research unit to examine which programs best prepared California inmates for life after prison. "We're spending a lot of money, and that gets you a very different discussion."

"Good programs is good security," explained Arizona correctional director Dora Schirro, one of the new breed of administrators, who made a name for herself as head of the Missouri system by paying prisoners to attend education classes. "If you can productively engage a population in pro-social activities, bad conduct drops off. Inmates need to be literate, get and keep jobs, become and stay sober. Our goal is to program every programmable inmate at least thirty hours every week." In 2003, about seven hundred of Arizona's prisoners received GED certification; the following year, more than fourteen hundred did likewise, and the department estimated that the number would double again in 2005. Since Schirro had begun reforming the state's prisons a couple years earlier, the department estimated that inmate-on-inmate assaults had dropped by about half, and that assaults by prisoners on guards had fallen by nearly a third.

"If you look at the history of corrections, it does go in cycles," Ault said in a slightly more optimistic moment. "It usually goes from overcrowding and scandal—like with Attica—to reform. Hopefully I'll live long enough that the pendulum will start swinging the other way."

———

Despite the subtle shift in emphasis within prison systems in many states, and marginally less shrill political rhetoric around incarceration, activist reformers are still a minority in U.S. correctional systems. Even in states such as Arizona, where the correctional bureaucracies have changed most dramatically, the new regimes are severely hampered by the policies and spending decisions of their predecessors, as well as the extremely conservative sentencing laws crafted by legislatures. Neither the infrastructure of supermax prisons and lockdown environments, the limits on programming that such environments dictate, nor the confrontational culture inculcated over the decades as the prison population swelled, will disappear overnight.

When I toured Connecticut's Northern Correctional Institution (NCI) in 2002, forty-nine-year-old warden Larry Myers presided over an inmate population just shy of five hundred and a staff of just over three hundred. With six mental-health professionals, a three-phase program offering inmates the possibility of returning to the general population within one year, and a relatively calm inmate-staff relationship, Myers prided himself on running a tight ship. His guards did not carry guns. Inmates who graduated from the lockdown conditions of Phase One—in which they were kept for a minimum of six months—were gradually given greater socializing rights. And, unlike in many supermaxes, once staff identified an inmate as psychotic, he was swiftly removed to another institution that catered more specifically to the needs of mentally ill prisoners. Since 1999, Myers claimed, in an attempt to avoid what he called a "ping-pong effect" in which inmates bounced back and forth between NCI and mental-health institutions, the prison had not accepted any inmates that staff identified as being severely disturbed.

But even in Myers's prison, where psychiatrist Paul Chaplin estimated that a relatively small percentage of the inmates were on antidepressants or antipsychotic drugs (10 percent, despite the official policy designed to remove mentally ill inmates from NCI), violent inmates had to be placed in four-point restraints several times a month, and guards frequently used mace on prisoners. No matter how progressive the intent of its administrators, the very structure of the prison, determined more by political expediency than by correctional expertise, seemed antithetical to the calm, ordered environment championed by old-time professionals such as Jim Estelle. As I walked around the pink steel tiers of level one, dozens of inmates, housed in barren concrete cells, prohibited from owning televisions, let out of their cells for less than an hour a day, began screaming often incoherent complaints in a raucous, bone-jarring cacophony of despair.

"Without a TV, it's stupid," shouted one thirty-one-year-old inmate. "We [his cellmate and he] just play cards, do push-ups, sit around. I read books every now and then, but I get tired of reading." And so, he said, he slept for over ten hours a day. "This is shitty. We ain't got no recreations, no space. If I try to sit back and motivate, you got people yelling. I have trouble concentrating." Another, twenty-one-year-old Edwin, shouted through the Plexiglas window in his cell door: "I'm in jail for behavior problems. My cellie has behavior problems. Why put two people with behavior problems in the same cell? I'm in cell twenty-three hours, with one hour rec. We are chained with shackles, can't get no exercise. Right now, this jail got me ready to kill somebody. My mind ain't focused right now."

———•———

In addition to tolerating a certain level of violence, Americans tend to view virtually all new technology as good technology, no matter how dangerous it might be. In many ways, we have been conditioned to uncritically equate technological innovation with cultural progress. Perhaps this state of mind is inevitable in the world's preeminent nuclear power; how else to create a comfortable national self-image while developing, and maintaining for more than six decades, a nuclear arsenal capable of unleashing Armageddon upon earth? Surely, we like to think, it can't be all bad. Surely we're creating something good here. Surely we're stumbling toward a new, better, more secure—and yet freer—way of living. Surely all the energy and brainpower we're using to create this ultra-high-tech system ties into a grand vision of progress.

In such a world, where individuals and organizations gain control according to the sophistication of their technologies, one-on-one human interactions—say, conversations between police officer and crime suspect—become quaint, almost antiquated, charming but irrelevant leftovers from the Norman Rockwell days. Replacing these interactions are gadgets of an age in which science fiction is often less strange than the realities. As the twenty-first century got under way, police departments around the country, for example, raced to deploy M26 TASER stun guns, capable of shooting barbs carrying a fifty-thousand-volt punch into the human body from over twenty feet away. The guns were marketed by their Arizona manufacturer as part of the inevitable march of progress—even the acronym TASER, standing for Thomas A. Swift Electric Rifle, was taken from an early-twentieth-century series of children's books in which the hero, Tom Swift, utilized futuristic gadgets such as an electric rifle. Critics of TASER use were routinely dismissed as naysayers and scaremongers. "With TASER devices, you can safely stop a threat from up to 15-feet or 4.5 meters," reads promotional material for the X26c, a version of the stun gun sold over the counter to civilian buyers in forty-three of the fifty states in the Union. "TASER technology has among the lowest injury rates of any force option. Test results indicate that the effects from TASER devices leave no lasting aftereffects."[29]

Despite the peppy language, however, the new technology does not come without a cost. Near Sacramento, for example, between mid-2004 and mid-2005, at least six individuals died shortly after being TASERed.[30] Unfazed, the county sheriff's department and the city police force continued to use the weapon. Many of the instances in which TASERs were deployed would be comic if they didn't have such devastating consequences.[31]

On December 22, 2004, thirty-one-year-old Ronnie Pino was making animal noises inside the intake room at the Heritage Oaks hospital, several miles south of downtown Sacramento. He had been released from the psychiatric ward of another hospital the day before, and now, on the advice of the family doctor, his mother, Marjorie, his aunt, and his cousin had brought him to Heritage Oaks to get his medications adjusted. Hard of hearing and mentally disabled, Ronnie took a bevy of powerful medications to control his seizures. His ailments were the legacy of a large brain tumor that had been diagnosed when he was only nine and removed when he was fifteen. He had a vagus nerve stimulator running from his heart up to his brain to try to limit the frequency of his fits, and despite his retardation he knew enough to know he wasn't even supposed to walk too close to a microwave oven in case the machine interfered with the stimulator. Pino lacked impulse control and got upset very easily, maddened that he couldn't read, angered that he didn't have a girlfriend. A big man with the mental age of a young child, he had been known to hit walls, even to attack his mother's car, when in a rage. Still, even after the trauma of seeing his father die of a heart attack before his eyes in a local restaurant in 1997, he did not express his frustrations through attacks on other people.

Now, as his animal noises got louder, Ronnie decided he needed to smoke a cigarette. But the intake room was a nonsmoking area, and the hospital staff feared that he'd flee if allowed outside. They locked the area down, and Pino's anxiety grew. He began begging the staff to let him out. Eventually, unable to take the pressure, Pino kicked and hit his way through a window and, covered with blood, blundered outside. There, with his cousin accompanying him, he began to chain-smoke his way through several cigarettes. The staff called the police department.

Months later, Pino's family would recall that he had always admired police officers. They were the good guys, people to turn to in an emergency. As his hallucinations got worse, Ronnie had repeatedly dialed 911, hoping the police could help him ward off his demons. "Ronnie liked cops," recalled his older brother Ryan. "He respected them."

But the officers who showed up outside Heritage Oaks weren't the heroes of Ronnie's imagination. Instead, they were confrontational, jittery people, apparently untrained to deal with a person as disturbed as Ronnie. "He would have listened to those cops," Ryan said later. "But the cops had the wrong impression of him because of his size."

The first to arrive on the scene at Heritage Oaks was a female officer. She ordered the now-sobbing Pino to get down on the ground. As he cried and shouted, she drew her TASER gun. Marjorie ran outside and begged her not to use the weapon, telling her that Ronnie had a vagus nerve stimulator and an electric shock could kill him. According to witnesses, the officer responded by threatening to TASER Marjorie as well unless she backed off. A few minutes into the confrontation, as other police officers milled around, a second police car raced onto the scene, its lights flashing as the male driver screeched to a halt just in front of Ronnie.

As the second officer began to approach Pino, the disoriented man shouted that the lights were going to give him a seizure. He reared up—inadvertently, his mother believes—and his arms struck the officer. The female deputy fired her TASER into Ronnie's chest. He fell, convulsing, to the floor and, according to the police, pulled the barbs out of his body. Then he rose again, shouting. A second blast from the TASER struck him in his abdomen, and as he lay immobilized, four or five additional police officers jumped him, cuffed him, and dragged him off to a squad car.

"Ronnie let out a death cry. He screamed, 'Oh Mom!'" Ryan remembered several months later, repeating the story Marjorie had told him shortly after the confrontation. "That drives you crazy. They're at Heritage Oaks. There were plenty of staff there to handle the situation. *I* could have handled it myself." The next day, suffering from grand mal seizures, Ronnie Pino died inside the Sacramento County jail. When his body was autopsied, the coroner found the cause of death to be sudden unexpected death syndrome. Buried on page three of the report was a reference to TASER injuries.[32]

If Ronnie Pino's case had been a one-off, it could have been dismissed as a freak tragedy, with no broader social ramifications. Sadly, there was nothing unique about this story. In November 2004, a man whom police were attempting to transport to hospital for a mental evaluation died after being TASERed in the Sacramento suburb of Elk Grove. In the same vicinity, in August 2005, a naked man throwing furniture and picture frames at some sheriff's officers died after being TASERed. In late September 2005, an agitated twenty-four-year-old named Timothy Torres died after being TASERed during a fight with six sheriff's deputies near his family home in another suburb, Rancho Cordova.

By the middle of 2005, more than six thousand police departments worldwide, including one-fifth of all police departments within the United States and forces in the U.K., Germany, South Africa, Saudi Arabia, and several other countries, had bought some TASER products. California, in particular, went for the new device with a vengeance. More than fifty departments up and down the Central Valley were using it, as was the LAPD and other big-city forces.[33] In Sacramento, it was first used on a large scale in June 2003, against protestors at an international conference on biotechnology.[34]

But soon after the weapons were introduced, reports started emerging of men and women who had been TASERed and died, either immediately or within a day or two, often in the county jails to which they had been transported. The *Arizona Republic* newspaper established a database to track these deaths, and by the fall of 2005 was reporting over 160 such deaths in the United States and Canada, more than a third of them in California and Florida.[35] The evidence in these cases did not unequivocally tie the stun gun to the deaths; it wasn't as causally obvious as a bullet going through a skull. In fact, as in Ronnie Pino's case, coroners generally ruled the deaths to be accidental, to be sudden and inexplicable. Still, the pattern was disturbing.

——•——

Assured by Taser International that the weapons were entirely safe, on a par with pepper spray, police departments had simply added TASERs to the standard arsenal designed to gain an edge on perceived criminals. Increasingly, TASERs became control tools of first resort. In Florida, officers in several incidents TASERed young children, including a six-year-old who was merely waving a piece of broken glass at them inside his school, and a twelve-year-old caught playing hooky from school. In Chicago, a fourteen-year-old boy almost died after being TASERed.[36] In Arizona, over twenty football fans were Tasered by Arizona State University security officers in fall 2004 after they failed to follow crowd-control instructions. And in South Carolina, a seventy-five-year-old woman was zapped after refusing to leave a nursing home in which she had been living temporarily.[37] In other words, once they were bought and approved by law-enforcement departments, TASERs were used in circumstances where guns would never have been drawn, where officers would once have used at most a baton or pepper spray, or would simply have spent more time talking a person, or a crowd, down through simple human interaction. As in the Zimbardo and Milgram experiments of the 1960s and 1970s, officers with a high level of discretionary control over people they were trying to apprehend or already had under their control grew rapidly accustomed to inflicting massive electric shocks on people.

While healthy people who are TASERed do not tend to experience a long-term adverse reaction, paradoxically it is often precisely the people most at risk of fatal complications who get TASERed. In the same way as secure housing units end up as a magnet for mentally ill prisoners, thus pushing those least able to withstand the rigors of isolation into the most isolated environments possible, so TASERs are frequently used on those least able to survive a massive electric shock. Law-enforcement officers in confrontational situations have no way of knowing up front whether they are TASERing someone healthy, someone with a seizure condition or a heart problem such as arrhythmia, or someone on powerful psychotropic medications. Like Ronnie Pino, many of those who find themselves in the kind of confrontation that police end up trying to defuse with a TASER are mentally unstable, so messed up by drugs that they cannot behave rationally or follow orders carefully, and/or physically weakened by years of living on the streets.

Like so much else in the modern American criminal-justice system, the widespread use and misuse of TASERs reflects good intentions gone awry. Intended to be "less lethal," TASERs are often used too casually; instead of merely immobilizing a prisoner, critics allege, they can contribute to a person's death. So, too, inside prisons, good intentions can produce bad consequences. High-security units were intended to isolate the worst of the worst and make general-population prisoners safer; instead, too often they serve as dumping grounds for the mentally ill. Antisuicide protocols were intended to prevent people from killing themselves; instead, they often result in deeply disturbed people being left naked and shivering for days on end. Mandatory sentences were intended to make communities safer; instead they have channeled thousands of offenders into rigid prison terms from which they will be released with no preparation for life on the outside.

With all the best intentions in the world, the criminal-justice system, whether the institutions of law enforcement, the courts, or the prisons and jails, would still have had difficulty handling a man as disturbed as Ronnie Pino. Yet it could have done a whole lot better than it did. The way in which it failed—the overreliance on high-tech control devices and the speed with which the situation spiraled out of control—speaks volumes about the current problems at the heart of America's vast law-enforcement and penal infrastructure.

CHAPTER 9

ADULT TIME

Mentally ill adults weren't the only new group experiencing the country's expansive penal hospitality by the last decade of the twentieth century. Increasingly, as prisons took center stage, teenagers were being removed from the purview of the juvenile courts, tried and sentenced as adults in adult courts, and sent to adult prisons. It was a startling development, a U-turn from over a century of juvenile-justice practice that had looked to create separate institutions for youngsters, based primarily on rehabilitation and education. Like so much else in the emotionally charged arena of crime and punishment, the shift grew out of an increasingly potent national sense of victimhood and public desire for revenge.

In a manner not too dissimilar to that of the notorious "hanging judges" of eighteenth- and early-nineteenth-century England, who were not averse to sentencing children to hang for crimes such as theft, or at least to ordering them deported to ferocious penal colonies in far-off lands,[1] so many contemporary American politicians, prosecutors, and judges seemed almost eager to deal with teenagers in as steely a manner as the U.S. Constitution would permit.

In the late winter of 2001, fourteen-year-old Lionel Tate was sentenced to life in prison in Florida for killing a six-year-old girl during a mock wrestling game a couple years earlier. So jarring was the image of a tear-stained, chubby-faced boy being told he would spend the rest of his life behind bars that it produced an almost instant national and international outcry. Within days, Tate had been moved from an adult prison to a secure unit in a juvenile facility. A clutch of high-powered appellate attorneys, led by the inimitable Johnnie Cochran, of O. J. Simpson notoriety, and Barry Scheck, of the New York–based Innocence Project, had clambered aboard the case. Soon Florida governor Jeb Bush was letting it be known that, while he generally favored a no-nonsense approach to criminals that he called "tough love," he might eventually be amenable to signing some sort of clemency deal for the boy.

Perhaps, Jeb Bush's intimations suggested, *the courts had gone slightly overboard this time.* It was, in a way, a bridge too far. Putting a fourteen-year-old in prison for life, without any possibility of parole, implied—as victims'-rights advocates such as Miriam Shehane had long argued, to the dismay of child-development experts—that young teenagers were already fully formed moral beings, and the acts of a person perched uncomfortably close to childhood could, and should, be dealt with in the exact same manner as those of a mature adult. For some youngsters, in short, the notion of redemption simply did not exist. This view came close to embracing the controversial religious idea that some people are simply born evil, possessed of the devil and, from their first breaths, predestined to be lost souls. These were the very ideas against which the modern juvenile justice system had fought since 1899, when Illinois created the country's first juvenile court as a way to divert young people from environments in which they would be surrounded by long-hardened criminals.[2]

Tate's sentence, in the full glare of the modern media spotlight, was the same as that meted out to Floyd Williams in rural Louisiana nearly forty years earlier. But Williams's sentence was, in a perverse way, an escape mechanism from the passions of the mob, the less severe legal option in a no-win situation. Tate's sentence, by contrast, was a peculiarly explicit pandering to popular passions in a state where prosecutors were aggressively moving to undermine a long-standing juvenile-justice system. There was nothing backwoods about Tate's punishment; on the contrary, it was intended to gain a high profile and set a new bar for the prosecution of dangerous teenagers. "Tate didn't have to wake up that morning and say, 'I'm going to kill Tiffany Emick,'" said prosecutor Ken Padowitz, who subsequently grew disgruntled with the district attorney's office, set up his own private practice, and eventually joined the campaign to grant Lionel Tate clemency. "All that is required is that he intended to act, not that he intended the result." Although the move backfired as public opposition to the sentence intensified, initially the district attorney's office clearly hoped that Tate's fate would be broadcast far and wide, signifying, in the starkest way possible, a break with a juvenile-justice system that had run parallel to the adult system in every state in America since the 1920s, and in some states since the end of the nineteenth century.

The formal mechanisms of the modern juvenile-justice system had their genesis in missionary work carried out by mid- to late-nineteenth-century reformers in the slums of New York, Chicago, Denver, and a host of other large and growing cities. Do-gooders established settlement houses, houses of refuge, and other institutions designed to take delinquent youngsters out of environments that were thought to corrode their moral well-being. Inside these buildings, they would be educated, fed, and taught trades; they would learn religion and imbibe the moral values of the middle-class reformers who had taken them under their wings. Later, from 1899 onward, municipalities began channeling juveniles into special courts created to deal with minors, the judges fashioning themselves more as stern surrogate parents than as imposers of criminal sanctions.

In its optimism, its belief in the potential for reform of even the most hard-nosed teen hoodlum, juvenile justice was a quintessentially American invention. Just as the initial impetus for Pennsylvania's prison system had come from radical social reformers, the creation of a massive network of juvenile courts, reformatories, and residential programs for troubled youths had come about as a result of the work of progressive criminologists, psychologists, and political reformers leery of placing teenagers in institutions that would further brutalize them. And just as the penitentiary model was exported from the United States to other countries in the nineteenth century, over the course of the twentieth century the juvenile-justice institutions and their philosophical underpinnings were pioneered in America and then adopted elsewhere.

Now the prosecutors in Florida seemed to be turning their backs on this history. Ironically, they were doing so at a time when increasingly advanced brain-imaging technology was leading large numbers of neurologists and psychologists to conclude that teenage brains lacked many of the neural connections and fatty deposits necessary for fully autonomous moral decision-making and reining in wayward impulses. In 2005, not long after it had banned the execution of severely mentally disabled individuals, the U.S. Supreme Court ruled that executing people for crimes committed before their eighteenth birthdays was also unconstitutional. This practice, the justices decided, flew in the face of evolving community standards of decency; and the reasons those standards were changing was, at least in part, because of the new scientific evidence regarding the physical state of the adolescent brain.[3] In an era when the Court was moving further and further to the right, the decision was a rare legal victory for progressive criminal-justice reformers.

After the hubbub, the Tate case was portrayed by many tough-on-crime figures as anomalous. In fact, however, the philosophy behind the prosecution was by no means exceptional. For in the 1980s, and more particularly the early 1990s, as the country battened down the hatches when it came to crime and punishment, it also began to dismantle a juvenile-justice system that had been carefully developed over the course of more than a century. Driven by the specter of what Princeton political scientist John J. DiIulio Jr. termed the unredeemable juvenile "superpredator,"[4] and by the fear of what representative Bill McCollum, chair of the House Subcommittee on Crime, in March 1997 called "tomorrow's wave of violent young people,"[5] forty-five states and the District of Columbia revamped their juvenile-justice systems in the 1980s and 1990s. The changes either mandated that certain crimes be tried in adult court, or shifted the decision to try a teenager in adult court from the juvenile-court judge to the prosecutor. Many states began allowing minors to be placed in adult prisons.

Teen superpredators, argued DiIulio—who was subsequently put in charge of President George W. Bush's faith-based charity initiative for an ill-fated few months, before resigning in August 2001—were the equivalent of a "generational wolf pack,"[6] gangsters lacking even elementary morality, who would kill for kicks and plunder and pillage without restraint. They were, he posited, the quintessential societal nightmare: progeny that had mutated into something altogether alien, something fierce and dark that could only be restrained through the use of brute force, through the full flexing of the muscle of the state. It was a stunning reversal of the optimistic theories and beliefs, concerning both delinquents and the role of the state in dealing with them, that had characterized the emergence of the juvenile-justice system a century earlier.

In schools, this meant employing "zero tolerance" rules, mandating suspension or expulsion for even trivial infractions such as smoking, swearing, and mocking teachers. One fourteen-year-old Texan girl faced five months in boot camp after bringing to school a soda mixed with a few drops of grain alcohol; in Alexandria, Louisiana, a second-grader was expelled for carrying a watch, owned by his grandfather, that had a tiny knife attached.[7] On public streets, it increasingly meant the enforcement of late-night curfews for teenagers; by 1997, a survey of 387 cities conducted by the U.S. Conference of Mayors found that 70 percent had curfews in place.[8] In the criminal-justice arena, it meant replacing the emphasis on rehabilitating young offenders—increasingly viewed as "coddling" thugs—with an approach emphasizing punishment. And yet DiIulio was ultimately attacking a straw man, for even as the Princetonian developed his superpredator theory, on the ground juvenile crime was finally, after decades of rising violence, starting to decline. That his arguments and prescribed solutions still carried such clout in the mid- to late 1990s, despite this data, indicates just how conservative—and how fearful—

large swaths of the fin de siècle populace and political leadership had become on the topic of crime and punishment.

———•———

Thus it was that two seemingly contradictory trends emerged in the mid-1990s. The first was that after years of rising juvenile-crime rates, and in particular the terrifying spike in violent crime that came with the crack epidemic and the intergang turf wars that followed in its wake, teenage crime rates began plummeting. The second was that, about a year *after* crime rates began to fall—as DiIulio's ideas hit the mainstream with a force comparable to that of Martinson's antirehabilitation arguments two decades earlier, and as politicians belatedly latched onto variants of the vote-winning slogan "adult time for adult crime"—the numbers of teens held in *adult* jails and prisons across the country began to skyrocket. After a decade and a half in which the numbers of minors tried and sentenced as adults had risen about 6 percent each year—a not entirely unreasonable increase given the severity of teen crimes in this period—in the mid-1990s, precisely when crime was becoming a *less* consuming problem, and a growing body of scientific evidence was showing that teenagers were *not* fully capable of understanding the consequences of their actions, that number began increasing at an annual average rate of 18 percent.

Nationally, the Bureau of Justice Statistics estimates that the total number of juvenile inmates held in adult prisons at any one moment peaked in 1995, at slightly over fifty-three hundred, and fell steadily in the years following, to fewer than twenty-five hundred by 2004. Still, the numbers admitted in any given year continued to increase: in 1997, seventy-four hundred adolescents under the age of eighteen were sentenced to state prisons. Of these, 61 percent were sent to prison for violent crimes; the rest were incarcerated for property crimes, drugs, and public-order offenses.[9] And while many of these teenagers served only a few months behind bars (which explains why far more were being admitted each year than were being held at any one moment), those convicted of violent crimes were expected to serve an average of five years. In addition, thousands more teenagers each year, close to three-quarters of them black or Hispanic, were being locked up in county jails.[10]

The extreme disparities in judicial treatment of white and nonwhite defendants were documented by the Center on Juvenile and Criminal Justice (CJCJ), which estimated that an astonishing 99 percent of juveniles transferred to adult court in Cook County, Illinois, in 1999 and 2000 were black and Latino. In Los Angeles County, CJCJ found that Hispanic and black youths were transferred to adult courts at six times the rate of whites, and that once in adult courts the black and Latino teenagers were far more likely to be sentenced to adult prison than their white peers. In Florida, three-quarters of teens in prison at century's end were nonwhite.[11] "The harsh attitudes towards kids right now in the United States," argued the CJCJ's Dan Macallair, "is a harsh attitude to black and Latino kids. Those *other* kids."

That harshness resulted in an erosion of the mission of juvenile-justice institutions. According to the Bureau of Justice Statistics, by 1997 only two states forbade the incarceration of those under sixteen in adult prisons; six other states required minors to be housed in separate units within adult prisons. The other forty-two states either segregated teens within the adult prison system, by placing them in protective custody cells originally designed for hard-to-control adults or those at risk of being attacked by fellow prisoners, or simply housed them with adults in the general prison population.[12]

The shift was most pronounced in Florida. In 1992, after a rash of high-profile teen crimes, then–Miami-Dade state attorney Janet Reno began pushing for more adult-court filings against violent juveniles; and in 1994, after gun-toting teenagers murdered several tourists, the state legislator gave prosecutors rather than juvenile judges the authority to choose whether to try offenders between fourteen and seventeen as adults. As with California's three-strikes law, however, this newfound prosecutorial freedom soon caught less-serious offenders in the punishment web. By the late 1990s, Palm Beach County state attorney Barry Krischer was prosecuting mentally disabled fifteen-year-old Anthony Laster in adult court for the crime of stealing lunch money from a schoolmate. "Depicting and treating this forcible felony, this strong arm robbery, in terms as though it were no more than a $2 shoplifting fosters and promotes violence in our schools," Krischer, a Floridian publicity hound in the Sheriff Arpaio mold who had prosecuted over six hundred juvenile crimes in adult courts the previous year, wrote in a February 1999 op-ed.[13] "There should be 'zero tolerance' for such acts. I believe that prosecuting this robbery in juvenile court would have diminished the seriousness of the crime." Until a *60 Minutes* investigative crew showed up on the scene, prompting Krischer to drop the charges, Laster was facing a thirty-years-to-life sentence if convicted. That a thirty-year sentence would, to all intents and purposes, shatter the life of the teenager—not to mention its cost to Florida's taxpayers—seemed of no consequence to the state attorney.

Six years later, in February 2005, Krischer's office again hit the headlines when it charged sixteen teenagers as adults for dealing drugs in their high schools. Most of the defendants were charged with selling marijuana, in some cases only ten dollars' worth. Those charged with dealing cocaine and ecstasy faced up to fifteen years in prison, according to the South Florida *Sun-Sentinel*. The marijuana dealers, their penalties enhanced because they had been caught selling within one thousand feet of a school, were looking at five years behind bars.[14] Perversely, had they and their buyers played hooky from school, gone on a walk, and conducted their transactions while ditching class, the pot dealers would have faced far less severe penalties. In labeling school-age drug dealers as hardened criminals, Krischer's office was in a very real way espousing a self-fulfilling prophecy. He was taking teenagers out of school, destroying any chance they'd have of creating careers for themselves, rendering them largely unemployable, and ensuring they spent their formative years behind bars with truly professional hoodlums. By every measure, his prosecutorial decisions were calculated to destroy whatever life chances these young people might have had. Down the road, these teenagers would indeed likely morph into much more dangerous criminals.

In 2001 Professor Paolo Annino of the Children's Advocacy Center at Florida State University estimated that, across Florida on any given day, close to 500 minors were incarcerated in adult prisons, and over 1,000 inmates were serving time for crimes committed when they were fifteen or younger. According to the Florida Department of Corrections, 251 prisoners from Dade County alone (of which Miami is a part) were serving time for crimes committed before their eighteenth birthdays. Thousands more were in jail or on probation. While the numbers of minors in adult prisons declined in subsequent years, Florida remained one of the harshest states in the country for teenage offenders.

All told, according to University of Minnesota law professor Barry Feld, a former prosecutor and author of *Bad Kids: Race and the Transformation of the Juvenile Court*, up to seventy thousand teens went through Florida's adult courts in the ten years straddling the turn of the century. Some of these juveniles ended up in adult prisons, while others were sent to what are known as youthful offender institutions. All inmates in YO are under twenty-six, but apart from that, from the razor-wire fencing to the burly guards and the almost stunningly casual violence, these institutions are prisons, places where fifteen-year-old muggers can end up sharing cells with hardened twenty-something killers.

In some ways, though, the YO lockups weren't dramatically different from the toughened-up juvenile institutions operating throughout much of the country. For, since local politicians and pundits had made it clear that teen thugs could expect as little public sympathy as adult inmates in adult prison facilities, so conditions had rapidly deteriorated. In Maryland, staff in the juvenile system were accused of beating up boys in the middle of the night, and of choking other kids. In California, Georgia, Michigan, Virginia, New Jersey, and a slew of other states, federal prosecutors launched investigations into allegations of systemic abuse in juvenile facilities. The creation of separate juvenile courts came about precisely because nineteenth-century reformers grew so disillusioned with stories of young people being brutalized and humiliated in adult prisons. And yet, a century after the birth of these courts and the institutions that developed to house delinquent minors, violence and despair once again characterize all too many of the interactions between troubled teens and the agencies and institutions responsible for housing and rehabilitating them.

———•———

Moreover, while the media—and, by extension, the general public and political leadership—could still muster a fair degree of outrage when scandals erupted around the beating and neglect of teens in juvenile facilities, generally no one paid attention when minors were sent to adult prisons and subjected to the coercion that is now routine in these institutions. The default assumption was that a significant level of coercion and pervasive lack of programming was the norm.

At the age of fifteen, in 1998, Atiba F. was put in prison for robbing a gas station with a friend and shooting the attendant in the arm. Over the next few years, he was shunted from institution to institution. Atiba had been sticking up local dope dealers and businesses for several years already; clearly he needed to be removed from society. But if he was ever going to change, this disturbed, hyperactive teenager, who had been on Prozac for years, also needed intensive counseling, a structured education—such as the mandatory GED education, delivered in a focused, intimate setting, required by the experimental juvenile system of early-twenty-first-century Missouri—and a sense of hope. He got none of that. Instead he found himself in adult prison.

When I met him in 2001, at the Zephyrhills Correctional Institution, twenty miles north of Tampa, Atiba was three years into a four-and-a-half-year sentence. He talked of wanting to study medicine or psychiatry...if he could ever get his GED. But everything in his life had conspired against such ambition. Instead of mandating that he enroll in school, or even encouraging him with incentives such as good-time credits, the prison authorities had put him to work raking leaves and mowing grass on the compound: make-work designed to fill his time rather than stimulate his mind and prepare him to return to the community. He was, in short, treated like an anonymous prisoner in a nineteenth-century London prison rather than a teenager in need of carefully tailored intervention from trained professional staff, the kind that was being implemented in states such as Missouri and counties such as Santa Cruz, California, and Multnomah County, Oregon. Because Atiba had been in and out of prison psychiatric wards, where overworked staff routinely prescribe powerful psychotropic drugs to deal with symptoms rather than causes of mental illness, he had over the previous few years been medicated rather than counseled. Often when his temper got the better of him he would get into fights or cuss out the guards. As a result, like so many of the mentally ill adults I interviewed in prisons around the country, Atiba would end up spending weeks in isolation in the prison wing colloquially known as the Box.

Atiba's parents were drug addicts. He had, he claimed, learned to rob and steal on the streets of Miami before he was ten, while living in a two-bedroom house with his grandmother, his aunt, several cousins, another uncle's family, and his own brothers and sisters. "In prison," the teenager told me, "I ain't really get no education. I get my learning from inmates. When I was on the street, I couldn't read well, or write; only thing I was good at was math. In prison, I learned to read and write. I learned from different inmates." The problem was that, in addition to familiarizing himself with the three R's, Atiba was also learning even more emphatically the ethos of the street: only the strong survive. "Prison's like a school and a gladiator prison," he explained, sitting in his prison-blue uniform in an interview room at Zephyrhills, where he lived with adult rapists, murderers, and other long-term inmates. "It's bad, because you've got to watch your back or you'll be killed in here. I've got beaten lots of times." One time, he said, when he was sixteen, an officer slammed his head against a Plexiglas window. Another time, at a youthful offender institution, a rival stabbed him in the chest with a shank. Inmates wielding socks filled with metal locks had hit friends of his on their heads at various times during his incarceration. "You're surrounded by different types of criminals," he said matter-of-factly. "People who know how to burgle houses, rob banks. You've got rapists here. Murderers. Young people, some don't have the mind I do. They'll listen to the older inmate: 'This is how you do a robbery.' He might go out there and try it again. He might get away, or he might end up dead, or back in here."

Atiba was scheduled to be released a year after my visit. He would return to the community barely nineteen years old, with no high school education, a felony record, and only the most dysfunctional of families on which to fall back. His father, the one relative who had kept in regular contact during his time behind bars, was apparently terminally ill with brain cancer. I suppose it wasn't entirely inconceivable that the teenager's dreams would come true, and he would one day be a doctor. Far more likely, though, according to the grim statistics surrounding teenagers who have spent time in adult prison, he would return to the Florida penal system not long after his release.

On the other side of the state, I visited a prison that housed only teenagers and twentysomethings. Twenty minutes drive from the Kennedy Space Center, at Cape Canaveral, from where astronauts soar to the very limits of human freedom, Brevard Correctional Institution and Work Camp is home to over a thousand youthful offenders, the majority of them black or Latino, from poor parts of Miami and other large Florida cities. Unlike those in juvenile institutions, the methods of confinement, punishment, and discipline employed here are firmly modeled on the adult penitentiary rather than the more rehabilitative framework developed by the juvenile courts. The crimes of Brevard's inmates range from drug violations to murder.

"I robbed," explained seventeen-year-old African American Ernest C., who had been in prison since his conviction for armed robbery at the age of fourteen, "because I ain't seen no other alternative. I went out there and did what I had to do." For the most part, Ernest recalled, the profits from the robberies he carried out when he was twelve and thirteen went to buy clothes, but sometimes he gave his mother money so she could pay the rent that month. It just seemed normal. Most of his friends were in and out of juvenile institutions, jail, and prison for every crime under the sun. His years running with the tough crowd were good preparation for life behind bars, he thought. Brevard was "really no different from the street. Just no guns. You've still got knives. You've still got drugs. When you go to sleep, you've got to keep one eye open, be prepared. You don't know who's gonna take you to the bathroom and rape you. It's real dangerous."

The young inmates at Brevard walked around the yard in blue uniforms with junior versions of the blank "prison stare" adorning their faces. They had some limited access to education—basic high school classes were available, though not mandatory—but the incarcerated youngsters mainly spent their time at make-work prison jobs or games with their friends. It was a world away from state-of-the-art juvenile justice in Missouri and elsewhere, developed toward the end of the twentieth century, that emphasized education and counseling, with teens housed in small, sometimes partly self-governing buildings and sessions held in lounges and family rooms in small, residential youth centers. The Missouri experiment had dramatically lowered the level of violence within the system and reduced the recidivism rates of teenagers who'd been through it.

Florida's youthful offender facilities showed none of the optimism of the Missouri system. At night, the Brevard inmates slept in semiprivate double rooms within larger dormitories inside the huge prison, prey to violent attack from their roommates. If they got into trouble with the guards, the teenagers were, like Atiba in the adult prison, hauled off for a spell of solitary confinement in the Box, hardly a therapy likely to improve the demeanor of an already disturbed, highly impulsive teenager. "Gunning" at female officers—an obscene prison sport in which inmates masturbate at passing guards—earned thirty days in isolation with no TV or radio, no recreation time, no visits, and no phone privileges, rather than a spell of mandatory counseling. When they misbehaved, or if a portion of the facility was on lockdown because of a riot, teenage prisoners were confined with a cellmate all day, every day. Not surprisingly, many resorted to violence.

"Every roommate I got," boasted sixteen-year-old Enrique E., imprisoned at fourteen after robbing a liquor store with what he says was an unloaded .357 Magnum, "I beat him up. I did fifty-nine days in confinement one time, because I got an assault charge after hitting my roommate lots of times, bruised him up."

Like those in adult prisons, inmates at Brevard reported that guards routinely resorted to physical force and the use of gas to subdue troublesome wards. "When they gas you," explained Enrique, who had experienced it several times at his previous prison, near Tampa, "you can't breathe. It goes in your pores. You can't see. I got used to it after the third time. I just got sprayed every day." Ernest C. remembered one guard slamming his right hand in a heavy door during a dispute. His palm still bore a jagged scar where twelve stitches closed the wound. In and out of the Box for fighting, Ernest said, his machismo momentarily peeled back, "It makes you feel like shit. Like the lowest of the low. If the officer don't like you, he spit in your food. Yeah, it make you angry!"

This seventeen-year-old hated prison so much that he had resolved, with almost childish fervor, never to come back. He hoped he wouldn't have to re-sort to crime when he was released, but, he added, you never can tell what you'll have to do to survive. "If I do have to go back to what I was doing," he explained slowly, deliberately, with an adolescent combination of awkward-ness and bravado, a lanky kid in a cheap blue uniform sitting deep within a maximum-security youthful-offender prison, "and the police come, it'll be me or them. I'll kill them. I won't come back. If I do have to do that, they're going to have to kill me."

———•———

While Florida was the bellwether state of harsh conditions for teens in the 1990s, by the turn of the century California was doing a pretty good job of catching up. In 2000 California voters passed Proposition 21, a significant measure that allowed prosecutors to charge teenagers arrested for relatively minor property and drug crimes in adult court; made it easier to detain youngsters charged in adult court while they awaited trial, either in jails or in juvenile-detention facilities; and drastically increased the sanctions for crimes carried out by gang members. Since local police departments and aggressive street-policing CRASH units (Community Resources against Street Hood-lums) had spent years building secret databases with the names of tens of thousands of alleged gang members—identified by signs as trivial as wearing certain forms of clothing, hanging out with known gang members, using gangs' hand signs, or gathering with three or more friends in a public space—the new law aroused major opposition among inner-city youths.

"Here," argued seventeen-year-old Maria Perez, of South Central Los An-geles's Youth United for Community Action group, "you're guilty until proven innocent. I'm walking down the street and they can stop me because of the way I'm dressed. Me, a straight-A student. Because of my pants, my makeup. Let's say I'm fifteen or seventeen and commit a crime. That record's going to stay. Let's say I'm nineteen or twenty-one and want to improve myself, that record's going to stay. They even check your record when you apply for a job at McDonald's. I'm going to just keep going back to jail."

Prop 21 also reduced the age at which teenagers could begin accumulating "strikes," which could ultimately force them to spend the rest of their lives in prison under the state's catchall three-strikes law. "It wasn't reform," said Los Angeles's newly elected district attorney, Steve Cooley, when I interviewed him in 2001 at his small suburban house one evening. "It was a power grab by po-lice and prosecutors. It's a reaction to violent juvenile crime. People take that fear and try and capitalize on it and end up with things like Prop 21. Bad law-making. An exploitation of people's legitimate fears."

Paradoxically, however, Prop 21 proved something of a turning point in the battles over juvenile justice in California. Not long after the law kicked in, a district court ruled, in response to a lawsuit filed by the parents of some white San Diego teenagers charged as adults for beating elderly Mexican migrant la-borers, that the discretionary aspects of Proposition 21 were unconstitutional. The ruling, combined with the reluctance of DAs such as Steve Cooley to take full advantage of the law, meant that Prop 21 never did result in thousands of teens being shunted into adult prisons. Moreover, as a slew of abuse allega-tions within California Youth Authority institutions (CYA is the controlling agency for the state's juvenile detention facilities) made headlines, political pressure built for an overhaul of the state's entire approach to juvenile crimi-nals. Nationally, however, despite increased scrutiny, alarming numbers of teens continued to be placed in either scandal-plagued juvenile institutions or adult prisons.

———•———

Youngsters in prison face daunting odds. Although they generally do not spend longer inside than those who are sent to juvenile facilities after com-mitting similar crimes, they *are* more likely to be raped or beaten than other prisoners, and according to research by the Center on Juvenile and Criminal Justice, they are eight times more likely than adult prisoners to attempt sui-cide. In November 2000 a sixteen-year-old girl named Cautia Spencer hung herself with her bedsheets in a Florida prison.[15] In July 2003 a seventeen-year-old boy serving three years in California's Tehachapi prison for robbery hung himself. That same summer, two teenagers tried to end their lives at the Cen-tral Jail in Los Angeles County. Meanwhile, in Mississippi, according to an August 2004 article in *U.S. News & World Report*, suicidal girl inmates were stripped naked and locked in a dark room, while other girl prisoners were forced to eat their own vomit.[16]

Unlike juvenile offenders housed in those few facilities specially designed for their needs, mandated to emphasize rehabilitation over punishment, teen-age prison inmates have only minimal access to education and job-training programs. Like the adults with whom they are incarcerated, they can get free education to the GED level, but the classes often have waiting lists; and adult inmates are generally not provided with either job training or drug treatment, both vital components of any meaningful strategy for prisoners who will one day return to the community. Where such programs exist, they often have waiting lists stretching for months or years. Because they are exposed to older and/or more sophisticated criminals while in prison, and because the adult felony convictions permanently etched in their records make it harder for them to find jobs upon release, teen criminals in adult facilities are more likely to return to crime upon their release than their peers held in juvenile facilities. To cap it all off, they are slower to "age out" of their criminal lifestyles. A research team led by Donna Bishop of the University of Central Florida compared pairs of teenagers matched for similar backgrounds and similar crimes, broken down into forty-six categories. Their study found that the teenagers processed through the adult courts and sent to prison (both youthful offender and general population) returned to crime sooner, committed more crimes, committed more serious crimes, and ended up back behind bars sooner than their peers who had gone through the juvenile system.[17]

Of course, this might have proved only that the prosecutors were successfully picking out the worst of the bad apples to prosecute as adults in the first place; but Bishop's team found no such evidence. Instead, they identified a pattern of living conditions that helped cement the teenagers' criminal identities during their time behind bars. "In the prisons, these kids were being warehoused. Very few were involved in any treatment programs. Some were at school, some were assigned to work tasks. But they weren't receiving vocational training," Bishop recalled in an interview with me. "In the adult system, the kids perceived [that] the correctional officers saw them as worthless, as nobodies, as people who were beyond redemption."

Another study, led by Jeffrey Butts of the University of Chicago's Chapin Hall Center for Children, found that more than 70 percent of teens who were transferred into adult courts received either comparable or less severe sentences than they would have received in the juvenile system. Many of these young people, Butts concluded, were either warehoused for short spells in prison, or put onto adult probation without receiving the monitoring and counseling for which they would have been eligible in juvenile court. Lacking such interventions, all too often they simply continued their lives of crime.[18] In other words, there is a paradox here: the "tough-on-crime" policies that ham-fistedly move teens into adult prisons may be tough on individual criminals, but if the measures of their success are decreases in both crime and the number of repeat offenders, they most assuredly have not been tough on crime. A study by Columbia University professor Jeff Fagan comparing New Jersey teenagers sent to the juvenile system with teenagers in the neighboring state of New York placed into that state's adult system came to the same conclusion.[19] Indeed, as far back as 1984, a panel of experts convened to study the effect of New York State's 1978 decision to lower to sixteen the age at which teens were automatically transferred into the adult system found that the policy was implemented in a selective manner, that it failed to provide adequate mental care, and that the adult court system was releasing onto probation large numbers of teens who would have benefited from institutional supervision in a juvenile facility.

"These kids come from backgrounds of family dysfunction, mental illness, a whole host of things. They need appropriate intervention," Miami public defender Steve Harper told me. "Most of the teenagers are going to get out. They went in damaged. The damage isn't addressed. It's worsened, because they're in a tough place. They'll be worse off when they come out than when they went in." Harper remembered a mentally ill teenager he had represented a decade earlier who was sent to prison rather than a secure mental institution, and killed someone after his release.

By undermining confidence in the already overburdened, malfunctioning juvenile-justice system, the policy changes proposed by "get tough" advocates did not lead to teenage thugs being sequestered from society for longer spells. Rather, they mainly resulted in more troubled teenagers spending short spells in prison without access to the specialized rehabilitation programs that juvenile facilities are supposed to provide. Coming out even worse than they were when they went in, they rapidly reoffended as adults. Prison, when used as a punishment rather than a place for rehabilitation, seems to act as a criminogenic toxin for teenagers, potentially leading not to less crime but to more.

"There are tremendous social costs of putting this number of people in prison," asserted James Milliken, chief judge in the San Diego juvenile court system. "I can't help but think the implications are those people will be far more of a risk when they're released than the population of ex-cons who went to prison as adults."

———

Any cold economic calculation shows that it makes more sense to provide less-serious young offenders with opportunities outside prison to turn their lives around than to spend over twenty thousand dollars a year to keep each one behind bars with hard-core adult offenders. Yet increasingly in the 1990s, as the tough-on-crime tsunami swept thousands of teens into adult jails, prisons, and parole and probation structures, that wasn't what was happening.

Under this system, all that many do upon their release is to screw up again. Similarly, providing dangerous teenage criminals with intensive counseling, mandatory education, and job training in a secure juvenile facility would probably prove more effective in the long term than merely incarcerating them in prison for a couple years and then spinning them through the revolving door. Lionel Tate was sent to prison for life, and, in the wake of the international outcry, released three years later into lifetime adult probation. By then, however, his mental condition had seriously deteriorated. In mid-2005 he held up a pizza deliveryman and stole four pizzas worth approximately thirty-three dollars. The gun crime landed him back behind bars, facing charges that would likely force him to spend the rest of his life in prison for violating the terms of his probation. Tate wrote to the judge saying that he was hearing voices and considering suicide. The teenager might have been one of those doomed individuals who would have spiraled into destruction even if he had not been placed in an adult prison at the age of fourteen and told he'd spend the rest of his days there; but it's entirely possible that his time in prison pushed him into the abyss.

At the end of the day, however, these outcome-based arguments for and against incarcerating teens in adult prisons largely miss the point. Beyond all the rhetoric, the revolution unleashed against the juvenile-justice system was never really about utilitarian, disinterested, criminal-justice policy. Rather, it was about a country's changing definition of childhood, shifting visions of redemption and rehabilitative potential, and an increasingly pre-Enlightenment vision of punishment as an emotional catharsis for victims and a theatrical response to violations of the moral code. Despite FBI statistics showing that nearly nine out of every ten U.S. counties experience no juvenile homicides in any given year, the public perception of crazed Uzi-toting teens roaming the countryside remains in place, and those whose families do fall victim to their actions acquire extraordinary political clout. And because teen robbers, burglars, car thieves, and vandals are far more prevalent than teen murderers, these lower-level offenders end up bearing the brunt of the new laws. "We're talking about one or two fifteen-year-olds who commit multiple murders," Judge Milliken stated, his voice brimming with passion. "We can't build public policy around these cases. Incarcerating too many people inappropriately is bad public policy."

LEVIATHAN CALLING

To say that prisons today are violent is not to romanticize the past. In the Middle Ages, it was not unheard of for thieves to have their heads shaved and boiling pitch poured on their scalps, or for those who fought in the presence of the king to have their hands chopped off and the stumps cauterized with red-hot irons. The British historian Christopher Hibbert, in his classic book *The Roots of Evil*, unearthed examples of murderers being buried alive next to the corpses of their victims; of men being hung, drawn, and quartered, their entrails burned, their heads promenaded on pikes; of defendants being subjected to religiously inspired tests known as "ordeals," involving such torments as sticking their arms in pots of boiling water or shoving their fists into near-molten iron gloves, their bodies' reactions seen as signs from God of their guilt or innocence. Throughout Europe, well into the eighteenth century, there was nothing out of the ordinary in seeing the rotting, often mutilated, corpses of executed criminals adorning city gates, bridges, and other public gathering places. In much of the world, public executions, generally surrounded by elaborate rituals, remained a staple into the modern era.

Today, while dictatorships still routinely torture criminals and political dissidents, devising new techniques such as burning victims with acid and using electric drills on them, the imagery of state-sponsored sadism is less exotic in democracies. But the desire, perhaps even the need, to terrify and subjugate through brute force remains strong. Within the massive human warehousing system that now passes for American criminal justice—an archipelago of prisons and jails not just for the hardened adult criminals, who most everyone agrees should be sequestered behind bars, but also for the mentally ill, disturbed teenagers, drug addicts, and homeless neighborhood nuisances—violence is all too common. Sometimes, as with the hazing of new inmates at Virginia's Wallens Ridge prison, or the racial abuse targeting black inmates in northern Florida prisons, it occurs *despite* official policies, sometimes even despite the best efforts of reform-minded correctional administrators and prison wardens. At other times, as with the gassing of inmates in Florida and the rampant use of isolation units to house unruly captives, it occurs with official blessing—violence by the book, in accordance with the burgeoning rules, regulations, and codes of conduct now in effect across the correctional spectrum.

The administrative and bureaucratic revolution that swept the correctional world in the latter half of the twentieth century *did* force correctional employees to adhere more strongly to written codes of conduct, *did* establish state and federal standards, *did* prepare better training programs for officers and better monitoring of those who employed them, and *did* allow prisoners and their advocates to sue the system if they felt they were subjected to cruel and unusual punishments. What the bureaucratic revolution failed to do— even before the political backlash and the tough-on-crime movement took off—was to eradicate the culture and climate of violence surrounding prisons and jails.

In some ways, the contemporary prison saga is the story of how violence has changed, rather than ebbed, to meet the new demands; how it has been codified and formalized, its practitioners relying more on high-technology weaponry than on the brute force of fists, boots, and leather straps. Like modern warfare, the violence has become colder, more detached, more professional, and yet it remains omnipresent. That is not to say that every prisoner is subjected to violence every day; but the *possibility* of sudden, overwhelming spasms of violence, perpetrated by inmates or guards or both groupings at once—the fragility of the moments of calm—forms the backdrop against which prison life is lived. And, it is worth repeating once again, because the prison boom has cycled so many millions of Americans through penal institutions, the numbers subjected to the new high-tech techniques of inmate control have risen exponentially.

Ultimately, given the equations in play today, the culture of violence affects not just the closed world of the prison or the jail, but entire communities. The acceptance—indeed, the expectations—of violence nurtured behind the high walls of the incarceration archipelago are amplified outward, ripping into the broader social fabric. Conversely, the tolerance of violence on the outside bounces back echo-like into the prisons. It is like the hall of mirrors in Versailles—a series of images ricocheting back and forth in an infinite regression, the behavioral norms of the free world and the cellblock reflecting tragically off each other.

————•————

Today, prisons are what we might call total environments: computerized, video-saturated Panopticons within which every inmate's actions are minutely scrutinized, and officers and prisoners alike are subject to mushrooming numbers of rules and regulations that too often give the nod to violence. Even when they don't, many prison administrators turn a blind eye to the violence within their institutions, and correctional officers, hewing to the informal code of silence, adopt a "see no evil, hear no evil" approach to the actions of their colleagues. This was most vividly demonstrated in California, where guards who turned whistleblower after a string of particularly violent incidents reported receiving threatening phone calls and being set up by fellow officers to be attacked by inmates.[1]

None of this should be a surprise. The United States has a far higher rate of violent crime than other first world democracies, and demonstrates an extraordinary willingness to tolerate officially sanctioned violence in response to crime. While much of the world has stopped using the death penalty, most American politicians favor capital punishment, and district attorneys in many states vie with one another to see how aggressively they can prosecute capital crimes. Moreover, at least until a series of recent scandals undercut support for capital punishment (allegations of torture by Chicago police officers looking for confessions in murder cases; flawed witness testimony landing innocent men on death row), supermajorities of the public also supported this ultimate sanction. When, in 1994, an American teenager was publicly caned in Singapore after being convicted of graffiti vandalism, a high percentage of Americans, according to opinion polls, not only supported the sentence but also said the American courts should hand out similar punishments.[2] Following the incident, legislators in Tennessee proposed the reintroduction of public caning, to be carried out on the courthouse steps, and then-governor of Mississippi Kirk Fordice supported a similar proposal. Even in the more liberal states of California and New York, calls for the introduction of "paddling" for juvenile graffiti artists were heard in the mid-1990s.

———•———

Thirty years after the United States began its unprecedented social experiment with mass incarceration, the country is at a moral crossroads. Will our political leaders continue to morally undercut the entity they govern—and cheapen the rhetoric of equality and fairness that has formed so vital a part of the American historical experience—by defending arrest techniques, sentencing policies, and prison conditions unheard of in other wealthy democracies? Or will they be brave enough to acknowledge the egregious failure that such policies represent?

For some, whatever the costs of mass incarceration, the alternatives would be worse. In late 2005 in California, Chuck Poochigian, the state senator in charge of the Public Safety Committee, launched a campaign to expand the state's already notoriously tough three-strikes law so that the crime of auto theft would count as a "serious" felony punishable by life in prison.[3] In Kentucky, commonwealth attorney Ray Larson, of Fayette County, informed readers of his Web site, "We can't afford not to incarcerate criminals! The problem is not too much incarceration. The problem is too much crime. The simple fact is that the best way to stop crime is to put criminals in prison."[4]

Others, however, have begun to reevaluate some of the policy shifts and cultural changes that have put so many people behind bars and so dramatically altered the conditions facing them there. In California, for example, Governor Arnold Schwarzenegger, along with Rod Hickman, then-director of the California Youth and Adult Correctional Authority (a coordinating body in charge of adult corrections, the juvenile system, and parole), began in 2004 a concerted effort to change the way in which the huge system was managed. After decades of relentless tough-on-crime posturing, California—home to the country's largest prison system—had, in many ways, come to represent the worst face of U.S. criminal justice: in the years after World War II, its correctional system had developed a massive bureaucracy that ultimately came to see institution building as a good in itself, regardless of whether or not the burgeoning bureaus and regulations reduced crime or improved the chances of rehabilitating inmates. The California prison guards' union had become a central player in the state's political process, and the correctional budget had soared to somewhere in the region of $5 billion per year, larger than the national budgets of some third world countries. The very moves toward professionalism, codification of rules of conduct, and bureaucratic centralization for which reformers had fought in the mid-twentieth century had morphed here into something different: a crime-and-punishment engine that was extraordinarily efficient not in establishing social safety and rehabilitating criminals, but in sucking ever more taxpayer dollars into its vast machinery.

Now, at Schwarzenegger's urging, the Department of Corrections was renamed the Department of Corrections and Rehabilitation—a symbolic change important in a state whose leadership had earlier declared rehabilitation obsolete as a function of the prison system—and a multimillion-dollar research wing, headed by parole and reentry specialist Joan Petersilia, was established to study which programs worked to lower recidivism rates. At the same time, Alan Glassman, a top-tier management consultant from Cal State Northridge was signed on to put together a comprehensive strategy to reform the entire correctional bureaucracy.

Glassman, a feisty man with a sparkle in his eyes, salt-and-pepper hair, and a striking resemblance to the comic actor Mel Brooks, hired a team of outside experts and, over the course of eighteen months, fundamentally re-designed the management structures of California's correctional system. He aimed to create a bureaucracy that would provide incentives for inmates to enroll in education, drug treatment, and vocational training programs, and would force prison wardens and their staff to take such programming seri-ously. "My only words for it," Glassman explained over a large sandwich in a San Fernando Valley deli: "We had a lot of swirl. It's very rare. You don't [often] get the coming together of new leadership committed to transforma-tional change with the support of a new governor for that change, and a prom-ise by the governor to blow up the boxes."

Glassman's hiring represented a belated acknowledgment by top correc-tional officials and political leaders that something had gone fundamentally wrong with the state's criminal-justice infrastructure. The evidence suggested that it was not making California safer; the state was sending a higher per-centage of its parolees back to prison than virtually any other state, and the Youth Authority had been rocked by a series of scandals after officers were filmed beating teenage prisoners to a pulp. "We can no longer do business the way we did it in the past," Glassman recalled YACA chief Hickman telling a meeting of senior prison managers in 2004. "What does public safety look like?" asked California Department of Corrections and Rehabilitation direc-tor Jeannie Woodford, brought in by Governor Schwarzenegger in 2004 to re-form the scandal-prone system. "It's really having an offender who leaves prison in better shape than they went in. Otherwise, they're just in, and when they get out there are people waiting to be victims." Woodford, who gained re-spect for being strong but fair during her tenure as warden of San Quentin, hoped that her legacy would be "greater public safety, reduced victimization. That we managed to put in place programs that have proven themselves to be effective. And that our prisons are smaller and less violent."

Of course, the results of these reforms will not be known for years. "In my world there are several areas of change you play with all the time, culture be-ing a major one," Glassman explained over lunch. "Estimates are, it takes seven to twelve years to change the culture of a major organization." The extent of the challenges facing Glassman's team became apparent in the spring of 2006, when Rod Hickman suddenly announced his resignation. Political support for systemic reform was, he argued, largely absent, so implementing durable changes had become all but impossible. Shortly afterward, Woodford, too, quit her job.

————•——•—

Even if reform-minded officials in some states succeed in transforming their bureaucracies and reinstating the notion of rehabilitation into the running of prisons, these changes in and of themselves won't reduce the enormous number of Americans who spend a significant portion of their lives locked up. Changing *that* number will involve a more fundamental shift in the nation's priorities.

Will conservative social legislation, regressive tax structures, and educational inequities—the results of decades of rightward, southern drift in U.S. politics—continue to expand the divide between wealth and poverty, opportunity and despair? And, in so doing, will these policy choices perpetuate the broader social conditions that lead to high levels of addiction and crime as well as high demand for tough incarceration practices? Or will we, as a society, finally make a commitment to grappling with the perennial issues of poverty and undereducation, urban decay, and the cascading sense of anomie that lies behind so much drug use and so many criminal acts?

These are far from idle questions. In past centuries, countries and political systems were esteemed for bringing glory to God and king; for conquest; for military triumphs. Today, in a democratic age, modern states are held to exist primarily for the good of their citizenry. While military triumphs clearly do still play a large role in national mythologies, we at least *claim* to fight only as a last resort, no longer valuing martial prowess as an end in itself. The American state is deliberately, and carefully, separated from religion, and we are governed by laws rather than the whims of potentates: it has been our democratic conceit that our legal system, combined with the political checks and balances delineated in the Constitution, prevents our descent into barbarism, into the bloodthirsty punitive practices that have characterized so many other ages and cultures. In the democratic era, as Alexis de Tocqueville wrote in *Democracy in America,* state structures ultimately hold value for their citizens only to the extent that they bring stability, security, economic mobility, and political inclusiveness, as well as a sense that everyone has equal opportunities and equal access to major institutions. If it doesn't deliver in these areas, the modern state fails the most basic democratic litmus tests.

Today, police officers routinely employ high-tech tools such as TASERs on America's streets, and companies such as the Enforcement Technology Group successfully hawk military-style control equipment, utilized in shadowy prisons in Afghanistan, Iraq, and Guantánamo Bay, for use inside state and federal prisons on American soil. With tens of billions of dollars a year channeled into the business of fighting crime, in addition to punishing and controlling a constantly expanding pool of social miscreants and convicts, the machinery of power is being profoundly recalibrated. It is, for the most part, occurring without the individual players' awareness of the scale of the shift. Myopic to the point of blindness, policymakers have sought to score cheap political points without stepping back to look at the broader picture, at the cumulative cultural costs of normalizing wholesale imprisonment.

Can a country's democratic institutions survive when the primary emotion underlying so much of its social policy, and determining the allocation of a sizable proportion of its annual revenues, is revenge? Dominated by mutual distrust, its social tensions temporarily controlled by mass incarceration, such a state must eventually but inevitably lose the noncoercive bonds vital for long-term stability. We will, in short, become a community in name only, an increasingly atomized continent in which the primary role of government is to instill fear of the law rather than respect for its integrity.

Such a beast is not dissimilar to that imagined by the seventeenth-century English political philosopher Thomas Hobbes, in his 1651 tract *Leviathan*, published barely two years after the beheading of King Charles I, and barely a decade after the collapse of social order and the outbreak of civil war. Absent the power of the state, Hobbes famously opined, life would be "nasty, brutish, and short." To avoid such a fate, individuals came together into a state of society, ceding their natural rights to an absolute sovereign whose primary function was to control and punish the violent, destabilizing, chaos-producing impulses of those within its sphere of influence. It was a vision overwhelmingly negative in its implications: the power of the sovereign was not used to better social circumstances, but rather to prevent the submersion of society by the selfish acts of inherently amoral individuals.

A century and a half later, the postrevolutionary French philosopher Joseph de Maistre offered a similarly authoritarian vision, advocating a social system based around strict hierarchies and the unquestioned power of the sovereign body. De Maistre lauded the hangman as the lodestone of social stability in a world in which man's default attitude was disregard for anything other than personal gain. "The whole earth," wrote de Maistre, a conservative Catholic, "perpetually steeped in blood, is nothing but a vast altar upon which all that is living must be sacrificed without end, without measure, without pause, until the consummation of things, until evil is extinct, until the death of death."⁵ His dark vision, wrote the British philosopher Isaiah Berlin in 1990, presaged the emergence of totalitarian fascist and communist regimes in the twentieth century.

While it is tempting to dismiss as peripheral both the numbers of people we now choose to incarcerate and the conditions of their confinement, the experience is too profound to long remain a footnote. In the same way as the Soviet gulag came to represent the values of the culture that created it, so America's network of jails and prisons will ultimately be viewed as a central pillar of the modern U.S. polity. The cultural values, political ideologies, and economic relationships that perpetuate mass incarceration and, increasingly, thrive off it will be understood as girds to this pillar.

After all, more Americans are now involved in the criminal-justice system —either behind bars or on parole or probation—than are employed in a civilian capacity by the federal government or are serving in the military. At some point soon, there will be even more "veterans" of the American prison system—carrying through their lives all of the political and economic handicaps that go with a felony conviction—than veterans of the armed forces. Already, in many parts of the country, far more young black men, especially in large urban ghettos, spend time behind bars than attend college. If current trends continue, in the not-too-distant future the same will be true for young black women as well. Latinos in many parts of the country also get sent to prison at alarmingly high rates. Factor in class as well as race and the picture is even bleaker: for poor young Americans—particularly poor young Americans of color—lacking the support structures and the opportunities that their middle-class peers take for granted, prison has become a commonplace rite of passage. And the brutalities of everyday life on the inside have, for these young Americans, become as formative of their characters as the intellectual climate of a good university is to those who spend the same years as students.

———

America's penitentiary system emerged as part of a "holy experiment," a counterpoint to the litany of physical torments, humiliation rituals, and wholesale executions that characterized the European criminal codes of the period. Over time, however, as the violence embedded in the laws of many other countries has ebbed, the worst aspects of the American incarceration experience have been allowed to flower. Beatings and gassings, racial harassment, sexual abuse, the catastrophic maltreatment of the mentally ill, and the use of solitary confinement as a punishment tool are all, in practice if not theory, mainstays of the modern correctional system. From an inmate eating his flesh in an isolation unit at Tamms prison, Illinois, to a blind man being gassed in his cell in a maximum-security prison in Florida, to guards in California's Corcoran prison organizing gladiatorial fights between prisoners, extraordinary stories abound.

While officials frequently denounce the violence, too often they do so halfheartedly, allowing abusive conditions to continue while removing the burden of responsibility from senior prison administrators and politicians. They denounce cruelty in the same nudge-nudge-wink-wink manner employed by federal officials when confronted with evidence of torture in military and intelligence facilities outside U.S. borders. Occasionally, if the abuse is particularly extreme or well documented, a few guards are prosecuted; even more occasionally, senior correctional administrators are fired for allowing the violence to continue under their watch. On the whole, however, once the doors to the prison click shut, the conditions inside are out of sight, out of mind to the rest of the population.

This does not imply that most guards are sadists, or that most prisoners are abused on a regular basis. Nor does it imply that most politicians are styling themselves as Grand Inquisitors. None of these is the case. Yet, as the Milgram experiments from the early 1960s showed, in certain circumstances perfectly good people will do perfectly beastly things. They will do them because they are told to do them, and they will do them because they genuinely believe—they have somehow been convinced—that their actions contribute to the greater good.

Using imprisonment so broadly and so casually is, in and of itself, an act of violence. This is arguably the clearest collateral impact of mass incarceration: with more than 2 million prisoners in America, and with hundreds of thousands of correctional employees working behind prison walls, conflict and abuse are almost inevitable. By extension, controlling so many people once they are locked away from the broader society cannot be done without the real and credible threat of force. Sentenced to life in prison on a low-level drug charge, an inmate like Dan Johnson, in California, or one of the life-without-parole prisoners at Angola prison, in the Louisiana countryside, has almost no incentive to abide by the rules. Neither do the tens of thousands of prisoners nationwide serving mandatory sentences—often decades in length —for drug crimes, prisoners who are not eligible for early parole and who thus have no motivation to do as they are told. The only way to make prisoners like these behave is to threaten them with pain and isolation, with humiliation and mental torment should they cross the lines laid down by the guards. And that, as Zimbardo's Stanford University volunteers found in the early 1970s, is precisely what ends up happening.

———•———

When the history books are written, specialists may be interested in how great social systems first emerged; but for the mass of humankind, the most gripping story is what those systems became, what they flowered into in full maturity. We are, as a species, always on the way somewhere, and for most the destination is usually more interesting than the route traveled. Scholars immerse themselves in the minutiae of democratic debates in the Roman republic, but laypeople tend to imagine the Rome of the Caesars, a great but brutal place defined by imperial ambitions and the cruel entertainment of the gladiatorial combats. Historians spend entire careers on the intellectual underpinnings of the French Revolution—the philosophical outpouring that led to the irresistible idea of *liberté, egalité, et fraternité*—but casual readers are likely to hold, as their dominant image of post-Bourbon France, the days of terror, the routine use of the guillotine, the armies sent to plunder Europe. Sovietologists enter Moscow's archives to gather documents on the chaotic public protests, the weariness with war, and the heady, utopian rhetoric of freedom that brought down the Romanov czars. But most people now recall the gulag, the deadening autocracy, and the drab culture of the Soviet Union.

The stakes are high. In play are the United States' sense of self and historical identity. Like a metastasized cancer, America's incarceration infrastructure—not only its domestic prisons and jails, but its growing web of overseas prisoner-of-war camps and secret facilities for holding terrorism suspects—has started to eat away the country's democratic institutions from the inside out. If the trend is not reversed, then eventually, when the annals of our era are written, the United States will, like the now-defunct Soviet Union, come to be defined as a prison state.

ACKNOWLEDGMENTS

American Furies is the culmination of nearly a decade of my reporting on criminal-justice issues, and on the interplay between notions of justice and broader political and cultural trends. Over these years, my work has been supported by newspaper, magazine, and publishing house editors; by foundations; and by think tanks interested in the ways in which mass incarceration has reshaped the American societal landscape. This book would certainly never have seen the light of day without their collective enthusiasm for the ideas and stories documented in it.

Particular thanks to *The American Prospect, Legal Affairs, The Nation,* and the *Sacramento News & Review* for granting me permission to adapt for inclusion in this book articles of mine that first appeared in those publications. Thanks also to Human Rights Watch for allowing me to quote from the report on mentally ill prisoners that I researched and cowrote for the organization. Similar thanks to the London *Independent, The Atlantic Monthly, Mother Jones, City Limits,* and *Blackbook* for assigning me stories the research for which subsequently made its way into my book files.

Were I to mention by name all of the people who have provided me with information, my acknowledgments would, quite literally, extend to the length of a chapter. I do, therefore, wish instead to proffer a collective expression of gratitude to the many hundreds of people, from prisoners to prison wardens, from prison abolitionists to victims'-rights advocates and elected politicians who have talked with me, written me letters, shared their ideas and their research, their experiences and their fears, during the course of my investigations.

Certain individuals, however, I owe a debt of gratitude of a different magnitude. Allen Beck, at the Bureau of Justice Statistics, has been more than patient in fielding my many requests for statistics and in generously referring me to sources of information. So too have Marc Mauer, at the Sentencing Project; my friend Jason Ziedenberg, of the Justice Policy Institute; and JoAnne Page, at the Fortune Society. David Garland, Francis Cullen, Nils Christie, Carla Crowder, Ralph Hendrix, Jennifer Trone and the folks at the American Correctional Association were magnificent in helping me set up lists of people to contact and in facilitating interviews with individuals from around the country and, ultimately, from points farther afield. Eyal Press, Adam Shatz,

Maura McDermott, Kim Gilmore, Carolyn Juris, George Lerner, Eric Klinen-burg, Eric Grodsky, and Theo Emery have all lent sympathetic ears during the writing of this book. And Dave Colburn has, once again, put in many hours getting my Web site into shape.

I want, also, to thank my editors at Beacon Press. Christopher Vyce, who commissioned this project before moving on, was adamant about the need for an overview book linking contemporary penal trends to broader political movements. Helene Atwan and Christine Cipriani helped coax the book to completion. My agent, Sam Stoloff, has sat through enough conversations about this and previous books of mine to have absorbed more knowledge about American prison mores than any layperson should rightfully have to know.

The Open Society Institute, JEHT Foundation, the Social Science Research Council, and, most recently Demos, have all, at various times, provided me with grants to further my research on America's overuse of incarceration, and on the ways in which crime, prisons, and the prison experience have become increasingly central elements of the American story, and, by extension, that of much of the rest of the world.

Last, but by no means least, I want to thank my family and friends. I have been extraordinarily lucky in being surrounded by loving, caring, questioning, and idealistic people my entire life. My grandparents—Chimen and Mimi, Mim and Bob—and parents—Lenore and Jack—helped instill in me a passion for justice and the self-confidence to pursue my dreams. My brother, Kolya, and my sister, Tanya, have always been there for me, during good times and bad, happy and sad. My wife, Julie Sze, my daughter, Sofia, and my son, Leo—born just days before this book went to press—make my home warm and full of life. Without them, my writing would wither on the vine.

Unless otherwise indicated, quotes from sources are from interviews I carried out while re-searching this book and occasionally while researching articles relating to the United States criminal-justice system. Most of the interviews were carried out in 2004 and 2005; a few date back as far as 2001.

INTRODUCTION: FROM OUT OF TARTARUS

1. In May 2004 the federal Bureau of Justice Statistics published *Prison and Jail Inmates at Midyear 2003,* by Paige Harrison and Jennifer Karberg. The report found that, as of June 30, 2003, Louisiana imprisoned 803 per 100,000 residents; Texas, 692; Mississippi, 688; Oklahoma, 645; and Alabama, 612. Nationwide, 238 per 100,000 were in jail at any one time. While the report didn't break down state jail numbers, assuming that the leading prison states also jail people at at least the national average, by mid-2003 Louisiana would have been incarcerating nearly 1,100 per 100,000 residents on any given day. Since the report was released, all of these states have seen their incarceration rates increase.

2. In the late 1990s the Bureau of Justice Statistics estimated that nearly one in three black men in their twenties was either in prison or jail or on parole or probation. The Bureau's report *Prison and Jail Inmates at Midyear 2001* estimated that the national rate of incarceration for black Americans, of all ages and both sexes, was 2,209 per 100,000, compared to 759 for Latinos and 366 for non-Latino whites. The bureau's *Prison Statistics: Summary Findings* for December 31, 2004, found that 3,218 per 100,000 black males were in prison, compared to 1,220 Hispanic males and 463 white males. In 2004 the Washington, D.C.–based Sentencing Project published numbers indicating even higher black incarceration rates in some states: 4,058 per 100,000 blacks of all ages and both sexes were incarcerated in Wisconsin; 3,302 in Iowa; 3,287 in Texas; 2,980 in Oklahoma; and 2,799 in Delaware.

3. The best study on this subject is Khaled Taqi-Eddin's *Class Dismissed: Higher Education vs. Corrections during the Wilson Years* (San Francisco: Justice Policy Institute, September 1998). The study shows that under Governor Pete Wilson, the state's higher-education budget had dropped by 3 percent while the corrections budget had grown by 60 percent. A follow-up article by Dan Reed, "Gap in Education, Prison Funds," appeared in the *San Jose Mercury News* on September 23, 1998. In 2003, at the end of Governor Gray Davis's gubernatorial term, journalist Mark Martin published similar findings in the *San Francisco Chronicle.* His article, "Davis Plan Spares Prisons—1% Funding Increase Proposed despite State's Hefty Deficits," reported that Davis was increasing spending on prisons while proposing a 4.2 percent cut in funding for the University of California system and a 4.5 percent reduction in spending on the California State University system.

4. Numbers provided by the Minnesota Department of Corrections.

5. Data from the Bureau of Justice Statistics.

6. Charles Murray, "The Hallmark of the Underclass," *Wall Street Journal,* October 2, 2005.

7. James Q. Wilson, *Thinking about Crime,* rev. ed. (New York: Vintage, 1983), p. 5. Wilson and Richard J. Hernstein, *Crime and Human Nature* (New York: Simon and Schuster, 1985).

8. The numbers in this paragraph are summarized and explained in the Center on Juvenile and Criminal Justice report *The Punishing Decade: Prison and Jail Estimates at the Millennium,* by Jason Ziedenberg and Vincent Schiraldi (San Francisco, 2000).

9. Bureau of Justice Statistics, *Correctional Populations: Key Facts at a Glance,* 2005.

10. Center on Juvenile and Criminal Justice, *America's One Million Nonviolent Prisoners,* by John Irwin, Vincent Schiraldi, and Jason Ziedenberg (2002). Numbers based on primary research data generated by the Bureau of Justice Statistics.

11. Stuart Grassian, statement to the Commission on Safety and Abuse in America's Prisons, in hearings held in Newark, New Jersey, July 19, 2005, www.prisoncommission.org/public_hearing_2.asp.

12. These numbers were released by the Bureau of Justice Statistics in the 2002 report *Justice Expenditure and Employment in the United States.*

13. Bureau of Justice Statistics report, *Census of State and Federal Correctional Facilities, 1995* (1997).

14. Bureau of Justice Statistics, *Justice Expenditure and Employment in the United States, 2001* (2004).

15. The numbers on Idaho are taken from my article "Is Idaho the Future?" published in *The Progressive* (September 2005). Data on food insecurity was gathered by the U.S. Department of Agriculture and released in November 2004.

16. Numbers from the Idaho Department of Corrections.

17. The report, released in May 2004, utilized data from the Texas Department of Criminal Justice, the Youth Commission, the Texas Juvenile Probation Commission, and Windham School District, the district responsible for education within Texas prisons. Five years earlier, in 1999, researchers from the University of Texas Medical Branch in Galveston had found that 41.5 percent of inmates scored low enough on literacy tests to suggest they were dyslexic.

18. The research team was headed by Steven Belenko. The report, released by Columbia University's National Center on Addiction and Substance Abuse in early 1998, was covered widely by the news media. On January 8, 1998, Joseph Califano, chair of the center, stated in an interview on PBS's *NewsHour,* "We have 1.7 million people in prison in this country; 1.4 million are there either because they violated drug and alcohol laws, because they were high at the time that they committed their crime, were on alcohol or drugs, because they stole money to buy drugs, or because they have a history of alcohol and drug abuse. So really we have prisons that are wall-to-wall with individuals with drug and alcohol problems."

19. 2005 Federal Interagency Forum on Child and Family Statistics. The biennial report, *America's Children: Key National Indicators of Well-Being 2005,* can be viewed online at www.childstats.gov/americaschildren/index.asp.

CHAPTER 1. THE HOLY EXPERIMENT

1. The section of this chapter on Waynesburg is adapted from my article "Seeds of Abu Ghraib," published in *The Nation,* December 26, 2005.

2. Information on Eastern State was gathered from the prison museum, from books about the prison, in particular Norman Johnston's *Eastern State Penitentiary: Crucible of Good Intentions* (Philadelphia: Philadelphia Museum of Art, 1994), and from the photographic and

manuscript archives across the street from the old penitentiary. While most nineteenth-century tourists-cum-observers left Eastern State with a favorable impression, Dickens recorded, in his 1842 book *American Notes,* his horror at the regime of silence and its impact on the minds of the prisoners.

3. So important was the notion of silence, along with that of solitude, that prison architects and administrators during these years went to extraordinary lengths to ensure a monastic tone in their buildings: architects designed chapels with individual cubicles carefully sealed and modified so that inmates could see the chaplain or priest but none of their fellow prisoners. Guards in many institutions wore felt coverings over their shoes to muffle the sound of their steps. A similar system seems to have been used for executions in nineteenth- and twentieth-century France: executioners would approach the condemned person's cell as quickly and quietly as possible, tell them their appeal had been denied, and whisk them off to the place of execution.

4. Robin Evans, *The Fabrication of Virtue: English Prison Architecture, 1750–1840* (Cambridge and New York: Cambridge University Press, 1982), p. 360.

5. A particularly detailed source of information on conditions at Eastern State Penitentiary during this period is [Thomas B. McElwee], *A Concise History of the Eastern State Penitentiary of Pennsylvania together with a Detailed Statement of the Proceedings of the Committee Appointed by the Legislature December 6th 1834* (Philadelphia: Neall and Massey, 1835). McElwee published the work anonymously, identifying himself only as a member of the Pennsylvania General Assembly. Charles Dickens also wrote about the methods utilized at Eastern State, and the prison administration itself kept fairly detailed files on its workings.

6. "Moral Instructor's Report," included in the 1877 annual report of the state penitentiary.

7. Michael J. Cassidy, *Warden Cassidy on Prisons and Convicts: Observation and Experience Gained during 27 Years Continuous Service in the Administration of the Eastern State Penitentiary, Pennsylvania* (Philadelphia: Patterson and White, 1897), pp. 27 and 93.

8. For more information on the intended occupancy of the original prison cells, see Norman Johnston, *Eastern State Penitentiary: Crucible of Good Intentions* (Philadelphia: Philadelphia Museum of Art, 1994). The annual reports of the state penitentiary also document the numbers admitted each year as well as the inmate population at the end of each year. Tour guides at the museum tell visitors the prison's population peaked in the early twentieth century at about 1,700 inmates.

9. The Pennsylvania Department of Corrections lists twenty-two prisons for adult males, two for adult females, one for youthful offenders, and a co-ed boot camp.

10. *The New Landscape of Imprisonment: Mapping America's Prison Expansion,* by Sarah Lawrence and Jeremy Travis (Washington, D.C.: Urban Institute, April 29, 2004).

11. Ibid.

12. The Bureau of Justice Statistics report *Prison and Jail Inmates at Midyear 2004,* by Paige Harrison and Allen Beck, listed the incarceration rate in Maine as 149 per 100,000 residents; Minnesota, 169; Rhode Island, 187; New Hampshire, 188; and North Dakota, 189.

13. I visited Huntsville prison's Estelle Unit while researching "When They Get Out," published in *The Atlantic Monthly,* June 1999.

14. I could find no comprehensive study on the number of escapes from supermax facilities over the years. Database searches on escapes from such facilities, however, revealed them to

be virtually nonexistent. When they did occur, they were generally the result of human error on behalf of guards rather than a successfully executed plan against a fully functioning system.

15. In 2002 and 2003 I conducted research for the Human Rights Watch study *Ill-Equipped: U.S. Prisons and Offenders with Mental Illness* (New York, October 2003). The study was coauthored with Jamie Fellner, director of the U.S. Program at Human Rights Watch.

16. The French sociologist Michel Foucault specialized in writings on punishment, sexuality, and the ways in which societies deal with madness. *Discipline and Punish: The Birth of the Prison* (first American edition published in 1977) explored the notion of the "carceral system" and its psychological relationship to the rise of the modern industrial state.

17. A good source on the rise of the modern British penal system is the historian David Garland, whose many books on the topic present an overview of the links between penal policy and other social and economic programs administered by modern bureaucracies.

18. Beaumont and de Tocqueville, *On the Penitentiary System in the United States and Its Application in France* (Carbondale: Southern Illinois University Press, 1979), p. 41.

19. A good overview of Penn's belief system is an article by Cato Institute senior fellow Jim Powell, "William Penn, America's First Great Champion for Liberty and Peace." It can be found online at www.quaker.org/wmpenn.html. Extracts from the Frame of Government of Pennsylvania can be found at www.constitution.org/bcp/frampenn.htm.

20. Benjamin Rush, "On Punishing Murder by Death," in *The Selected Writings of Benjamin Rush,* ed. Dagobert D. Runes (New York: Philosophical Library, 1947), p. 40.

21. Speech reproduced as an essay, "The Influence of Physical Causes upon the Moral Faculty," quoted in David Barton's *Benjamin Rush: Signer of the Declaration of Independence* (Aledo, Tex.: WallBuilder, 1999).

22. Cesare Beccaria, *On Crimes and Punishments* (Boston: Branden, 1983).

23. Bentham compiled his ideas on the model prison in a series of letters written from Russia to "a friend in England" in 1787, with postscripts added in 1790 and 1791. Jeremy Bentham, *Panopticon Writings* (New York: Verso, 1995). I quote from Letter 5, p. 43.

CHAPTER 2. A RISING TIDE OF VIOLENCE

1. [McElwee], *A Concise History of the Eastern State Penitentiary.*

2. Milgram detailed his work in his 1974 book *Obedience to Authority.* By the time of his death, in 1984, at age fifty-one, Milgram's study had become one of the most quoted psychological experiments of all time. He was widely honored for his research, with awards including a Ford Foundation Fellowship and a Guggenheim Fellowship.

3. Stanley Milgram, *Obedience to Authority,* repr. (New York: Perennial Classics, 2004), p. 5.

4. Kathleen O'Toole, "The Stanford Prison Experiment: Still Powerful after All These Years," Stanford News Service, January 8, 1997.

5. "Transforming People into Perpetrators of Evil: Why Does Genocide Continue to Exist?" Lecture given by Zimbardo at Holocaust Studies Center, Sonoma State University, Rohnert Park, California, March 9, 1999.

6. This quote is taken from an online American Psychological Association Q&A titled "How Psychology Can Help Explain the Iraqi Prisoner Abuse," posted in 2005, www.apa.org/topics/iraqiabuse.html. The answers, according to the Web site, were compiled from expert

interviews and news sources including *The NewsHour with Jim Lehrer,* the *Washington Post,* the *New York Times,* and *USA Today.* The site does not identify where Zimbardo's quote was originally published.

7. Blake McKelvey, *American Prisons: A Study in American Social History prior to 1915* (Chicago: University of Chicago Press, 1936), p. 20.

8. John Howard, *The State of the Prisons,* ed. Kenneth Ruck (London and New York: J. M. Dent & Sons, 1929), p. 1.

9. McKelvey, *American Prisons,* p. 180.

10. David Oshinsky, *Worse Than Slavery* (New York: Free Press, 1996), quoted by James McPherson in "Parchman's Plantation," *New York Times Book Review,* April 28, 1996.

11. McKelvey, *American Prisons,* p. 182.

12. Ray March, *Alabama Bound: Forty-Five Years inside a Prison System* (Tuscaloosa: University of Alabama Press, 1978), p. 76.

13. Elias theorized that the cultures of Europe, and by extension much of the rest of the world, changed over several centuries with regard to the kinds of violence, and the social mores in general, that populations and governments would tolerate. The rough edges of life, he posited, were smoothed out during this process, resulting in fundamental changes in manners, sexual mores, notions of privacy, and systems of crime and punishment. As private actions were circumscribed by this process, so the power of the state grew, and as it did, its institutions demanded more control over populations, further limiting the actions permissible by private individuals. In the sphere of criminal justice, the "civilizing process" led to a decline in private vengeance, the demise of officially sanctioned torture, a reduction in use of the death penalty and other physical punishments, and eventually the emergence of large state-run bureaucracies to deal with malfeasants.

14. Ida B. Wells was a leading African American journalist in the late nineteenth and early twentieth centuries. In addition to writing newspaper articles and books on lynching in the South, she co-owned and edited the Memphis journal *Free Speech.* Many of her writings on lynching have been collected in *Southern Horrors and Other Writings: The Anti-Lynching Campaign of Ida B. Wells, 1892–1900,* ed. Jacqueline Jones Royster (Boston: Bedford Books, 1996).

15. Lon Bennett Glenn, *Texas Prisons: The Largest Hotel Chain in Texas* (Austin, Tex.: Eakin, 2001), p. 206.

16. Ibid., p. 204.

17. For a good history of this phenomenon, see Jack K. Williams's *Dueling in the Old South: Vignettes of Social History* (College Station: Texas A&M University Press, 1984).

18. For details on South Carolina's antidueling laws, I relied on Francis W. Dawson's lecture, "Dueling with the Code of Honor," at the 1999 Symposium on the Nineteenth-Century Press, the Civil War, and Free Expression, at the University of Tennessee at Chattanooga.

19. I wrote about Chicago's torture scandal in "The Serious Torture Squad," a cover story in London's *The Independent* magazine published on December 12, 1999. Lieutenant Jon Birge, the head of a violent-crime investigative unit on Chicago's South Side, had allegedly instituted a regime of systematic torture involving mock executions, beatings, burnings, suffocation, and the electric-shock "telephone" that had been widely used by U.S. military interrogators and military police (of which Birge was one) during the Vietnam War. Most

of the victims of these interrogations were poor and had indifferent legal representation, and many were guilty of other crimes. The scandal came to light after the People's Law Office began collecting information on torture allegations made over the course of more than a decade. Ultimately Birge's unit was investigated and he was forced into retirement. He was not, however, prosecuted for his activities.

A good summary of the thinking behind Governor Ryan's imposition of a death-penalty moratorium can be found in Bill Kurtis's *The Death Penalty on Trial: Crisis in American Justice* (New York: Public Affairs, 2004).

20. Cindy Struckman-Johnson and David Struckman-Johnson, "Sexual Coercion Rates in Seven Midwestern Prisons for Men," *Prison Journal* 379 (2000).

21. Glenn, *Texas Prisons*, p. 18.

22. These are just two of the many examples reported by investigators during the litigation against the Texas Department of Criminal Justice, and ultimately included in the court files on the case.

23. Enoch Cobb Wines's *The State of Prisons and of Child-Saving Institutions* (1880) and George Washington Cable's *The Convict Lease System in the United States* (1883) and *The Silent South* (1885) provided graphic details and statistics on prison conditions, disease and mortality rates among prisoners, and the generally corrupt nature of the southern court system.

CHAPTER 3. USING A SLEDGEHAMMER TO KILL A GNAT

1. Robert Martinson. "What Works?—Questions and Answers about Prison Reform." *Public Interest* 35 (spring 1974).

2. Ibid., p. 38.

3. Ibid., pp. 25, 49.

4. Quotes taken from *60 Minutes* transcript.

5. James Q. Wilson, "'What Works' Revisited: New Findings on Criminal Rehabilitation," *Public Interest* 61 (fall 1980), p. 4.

6. Wilson's *Atlantic Monthly* article, "Broken Windows," coauthored by George L. Kelling, appeared in March 1982. In 2001, I flew to Los Angeles to interview Wilson for an article I was writing for *The American Prospect*. We met at a restaurant near Wilson's house in Malibu. Although the article did not ultimately appear in print, I have used the research from that article in writing about Wilson here.

7. For more details on the treatment of transported convicts in Australia, see Christopher Hibbert's excellent history of punishment, *The Roots of Evil* (London: Weidenfeld & Nicholson, 1963).

8. These quotes were taken from "Research in Correctional Rehabilitation," by the Joint Commission on Correctional Manpower and Training, transcripts from a seminar held in December 1967 in Washington, D.C. The commission subsequently published the transcripts as a booklet.

9. A particularly interesting profile of Joseph E. Ragen can be found in James Jacob's 1977 text *Statesville: The Penitentiary in Mass Society.* Jacobs documents the almost feudal powers Ragen excercised, running his prison for thirty years as an "efficient paramilitary organization famous and infamous throughout the world." Prisoners who challenged conditions in the prison, Jacobs writes, were beaten and "salted away" in isolation for years at a stretch.

10. Robert Martinson, "Symposium on Sentencing, Part II. New Findings, New Views: A Note of Caution Regarding Sentencing Reform," *Hofstra Law Review* 7, no. 12 (1979).

11. While thousands of articles have been written over the years on Martinson's "Nothing Works" theory, there is a paucity of information on his death. A *Washington Post* article published several years afterward details some of the circumstances. Alumni listings for the Berkeley Sociology Department give only the date of Martinson's death. I reconstructed many of the events from interviews with academics and criminologists who knew Martinson or were familiar with his life story.

12. The defendants at Nuremberg were tried in two separate stages. The first dealt with twenty-four first-tier Nazi war criminals, most of whom were either sentenced to death or sentenced to prison for anywhere from fifteen years to life. A few committed suicide before they stood trial, and three were acquitted. A follow-up trial of nearly two hundred other high-ranking Nazis resulted in a few death sentences, but most were sentenced to prison terms.

13. Details on the numbers of state inmates serving finite sentences of more than twenty years, as well as those serving life, those serving life without parole, and those on death rows around the country were generated by the Bureau of Justice Statistics in January 2006 at my request, and sent as personal correspondence. As of December 2002, 24 percent of state inmates were serving finite sentences of at least twenty years, and 11 percent were serving life or were on death row.

14. Bureau of Justice Statistics, BJS *Sourcebook* (Washington, D.C.: U.S. Government Printing Office), p. 20.

15. FBI, *Uniform Crime Reports,* 1990–1997.

16. Commission on Safety and Abuse in America's Prisons, public hearing, April 19–20, 2005, Tampa, Florida.

17. *No Escape: Male Rape in U.S. Prisons* (New York: Human Rights Watch, 2001), p. 130. Authored by Joanne Marine, deputy director of the Americas Division of Human Rights Watch, *No Escape* relied on data collated by a research team led by Professor Cindy Struckman-Johnson in "Sexual Coercion Reported by Men and Women in Prison," *Journal of Sex Research* 33, no. 1 (1996).

18. *Wyoming: Report on Violence at Wyoming State Penitentiary* (Portland, Ore.: Western Prison Project, September 19, 2005).

19. These allegations are included in the 2003 report I coauthored with Jamie Fellner for Human Rights Watch, *Ill-Equipped: U.S. Prisons and Offenders with Mental Illness,* pp. 83–84.

20. Ibid., p. 82.

21. Charlie Frago, "Data: Use of Force up in State Prisons," *Arkansas Democrat Gazette,* December 26, 2005.

22. Fukuyama's ten-thousand-word essay, "The End of History?" appeared in summer 1989 in *The National Interest.*

23. A similar argument about the cultural shift rightward and its impact on economic and social policy was made by the author Thomas Frank in *What's the Matter With Kansas?: How Conservatives Won the Heart of America* (New York: Metropolitan, 2004).

CHAPTER 4. VICTIMS, FUNDAMENTALISTS, AND RANT-RADIO HACKS

1. For a time line of the victims'-rights movement, see "The History of Crime Victims' Rights in America," published by the Maryland Crime Victims' Resource Center, Inc. (www.mdcrimevictims.org/_pages/e_legislation_policy/e2_legis_federal.htm). The National Organization for Victim Assistance hosts an annual North American Victim Assistance Conference, and the National Center for Victims of Crime collates data on crime victimization and local victims'-rights movements. Two essays I found particularly useful were: "The Victims Movement: A Confluence of Forces," by Marlene Young, executive director of the National Organization for Victim Assistance, originally delivered as an address to the first National Symposium on Victims of Federal Crime, in Washington, D.C., February 10, 1997; and Steven Walker's "History of the Victims' Movement in the United States," *Journal of the American Association of Behavioral and Social Sciences* 3 (fall 2000).

2. The U.S. Supreme Court heard arguments in the *Roper v. Simmons* case, in which Missouri resident Christopher Simmons was convicted of kidnapping and murdering a woman when he was seventeen. Simmons was sentenced to death. The Missouri Supreme Court struck down the death sentence, citing a 2002 decision by the U.S. Supreme Court barring execution of the mentally retarded, and arguing that a similar rationale should apply in juvenile death-penalty cases. The U.S. Supreme Court agreed to hear arguments on the constitutionality of the juvenile death penalty. On March 1, 2005, the Court ruled 5–4 that the juvenile death penalty was unconstitutional, and in so doing, it reversed the death sentence of seventy-two convicts nationwide who had committed their crimes before their eighteenth birthdays.

3. *Alabama Prison Crisis: A Justice Strategies Policy Report,* by Judith Greene and Kevin Pranis (New York: Justice Strategies, October 2005).

4. There were two presidential debates in 1988. The first was held on September 25, 1988, in Winston-Salem, North Carolina, and the second took place on October 13, 1988, at the University of California, Los Angeles. Shaw moderated the debate, and this was the first question he asked Governor Dukakis.

5. Greene and Pranis, *Alabama Prison Crisis.*

6. Pat Robertson, *The New World Order* (Dallas: Word, 1991), p. 227.

7. Falwell made this statement on September 13, 2001, in an interview with Pat Robertson on Robertson's television show.

8. Bennett made the statement on CNN's *Larry King Live* show in late 1989.

9. The numbers quoted here are taken from Michael Massing's "The End of News?" *New York Review of Books* 52, December 1, 2005.

10. Numbers in this paragraph were provided by state departments of corrections, the federal Bureau of Prisons, and the Bureau of Justice Statistics.

11. Bill Clinton, *Between Hope and History: Meeting America's Challenges for the 21st Century* (New York: Times Books, Random House, 1996).

12. Reported by Stephen G. Bloom in "Iowa: Setting the Scene," *Mother Jones,* www.motherjones.com/news/special_reports/election_96/iacauc.html.

13. *Honolulu Star-Bulletin,* candidates' forum, August 26, 1996.

CHAPTER 5. REDUCTIO AD ABSURDUM

1. Articles on Sheriff Arpaio have appeared in newspapers and magazines around the world, often detailing the investigations he has faced. A fairly comprehensive overview can be found in Tony Orteg, "Blowing His Cool," *Phoenix New Times,* May 27, 1999.

2. The ban on coffee went into effect in 1994. In an interview with CNN, aired on July 27, 1999, Arpaio claimed the policy was saving his jails $150,000 per year. The use of videotaped visits goes back to 1998, when voters approved a 0.2-cent sales tax for use in the jail system. The tax was extended for twenty years in 2002. On November 3, 2005, the Associated Press reported that there were 126 video booths spread over three facilities for visitors, and 280 booths for inmates.

3. In 2000, facing three opponents, Arpaio garnered 70 percent of the vote. In 2004 he faced a primary challenge and received 56.4 percent, versus 30.9 percent and 12.5 percent for his opponents. In the general election, he defeated Saban by 14 percent.

4. Joe Arpaio and Len Sherman, *America's Toughest Sheriff: How We Can Win the War against Crime* (New York: Summit, 1996), pp. xxi–xxii.

5. *The Foucault Reader,* p. 182; text originally published in *Discipline and Punish.*

6. An excellent book on the ways in which public suffering, and the meting out of humiliation and violence against criminals, were used as tools of social control is Pieter Spierenburg's *The Spectacle of Suffering: Executions and the Evolution of Repression: From a Preindustrial Metropolis to the European Experience.* Interestingly, Spierenburg notes that in preindustrial Europe, the term "execution" was frequently used to signify any public sentence, not just those involving death. Spierenburg links the rise of public "executions" with the rise of the nation-state, and notes that, from the late thirteenth century onward, most municipalities employed executioners, whose wages were paid out of public funds.

7. Nietzsche's words are quoted by David Garland in *Punishment and Modern Society* (Chicago: University of Chicago Press, 1993), p. 63.

8. Paul Harris, "Champion of the Chain Gang," *Daily Mail,* May 21, 2005.

9. The paragraphs on JoAnne Page and the Fortune Society's residential program are adapted from my article "Return Address," *City Limits,* June 2004.

10. Hege's regime was documented by Elsner in *Gates of Injustice* (New York: Prentice Hall, 2004). Chapter 1, "The Second Toughest Sheriff in America," was largely about Sheriff Hege.

11. Reported in the summer 2003 issue of *Fortune News,* the newsletter of the Fortune Society.

12. The text of Gingrich's remarks in the House of Representatives, March 20, 1990, can be found online at http://thomas.loc.gov/cgi-bin/query/z?r101:E20MR0–168.

13. Phil Gramm for President campaign brochure, "Restoring the American Dream," 1996.

14. Weld apparently used similar phraseology throughout his career. A November 1995 article in *The Atlantic Monthly* (Robert Worth's "A Model Prison") quotes the politician as saying that prison should be "a tour through the circles of hell."

15. For good analyses of how poverty, joblessness, decrepit urban infrastructures, and inadequately funded social programs come together to create desperate conditions, see William Julius Wilson, *When Work Disappears: The World of the New Urban Poor* (New York: Vintage, 1997), and Michael Tonry, *Malign Neglect: Race, Crime, and Punishment in America* (Oxford and New York: Oxford University Press, 1996).

16. U.S. Conference of Mayors, *Hunger: The Problem: Emergency Food Assistance Requests,* 2004. In Boston, Project Bread reported that requests for food aid rose 24 percent from 2002 to

2003, and in some of the city's poorest neighborhoods, food pantries reported 100 percent increases.

17. U.S. Conference of Mayors, *Hunger: The Problem.* In Charleston and San Antonio, 79 percent of adults requesting food aid had jobs; in Detroit, the figure was roughly half; and in New Orleans, 40 percent. Nationally, the study estimated that 39 percent of adults requesting emergency food assistance were employed.

CHAPTER 6. OPEN FOR BUSINESS

This chapter borrows extensively from my article "Incarceration, Inc.," *The Nation*, July 19, 2004.

1. U.S. Department of Agriculture, *Rural Conditions and Trends* 7, no. 1 (July 1996).
2. Numbers provided by Arizona Department of Corrections.
3. The *World Prison Brief* (www.kcl.ac.uk/depsta/rel/icps/worldbrief/world_brief.html), compiled by researchers at the International Center for Prison Studies at King's College, London, breaks down state incarceration rates in great detail and compares American incarceration rates to those of other countries around the world.
4. The $87-billion supplemental request was submitted to Congress in September 2003, and lawmakers on both sides objected to its pork-barrel elements. On September 30, 2003, Massachusetts senator Edward Kennedy said on the floor of the Senate that "this is worse than fuzzy math, and the American people have a right to be furious about it. And they will be even more furious about it as they learn what we are being asked to fund." First on the list, according to Kennedy, was "four hundred million dollars for maximum-security prisons. That's $50,000 a bed." The high-cost prisons were widely reported on by the American media. Ultimately, despite the unease, the supplemental request was approved.
5. The hiring of "advisers" such as Stewart and McCotter preceded the $87-billion supplemental request by several months. On May 20, 2003, less than three months after the war in Iraq commenced, Attorney General John Ashcroft announced that the U.S. Department of Justice would be sending twenty-five advisers to Iraq. A year later, after repeated prodding from New York senator Charles Schumer, the inspector general's office of the Department of Justice announced that it would open an investigation into the hiring of Stewart, McCotter, and one other ex-correctional director, all three of whom, according to Schumer, had "checkered records." Schumer stated that their tenures as correctional directors were "marred with scandal, including incidents involving tolerating of prisoner abuse." He singled Stewart out for particular criticism, alleging that he "had come under scrutiny for numerous incidents involving the mistreatment of inmates while serving as head of the Arizona Department of Corrections from 1995–2002."
6. In states where powerful correctional guards' unions represent employees, salaries within the prison system allow guards to live middle-class lives: well over $50,000 a year including overtime, and in some states significantly more. In states where prisons are not unionized, salaries for correctional officers can start at less than $20,000 a year. Hourly rates for guards in some private prisons barely hit $10 per hour.
7. Kopczynski began researching the for-profit, private prison industry in the mid-1990s. His book, *Private Capitol Punishment: The Florida Model—A True Story of Corruption, Politics, and the For-Profit Private Prison Industry* (La Vergne, Tenn.: Lightning Source,

2004), detailed the inroads that corporations such as Wackenhut had made within Florida's criminal-justice system.

8. In the first years of the twenty-first century, legislators in Arizona approved the building, in Kingman, of a fourteen-hundred-bed prison for those convicted of DUI; a one-thousand-bed private facility for sex offenders; and several other facilities. The proposal for a thirty-two-hundred-bed private prison for female inmates was withdrawn after a national campaign against it. But in the Private Corrections Institute, Inc., report, *Cost-Saving or Cost-Shifting: The Fiscal Impact of Prison Privatization in Arizona* (2005), researcher Kevin Pranis notes that "even without the women's prison, the number of private beds will have nearly tripled between 2003 and 2005."

9. More details on the MTC scandal in Santa Fe can be found in *Prison Privatisation Report International* 58 (October 2003), Public Services International Research Unit (PSIRU), University of Greenwich, London, U.K.

10. Letter from Barbara Mikulski and Paul Sarbanes to Attorney General John Ashcroft, November 17, 2003.

11. In December 2003 the *Laredo Morning Times* reported on growing local opposition to the facility, coordinated by a group calling itself South Texans Opposing Private Prisons (STOPP). Tricia Cortez, "Group Opposes Superjail," *Laredo Morning Times,* December 22, 2003.

12. Data on CCA and Wackenhut annual revenues contained in the Open Society Institute report *The Rise and Decline of Private Prisons* (2001).

13. ALEC was founded in 1973 by Paul Weyrich of the Free Congress Foundation. Over the years, Weyrich has been instrumental in creating a network of right-wing foundations and think tanks, including the influential Heritage Foundation. ALEC claims over twenty-four hundred state legislators as members—more than one-third of all state legislators in the country.

14. Brigette Sarabi and Edwin Bender document these political links in *The Prison Payoff: The Role of Politics and Private Prisons in the Incarceration Boom* (November 2000), a report commissioned by the Western States Center and the Western Prison Project. New Mexico's house majority leader Michael Olguin was paid ten thousand dollars by Wackenhut to lobby New Mexico legislators during the thirty-day legislative session in 2000. The researchers also identified lobbyists in Alabama, Washington, D.C., Florida, New Mexico, Tennessee, Idaho, and Texas who were working for CCA and Wackenhut.

15. In April 1999, Charles Thomas agreed to accept a finding by the Commission on Ethics that he was involved in a conflict of interest, since he owned corporate corrections stock at the same time that he produced an annual report used by investment firms to determine the value of the stock. He had also been paid $3 million for consulting work around the merger of the Corrections Corporation of America and the Prison Real Estate Investment Trust. After retiring from the University of Florida, Thomas joined the Homeland Security Corporation. In 2005 he revisited the private-prison issue, publishing "Recidivism of Public and Private State Prison Inmates in Florida: Issues and Unanswered Questions," *Criminology & Public Policy* 4, no. 1 (2005). The Vanderbilt University researchers James Blumstein and Mark A. Cohen coauthored *The Interrelationship between Public and Private Prisons: Does the Existence of Prisoners under Private Management Affect the Rate of Growth in Expenditures on Prisoners under Public Management?* (April 2003).

16. Amy Cheung, *Prison Privatization and the Use of Incarceration* (Washington, D.C.: Sentencing Project, January 2002).

17. Ibid.

18. This quote is from "Highlights of Private Prison Scandals in Texas" (February 28, 2003), a paper prepared by attorney Michele Deitch, who was working as a consultant investigating Texas prison conditions during a period of prolonged litigation against the Texas Department of Criminal Justice.

19. For an exhaustive study of CCA, see the Grassroots Leadership report *Corrections Corporation of America: A Critical Look at Its First Twenty Years* (December 2003), written by Philip Mattera, Mafruza Khan, and Stephen Nathan.

20. The Governor's Efficiency Commission was created by New Hampshire House Bill 171, passed into law March 20, 2003.

21. Calvin Beale, "Cellular Rural Development: New Prisons in Rural and Small Town Areas in the 1990s," paper presented at annual meeting of Rural Sociological Society, Albuquerque, New Mexico, August 18, 2001.

22. The locations of New York State's new prisons are indicated in a report by the Sentencing Project titled *Big Prisons, Small Towns: Prison Economics in Rural America* (February 2003), authored by Ryan S. King, Marc Mauer, and Tracy Huling.

23. County officials helped me calculate the total value of the prison bonds while I was researching my *Nation* article "Incarceration, Inc." Similar numbers are quoted by Smokey Briggs in "Aide to Bonilla Blames Galindo for RCDC Woes," *Pecos Enterprise,* June 26, 2003.

24. I did not see the original contract. My information came from Lynn Owens.

CHAPTER 7. TILL THE END OF TIME

1. The section of this chapter on Louisiana is modified from my article "Lifers," originally published in *Legal Affairs,* March 1, 2004. I conducted the interviews inside the prisons in November 2003.

2. Data from Angola penitentiary and Louisiana Department of Public Safety and Corrections.

3. *Schick v. Reed,* 419 U.S. 256 (1974). Certiorari to the United States Court of Appeals for the District of Columbia Circuit, No. 73–5677. Argued before the U.S. Supreme Court on October 23, 1974. Decided in a 6–3 majority opinion December 23, 1974. Chief Justice Burger delivered the opinion for the Court.

4. *Simmons v. South Carolina,* 512 U.S. 154 (1994). The case was argued before the Supreme Court on January 18, 1994, and was decided June 17, 1994.

5. Numbers provided by the Death Penalty Information Center.

6. Numbers on Louisiana's LWOP population are contained in "What is the Meaning of Life: The Evolution of Natural Life Sentences in Louisiana, 1973–1994," a paper by Burk Foster, a professor of criminal justice at Saginaw Valley State University, Michigan, presented at the Academy of Criminal Justice Sciences annual meeting on March 9, 1995.

7. Numbers generated by the Louisiana Department of Public Safety and Corrections.

8. The 650-lifer law was passed in 1978, during a popular panic about rising rates of heroin and cocaine addiction. In 2002, a reform package known as the McConico Package, gained political traction. On Christmas Day 2002, Governor John Engler signed into law Public Acts 665, 666, and 670, repealing the mandatory sentences, reestablishing judicial discretion, and

allowing twelve hundred prisoners, who had served decades under the old laws, to apply for parole.

9. In December 1997, in an episode on marijuana prosecutions, PBS's *Frontline* aired an interview with journalist Eric Schlosser, who went on to write *Reefer Madness,* a book on the criminal-justice system's approach to marijuana. According to Schlosser, fifteen states provide for the possibility of a life sentence for marijuana offenses, and Oklahoma is one of the worst. He detailed the case of one man, convicted of selling 0.005 grams of marijuana (far less than one joint's worth), who was sentenced to life without parole; and another man, a paraplegic who used marijuana for medicinal purposes, who was sentenced to life plus fifteen years for possession of two ounces.

10. Numbers from Alabama Department of Corrections. While reporting on an article for the Review section of the London *Independent* ("No Way Out. Throw Away the Key," May 18, 1999), I interviewed three middle-aged men in prison at St. Clair, Alabama, who were serving life sentences as habitual offenders after being caught selling marijuana in undercover sting operations.

11. I reported on Tulia for *Blackbook* magazine ("Busted," summer 2002). For a more comprehensive look at the events in Tulia, see *Texas Observer* journalist Nate Blakeslee's book *Tulia: Race, Cocaine, and Corruption in a Small Texas Town* (New York: Public Affairs, 2005).

12. Numbers provided to me by researchers at the Bureau of Justice Statistics, while I was working on "Lifers" for *Legal Affairs* in late 2003. The numbers were updated in private e-mail correspondence in January 2006.

13. Ibid.

14. Numbers provided by the District Attorney's Office and by the Orange County chapter of Families to Amend California's Three Strikes.

15. Bureau of Justice Statistics data, quoted in the Center for Juvenile and Criminal Justice report *Poor Prescription: The Costs of Imprisoning Drug Offenders in the United States* (2000), by Phillip Beatty, Barry Holman, and Vincent Schiraldi.

16. Ibid.

17. Ibid.

18. This section of the chapter, including the information on New Mexico, is adapted from my article "The Drug War Goes Up in Smoke," published in *The Nation,* August 18, 2003. Quote from John Conyers is from a June 14, 2005, briefing at the Public Safety, Sentencing and Incarceration Reform Caucus.

19. Nell Bernstein's book *All Alone in the World* (New York: New Press, 2005) details the extraordinary impact of the war on drugs on families. Bernstein reported that one in thirty-three American children has an incarcerated parent, and one in ten children has a parent either in prison or on probation or parole.

20. On October 17, 2001, for example, in Washington, D.C., the House Subcommittee on Coast Guard and Maritime Transportation held hearings on drug interdiction. The Office of National Drug Control Policy estimated that, while the numbers of those regularly using illegal drugs had peaked in 1979, there had been a resurgence of drug use in the 1990s. From 1992 to 1997 the rate rose significantly, and then it stabilized. But the number of teens reporting use of illegal drugs continued to rise. In 1998 the National Center for Addiction and Substance Abuse reported that teens' use of marijuana had gone up a startling 300 percent since 1992.

21. Drug Enforcement Agency Congressional Testimony. Asa Hutchinson, statement to United States Senate Caucus on International Narcotics Control, April 11, 2002.

22. Data on needle exchange was provided by YDI and public health officials in New Mexico.

23. Centers for Disease Control morbidity data, reported on the heroin information Web site www.heroinaddiction2.com/heroin-facts.htm.

24. In 1997, Steve Jenison, physician-administrator for the Infectious Diseases Bureau, testified before the New Mexico legislature on the issue of needle exchange. He reported that his team had found 82 percent of IV-drug users carried hepatitis C, but fewer than 1 percent had HIV. This was reported on by Barbara Ferry, in the *Santa Fe Reporter,* and reprinted online on *AlterNet,* posted August 22, 2002.

25. Information provided by New Mexico Department of Health officials during reporting I conducted for "The Drug War Goes Up in Smoke," *The Nation,* August 18, 2003.

26. Data from the California Legislative Analyst's Office and the Drug Policy Alliance.

27. Pew Research Center, March 2001. The sample size of the poll was 1,513.

28. Bureau of Justice Statistics, *Felony Sentences in State Courts, 2002.*

29. Bureau of Justice Statistics, *Prison and Jail Inmates at Midyear 2004.*

30. Data in this paragraph is from the Bureau of Justice Statistics reports *Federal Drug Offenders, 1999 with Trends 1984–99* and *Compendium of Federal Justice Statistics, 2003.*

31. Bureau of Justice Statistics, *Prison and Jail Inmates at Midyear 2004.*

CHAPTER 8. STOREHOUSES OF THE LIVING DEAD

Sections of this chapter are adapted from my article "Return of the Madhouse," *The American Prospect,* February 2002.

1. The hunger strike was covered by the journals and Web sites of many prisoner activist organizations. For details see www.pelicanbayprisonproject.org/features.htm; *Prison Focus* 16 (summer 2002), viewable online at www.prisons.org; or www.prisonactivist.org.

2. From the 1995 procedural manual prepared by the Florida Department of Corrections' Adult Services Programs Office. The reform was quietly instituted through an internal departmental memo in 2001, following the filing of the class-action lawsuit *Osterback v. Moore* by mentally ill prisoners.

3. *Madrid v. Gomez,* 889 F. Supp. 1146 (N.D. Cal. 1995).

4. Findings of fact, January 10, 1995. Case C90–3094 T.E.H., U.S. District Court of California.

5. Some sources say nine prisoners were killed. The *San Francisco Chronicle* documented eight such killings between 1996 and 1998; see Susan Sward, "Pelican Bay Killings Linked to Supremacists," *San Francisco Chronicle,* February 28, 1998.

6. Roy D. King, "The Rise and Rise of Supermax: An American Solution in Search of a Problem?" *Punishment and Society* 1 (1998), pp. 163–86. See also Daniel Mears and Michael Reisig, "The Theory and Practice of Supermax Prison," *Punishment and Society* 8 (2006), pp. 33–57.

7. *Supermax Housing: A Survery of Current Practice,* U.S. Department of Justice, National Institute of Corrections, March 1997.

8. The Florida Corrections Commission's annual reports are viewable online at www.fcc.state. flo.us/fcc/reports/report.html.

9. The lawsuit was filed as a class action in June 2001, *Jones 'El v. Litscher* (00–C–421–C). The parties entered into a settlement agreement on March 8, 2002.

10. *Cold Storage: Super-Maximum Security Confinement in Indiana,* Human Rights Watch, October 1997. The report was coauthored by Jamie Fellner, then associate counsel of Human Rights Watch, and Joanne Mariner, associate counsel of Human Rights Watch.

11. Information on the ruling is contained in the American Civil Liberties Union press release "District Court Approves ACLU Settlement, Orders Improvement at Wisconsin's 'Supermax,'" March 8, 2002.

12. I subsequently researched and coauthored with Jamie Fellner a report on the mentally ill in American prisons, *Ill-Equipped: U.S. Prisons and Offenders with Mental Illness,* for Human Rights Watch (2003). Several of the details on mental illness in this chapter rely on research I carried out for this report in 2002 and 2003.

13. Haney delivered this lecture as a paper, "The Psychological Impact of Incarceration: Implications for Post-Prison Adjustment," at a Health and Human Services conference in Washington, D.C., in December 2001.

14. The CCPOA funds were distributed to leading political figures via four political-action committees: the CCPOA PAC; the Issues Committee; the Local PAC; and the Independent Expenditures Committee. An undated report by the Center on Juvenile and Criminal Justice, *Political Power of the CCPOA,* reports that in October 1998, the Independent Expenditures Committee gave Gray Davis's campaign $946,000. Throughout the 1990s, the PACs gave Governor Pete Wilson's campaigns approximately $2 million. In addition to the funding of top political figures in California, the union also helped set up the Doris Tate Crime Victims Bureau and Crime Victims United of California, and it was one of the largest backers of the Proposition 184 campaign, the 1994 ballot initiative that locked Three Strikes and You're Out into place.

15. Alan Bernstein, *The Formation of Hell: Death and Retribution in the Ancient and Early Christian Worlds* (Ithaca, N.Y.: Cornell University Press, 1993), p. 11.

16. National Institute of Corrections, *Supermax Housing: A Survey of Current Practice,* March 1997.

17. Florida Corrections Commission, 2000 annual report.

18. State of Texas, "Intervention Plan for Seriously Mentally-Ill Offenders in Administrative Segregation," *Ruiz v. Johnson,* Civil Action H-78-987, December 15, 2001.

19. The *Los Angeles Times* obtained thousands of pages of internal corrections reports and interviewed large numbers of guards and DOC investigators in 1996. The stories ran from the fall of 1996 through 1998. Alexander Cockburn, "California's Gulag on Trial," *The Nation,* November 22, 1999.

20. The report was filed in August 1998, and focused on suicide attempts and self-mutilation in the Estelle Unit. Conklin's conclusions were referenced in a letter from Dr. Jeffrey Metzner to San Francisco–based attorney Donna Brorby, December 31, 1998, about Texas mental health services.

21. The survey, which is unpublished, was sent to fifteen prisoner-rights groups including Human Rights Watch. Staughton and Alice Lynd, "Compilation of Statements by Prisoners at Ohio State Penitentiary, Received between July 20 and July 31, 1999."

22. David Lovell et al., "Who Lives in Supermaximum Custody? A Washington State Study," *Federal Probation* 64, no. 2 (December 2000), reported 29 percent of inmates in internal management units as mentally ill, with 15 percent qualifying as seriously mentally ill.

23. The psychologist who appraised the mental-health care available in Texas prisons, Keith Curry, detailed his findings in correspondence with Donna Brorby, lead attorney for the plaintiffs. Of particular interest is the information contained in a long letter dated March 19, 2002, which I read during the course of my research into mental illness in prisons.

24. These details are contained in the amended complaint to *Boyd v. Snyder*, No. 99 C 0056 (N.D. Illinois, February 1999).

25. James Gilligan, *Violence: Reflections on a National Epidemic* (New York: Vintage, 1997), pp. 97, 110, and 149–50.

26. *Ill-Equipped*, pp. 161–62.

27. The article, "When They Get Out," was published in *The Atlantic Monthly* (June 1999). Most of the research was conducted in 1998.

28. Joel Dyer, *The Perpetual Prisoner Machine: How America Profits from Crime* (Boulder, Colo.: Westview, 2000).

29. This can be accessed online at www.impactguns.com/store/796430260090.html.

30. This number was reported by the *Sacramento Bee*, and also was widely quoted during press conferences held by the American Civil Liberties Union. In particular, see "Deaths Spur Two Taser Lawsuits," by Crystal Carreon, *Sacramento Bee*, November 1, 2005.

31. The section on TASER gun usage in Sacramento is adapted from my article "50,000 Volts: Why Has Sacramento Become One of the Most Lethal Taser-Gun Hot Spots in the World?" published as a cover story in the *Sacramento News & Review*, November 17, 2005.

32. I was shown a copy of this report by Marjorie Pino, when I interviewed her at her house on October 12, 2005. The case number is listed as 04–6432. The pathologist was Dr. Super. The investigator was A. Rogers. The postmortem on Ronnie Pino was carried out on December 27, 2004.

33. Information from the TASER company Web site.

34. Details on the use of TASERs on protestors in Sacramento were documented in *Z Magazine*'s September 2003 issue. The article, "Countering Biotech and 'Free Trade' in Sacramento," was written by Brian Tokar and Doyle Canning of the Institute for Social Ecology Biotechnology Project.

35. The *Arizona Republic* database is continually updated as new deaths are reported. Periodically the newspaper publishes articles on the numbers of fatalities. See, for instance, Robert Anglen, "144 Cases of Death Following Stun-Gun Use," May 26, 2005.

36. Monica Davey and Alex Berenson, "Chicago Rethinks Its Use of Stun Guns," *New York Times*, February 12, 2005.

37. These, and other instances of inappropriate TASER usage, are documented in Anne-Marie Cusac's article "The Trouble with Tasers," originally published in *The Progressive* and posted on AlterNet on April 11, 2005.

CHAPTER 9. ADULT TIME

This chapter is adapted from "Hard-Time Kids," a cover story I wrote for the August 2001 issue of *The American Prospect*.

1. The historian Christopher Hibbert, in his book *The Roots of Evil*, documents instances in which preteen-age children, convicted of such crimes as theft, were publicly hung. Such practices, though relatively rare, continued into the early nineteenth century.

2. The Illinois Juvenile Court Act of 1899 established a special court for neglected, dependent, or delinquent children under the age of sixteen. Explicitly intended to be rehabilitative rather than punitive, the act mandated that juvenile-court records would be kept confidentially, separate from adult criminal records, and barred children under the age of twelve from being housed in jails under any circumstances. The Illinois system was the first juvenile court in the country; the philosophy behind it was expanded upon in Denver, in the early twentieth century, when judge Ben Lindsey began counseling teenage delinquents brought before him. From that point on, the system spread rapidly across the country.

3. *Roper v. Simmons*, 543 U.S. 551 (2005). In a 5–4 ruling, the Court found that the juvenile death penalty violated the Eighth and Fourteenth Amendments. Among the individuals and groups who filed amicus briefs urging the justices to make such a ruling were former president Jimmy Carter, the American Medical Association, the European Union, and the U.S. Conference of Catholic Bishops.

4. DiIulio coined this phrase in a book he coauthored with William Bennett and John P. Walters titled *Body Count: Moral Poverty—and How to Win America's War against Crime and Drugs* (New York: Simon & Schuster, 1996). Although the book was coauthored, the phrase is generally attributed to DiIulio. Ironically, on many issues relating to the adult criminal-justice system, DiIulio was far more moderate than Bennett and others with whom he is linked. He did not support the notion of mass incarceration, opposed long mandatory-minimum sentences, and made statements calling for "zero prison growth."

5. Bill McCollum made this statement before the subcommittee hearing on Reforming Juvenile Justice in America, March 20, 1997. His statement continued: "Only by taking decisive action now, can America prevent this wave of young people from committing unprecedented numbers of violent crimes." The entire statement can be viewed online at http://judiciary.house.gov/legacy/322.htm.

6. DiIulio's views on juvenile justice, including references to this quote, were explored in detail by journalist Bruce Shapiro in his *Salon* article "Bringing Faith to the West Wing" (February 1, 2001). Another good source here is Bill Berkowitz's "Tilting at Faith-Based Windmills: Over a Year in the Life of President Bush's Faith-Based Initiative" (PublicEye.org, Political Research Associates, undated).

7. Dennis Cauchon, "Zero-Tolerance Policies Lack Flexibility," *USA Today*, April 13, 1999.

8. Quoted in Kenneth Adams, "The Effectiveness of Juvenile Curfews at Crime Prevention," *Annals of the American Academy of Political and Social Science* 587 (May 2003).

9. Kevin Strom, *Profile of State Prisoners under Age 18, 1985–1997* (Washington, D.C.: Bureau of Justice Statistics, February 2000).

10. Information on the number of juveniles in adult correctional settings can be found in the Bureau of Justice Statistics reports *Justice Expenditure and Employment in the United States, 1995* (1999); *Juveniles in Adult Prisons and Jails: A National Assessment* (October 2000); and *Profile of State Prisoners under Age 18, 1985–1997* (2000). The numbers of these juveniles who were members of racial minorities are presented in the Center on Juvenile and Criminal Justice briefing paper, "Myths and Facts about Youth and Crime," www.cjcj.org/jjic/myths_facts.php.

11. For specific data on minority youth in adult correctional settings, see the Building Blocks for Youth report *The Problem of Overrepresentation of Minority Youth in the Justice System* (undated). This report details that 52 percent of all juveniles transferred to adult court are

African American, and about one-quarter are Hispanic and members of other racial mi-
norities. For specific information on the Illinois experience, see the Building Blocks for
Youth report *Drugs and Disparity: The Racial Impact of Illinois' Practice of Transferring
Young Drug Offenders to Adult Court.*

12. Bureau of Justice Statistics, *Profile of State Prisoners under Age 18, 1985–1997.*

13. The number of teens prosecuted as adults by Krischer is quoted by Megan Twohey in "The
Wrong Answer to Littleton," *Washington Monthly,* June 1999. Krischer's op-ed was published in the *Palm Beach Post.*

14. Shahien Nasiripour and Bill Lucey, "Students Could Face up to Fifteen Years in Jail," *Sun-
Sentinel,* January 29, 2005.

15. Florida Department of Corrections press release, November 8, 2000.

16. Angie Cannon, "Special Report: Juvenile Injustice," *U.S. News & World Report,* August 3,
2004.

17. Donna Bishop et al., "The Transfer of Juveniles to Criminal Court: Does It Make a Difference?" *Crime and Delinquency* 42, no. 2 (April 1996).

18. Jeffrey Butts has studied the juvenile court system over many years. This reference is from
"How Severe Is America's Juvenile Crime Problem?" a fact sheet produced in 2002 by the
Washington, D.C.–based American Youth Policy Forum. In 2000, Butts published the
influential article "Can We Do Without Juvenile Justice?" in *Criminal Justice* 15 (spring
2000). He argued that, while there were serious flaws in the juvenile-justice system, the
practice of transferring larger numbers of juveniles into adult courts denied these teenagers
access to those professionals best qualified to design a program to help them.

19. Jeff Fagan, "The Comparative Advantage of Juvenile versus Criminal Court Sanction on Recidivism Among Adolescent Felony Offenders," *Law and Policy* 18, nos. 1 and 2 (January and
April 1996).

CONCLUSION: LEVIATHAN CALLING

1. These allegations were reported by Stephen James in "The Code Of Silence," *Sacramento
News & Review,* May 13, 2004.

2. Eighteen-year-old Michael Fay, a student at the Singapore American School, was arrested
for vandalizing upmarket cars by pelting them with eggs and spray-painting them. He was
sentenced to four months in jail, a fine equal to $2,233, and six lashes of the cane. After Pres-
ident Bill Clinton appealed for clemency, and twenty-four U.S. senators signed a letter to
the same effect, the number of lashes was reduced to four. Fay was publicly caned on May
5, 1994.

3. See Chuck Poochigian's opinion piece in the November 8, 2005, edition of the *Modesto Bee,*
titled "Bad Guys Lured by Light Penalties for Auto Theft."

4. The Web site is www.lexingtonprosecutor.com.

5. This first appears in de Maistre's *Les Soirées de Saint-Pétersbourg* (1821). It is quoted in Isaiah Berlin's *The Crooked Timber of Humanity: Chapters in the History of Ideas* (New York:
Knopf, 1991), p. 111.

SELECTED BIBLIOGRAPHY

This bibliography lists the books I have found the most useful during the decade that I have worked on the subject of crime and punishment in America. It is not intended to be comprehensive. In addition to the books listed here, I referenced numerous articles—in academic journals, newspapers, and magazines—during the course of my research. For the sake of brevity, I have chosen not to list the great majority of these articles in the bibliography. Where an article is listed, it is because the article entered the literature and became a critical part of the broader policy debate.

Abramsky, Sasha. *Conned: How Millions Went to Prison, Lost the Vote, and Helped Send George W. Bush to the White House.* New York and London: New Press, 2006.

————. *Hard Time Blues: How Politics Built a Prison Nation.* New York: Thomas Dunne Books, St. Martin's, 2002.

Abramsky, Sasha, and Jamie Fellner. *Ill-Equipped: U.S. Prisons and Offenders with Mental Illness.* New York, Washington, London, Brussels: Human Rights Watch, 2003.

American Friends Service Committee. *Struggle for Justice: A Report on Crime and Punishment in America.* New York: Hill and Wang, 1971.

Applebaum, Anne. *Gulag: A History.* New York: Doubleday, 2003.

Arendt, Hannah. *Eichmann in Jerusalem: A Report on the Banality of Evil.* 1963. New York: Penguin, 1994.

Arendt, Hannah. *The Origins of Totalitarianism.* New York: Harvest, 1973.

Arpaio, Joe. *America's Toughest Sheriff: How We Can Win the War against Crime.* Arlington, Tex.: Summit, 1996.

Barton, David. *Benjamin Rush: Signer of the Declaration of Independence.* Aledo, Tex.: Wallbuilder, 1999.

Baum, Dan. *Smoke and Mirrors: The War on Drugs and the Politics of Failure.* Boston: Little, Brown, 1996.

Beaumont, Gustave de, and Alexis de Tocqueville. *On the Penitentiary System in the United States and Its Application in France.* 1833. Carbondale: Southern Illinois University Press, 1964.

Beccaria, Cesare. *On Crimes and Punishment.* Translated by David Young. Indianapolis: Hackett, 1986.

Beecher, Edward. *History of Opinions on the Scriptural Doctrine of Retribution.* New York: D. Appleton, 1878.

Bellesiles, Michael, ed. *Lethal Imagination: Violence and Brutality in American History.* New York: New York University Press, 1999.

Bender, John. *Imagining the Penitentiary: Fiction and the Architecture of Mind in Eigtheenth-Century England.* Chicago and London: University of Chicago Press, 1987.

Bennett, William. *The Book of Virtues: A Treasury of Great Moral Stories.* New York: Simon & Schuster, 1993.

————. *The De-Valuing of America: The Fight for Our Culture and Our Children.* New York: Summit, 1992.

———. *The Index of Leading Cultural Indicators: Facts and Figures on the State of American Society.* New York: Broadway, 1999.

Bentham, Jeremy. *The Correspondence of Jeremy Bentham.* London: Athlone, 1968.

———. *An Introduction to the Principles of Morals and Legislation.* 1823. New York: Hafner, 1948.

———. *The Panopticon Writings.* 1791. Edited by Miran Božovič. London and New York: Verso, 1995.

Berlin, Isaiah. *The Crooked Timber of Humanity.* London: John Murray, 1990.

Berman, Greg, and John Feinblatt. *Good Courts: The Case for Problem-Solving Justice.* New York: New Press, 2005.

Bernstein, Alan. *The Formation of Hell: Death and Retribution in the Ancient and Early Christian Worlds.* Ithaca, N.Y.: Cornell University Press, 1993.

Bernstein, Nell. *All Alone in the World: Children of the Incarcerated.* New York and London: New Press, 2005.

Blakeslee, Nate. *Tulia: Race, Cocaine, and Corruption in a Small Texas Town.* New York: Public Affairs, 2005.

Blass, Thomas. *The Man Who Shocked the World: The Life and Legacy of Stanley Milgram.* New York: Basic Books, 2004.

———, ed. *Obedience to Authority: Current Perspectives on the Milgram Paradigm.* Mahwah, N.J.: Lawrence Erlbaum Associates, 1999.

Blomberg, Thomas, and Stanley Cohen, eds. *Punishment and Social Control.* 2nd ed. New York: Aldine de Gruyter, 2003.

Blomberg, Thomas, and Karol Lucken. *American Penology: A History of Control.* New York: Aldine de Gruyter, 2000.

Bogira, Steve. *Courtroom 302: A Year Behind the Scenes in an American Criminal Courthouse.* New York: Knopf, 2005.

Browning, Frank, and John Garassi. *The American Way of Crime.* New York: Putnam, 1980.

Burton-Rose, Daniel, Dan Pens, and Paul Wright, eds. *The Celling of America: An Inside Look at the U.S. Prison Industry.* Monroe, Maine: Common Courage, 1998.

Cable, George Washington. *The Convict Lease System in the United States.* New York: Scribner, 1883.

———. *The Silent South.* New York: Scribner, 1885.

Clark, Phyllis Elperin, and Robert Lehrman. *Doing Time: A Look at Crime and Prisons.* New York: Hastings House, 1980.

Cook, John Raymond. *Asphalt Justice: A Critique of the Criminal Justice System in America.* Westport, Conn., and London: Praeger, 2001.

Corlett, J. Angelo. *Responsibility and Punishment.* 2nd ed. Dordrecht and Boston: Kluwer Academic, 2004.

Culbertson, Robert, and Ralph Wershiet, eds. *Order Under Law: Readings in Criminal Justice.* 6th ed. Long Grove, Ill.: Waveland, 2001.

Cullen, Francis, and Brandon Applegate, eds. *Offender Rehabilitation: Effective Correctional Intervention.* Aldershot, U.K.: Ashgate/Dartmouth, 1997.

Cullen, Francis, and Karen Gilbert. *Reaffirming Rehabilitation.* Cincinnati: Anderson, 1982.

Cummins, Eric. *The Rise and Fall of California's Radical Prison Movement.* Stanford, Calif.: Stanford University Press, 1994.

Currie, Elliott. *Confronting Crime: Why There Is So Much Crime in America & What We Can Do About It.* New York: Pantheon, 1985.

Danner, Mark. *Torture and Truth: America, Abu Ghraib, and the War on Terror.* New York: New York Review of Books, 2004.

DiIulio, John J., Jr. *Governing Prisons: A Comparative Study of Correctional Management.* New York: Free Press, 1987.

Donziger, Steven, ed. *The Real War on Crime: The Report of the National Criminal Justice Commission.* New York: Harper Perennial, 1996.

Duke, Steven, and Albert Gross. *America's Longest War: Rethinking Our Tragic Crusade against Drugs.* New York: Putnam, 1993.

Dumm, Thomas. *Democracy and Punishment: Disciplinary Origins of the United States.* Madison, Wis.: University of Wisconsin Press, 1987.

Dyer, Joel. *The Perpetual Prisoner Machine: How America Profits from Crime.* Boulder, Colo.: Westview, 2000.

Eddy, Paul, Hugo Sabogal, and Sara Walden. *The Cocaine Wars.* New York: Norton, 1988.

Elias, Norbert. *The Civilizing Process: The History of Manners and State Formation and Civilization.* New York: Pantheon, 1982.

———. *The Civilizing Process: Sociogenetic and Psychogenetic Investigations.* New York: Pantheon, 1978.

Elsner, Alan. *Gates of Injustice: The Crisis in America's Prisons.* Upper Saddle River, N.J.: Financial Times Prentice Hall, 2004.

Evans, Robin. *The Fabrication of Virtue: English Prison Architecture, 1750–1840.* Cambridge and New York: Cambridge University Press, 1982.

Feld, Barry. *Bad Kids: Race and the Transformation of the Juvenile Court.* Oxford and New York: Oxford University Press, 1999.

Fellner, Jamie. *Collateral Casualties: Children of Drug Offenders.* New York, Washington, London, Brussels: Human Rights Watch, 2002.

———. *Cruel and Unusual: Disproportionate Sentences for New York Drug Offenders.* New York, Washington, London, Brussels: Human Rights Watch, 1997.

Fellner, Jamie, and Joanne Mariner. *Cold Storage: Super-Maximum Security Confinement in Indiana.* New York, Washington, London, Brussels: Human Rights Watch, 1997.

Foucault, Michel. *Discipline and Punish: The Birth of the Prison.* London: Allen Lane, 1977.

———. *The Foucault Reader.* Edited by P. Rabinow. New York: Pantheon, 1984.

———. *Madness & Civilization: A History of Insanity in the Age of Reason.* New York: Random House, 1965.

Frank, Thomas. *What's the Matter With Kansas? How Conservatives Won the Heart of America.* New York: Holt, 2004.

Friedman, Lawrence. *Crime and Punishment in American History.* New York: Basic Books, 1993.

Garland, David. *The Culture of Control: Crime and Social Order in Contemporary Society.* Oxford and New York: Oxford University Press, 2001.

———. *Punishment and Modern Society: A Study in Social Theory.* Oxford: Clarendon Press, 1990.

———. *Punishment and Welfare: A History of Penal Strategies.* Aldershot, U.K.: Gower, 1985.

Gest, Ted. *Crime & Politics: Big Government's Erratic Campaign for Law and Order.* Oxford and New York: Oxford University Press, 2001.

Gilligan, James. *Violence: Reflections on a National Epidemic.* New York: Random House, 1996.

Glenn, Lon Bennett. *Texas Prisons: The Largest Hotel Chain in Texas.* Austin: Eakin, 2001.

Gonnerman, Jennifer. *Life on the Outside: The Prison Odyssey of Elaine Bartlett.* New York: Farrar, Straus and Giroux, 2004.

Gordon, Diana. *The Return of the Dangerous Classes: Drug Prohibition and Policing Politics.* New York: Norton, 1994.

Gray, Mike. *Drug Crazy: How We Got Into This Mess and How We Can Get Out.* New York: Random House, 1998.

Greenberg, Karen, and Joshua Dratel, eds. *The Torture Papers: The Road to Abu Ghraib.* Cambridge and New York: Cambridge University Press, 2005.

Hallinan, Joseph. *Going Up the River: Travels in a Prison Nation.* New York: Random House, 2001.

Haney, Craig. *Death by Design: Capital Punishment as a Social Psychological System.* Oxford and New York: Oxford University Press, 2005.

Harris, David. *Good Cops: The Case for Preventive Policing.* New York and London: New Press, 2005.

———. *Profiles in Injustice: Why Racial Profiling Cannot Work.* New York: New Press, 2002.

Henberg, Marvin. *Retribution: Evil for Evil in Ethics, Law, and Literature.* Philadelphia: Temple University Press, 1990.

Herival, Tara, and Paul Wright, eds. *Prison Nation: The Warehousing of America's Poor.* New York and London: Routledge, 2003.

Hibbert, Christopher. *The Roots of Evil: A Social History of Crime and Punishment.* London: Weidenfeld & Nicolson, 1963.

Howard, John, *The State of the Prisons.* Edited by Kenneth Ruck. London and New York: J. M. Dent & Sons, 1929.

Hudson, Barbara. *Justice through Punishment: A Critique of the 'Justice' Model of Corrections.* London: Macmillan Education, Ltd., 1987.

Jacobs, James B. *Stateville: The Penitentiary in Mass Society.* Chicago and London: University of Chicago Press, 1977.

Jacobson, Michael. *Downsizing Prisons: How to Reduce Crime and End Mass Incarceration.* New York and London: New York University Press, 2005.

Johnson, Robert. *Hard Time: Understanding and Reforming the Prison.* London: Wandsworth, 2001.

Johnston, Norman. *Eastern State Penitentiary: Crucible of Good Intentions.* Philadelphia: Philadelphia Museum of Art, 1994.

Joint Commission on Correctional Manpower and Training. *Research in Correctional Rehabilitation: By the Joint Commission on Correctional Manpower and Training.* Washington, D.C.: Joint Commission on Correctional Manpower and Training, 1967. Transcript of seminar.

Justice Policy Institute. *Second Chances: 100 Years of the Children's Court.* Washington, D.C.: Justice Policy Institute, 1999.

Kelling, George, and Catherine Coles. *Fixing Broken Windows: Restoring Order and Reducing Crime in Our Communities.* New York: Touchstone, 1997.

Kennedy, Randall. *Race, Crime, and the Law.* New York: Pantheon, 1997.

King, Roy, and Kathleen McDermott. *The State of Our Prisons.* Oxford: Clarendon, 1995.

Kupers, Terry. *Prison Madness: The Mental Health Crisis behind Bars and What We Must Do about It.* New York: Jossey-Bass, 1999.

Lewis, Orlando. *The Development of American Prisons and Prison Customs, 1776–1845: With Special Reference to Early Institutions in the State of New York.* 1922. Montclair, N.J.: Patterson Smith and the Prison Association of New York, 1967.

Lind, Michael. *Made in Texas: George W. Bush and the Southern Takeover of American Politics.* New York: Basic, 2003.

Linebaugh, Peter. *The London Hanged: Crime and Civil Society in the Eighteenth Century,* 2nd ed. London and New York: Verso, 2003.

Lipton, Douglas, Robert Martinson, and Judith Wilks. *The Effectiveness of Correctional Treatment: A Survey of Treatment Evaluation Studies.* New York: Praeger, 1975.

Males, Mike. *Framing Youth: 10 Myths about the Next Generation.* Monroe, Maine: Common Courage, 1999.

March, Ray. *Alabama Bound: Forty-Five Years inside a Prison System.* Tuscaloosa: University of Alabama Press, 1978.

Mariner, Joanne. *No Escape: Male Rape in U.S. Prisons.* New York, Washington, London, Brussels: Human Rights Watch, 2001.

Martinson, Robert. "New Findings, New Views: A Note of Caution Regarding Sentencing Reform." *Hofstra Law Review* 7 (1979): 243–58.

———. "What Works? Questions and Answers about Prison Reform." *Public Interest* 35 (1974): 22–54.

Massing, Michael. *The Fix.* New York: Simon & Schuster, 1998.

Matthews, Rogers, and Jock Young, eds. *Confronting Crime.* London and Thousand Oaks, Calif.: Sage, 1986.

Mauer, Marc, and Meda Chesney-Lind, eds. *Invisible Punishment: The Collateral Consequences of Mass Imprisonment.* New York: New Press, 2002.

Mauer, Marc, and the Sentencing Project. *Race to Incarcerate.* New York: New Press, 1999.

May, John, and Khalid Pitts, eds. *Building Violence: How America's Rush to Incarcerate Creates More Violence.* London and Thousand Oaks, Calif.: Sage, 2000.

McKelvey, Blake. *American Prisons: A Study in American Social History Prior to 1915.* Chicago: University of Chicago Press, 1936.

McWhiney, Grady. *Cracker Culture: Celtic Ways in the Old South.* Tuscaloosa: University of Alabama Press, 1988.

Menninger, Karl. *The Crime of Punishment.* New York: Penguin, 1968.

Milgram, Stanley. *Obedience to Authority.* New York: Harper Perennial, 1983.

Miller, Jerome. *Search and Destroy: African-American Males in the Criminal Justice System.* Cambridge and New York: Cambridge University Press, 1996.

Morris, Norval. *The Future of Imprisonment.* Chicago: University of Chicago Press, 1974.

Morris, Norval, and David Rothman. *The Oxford History of Prison: The Practice of Punishment in Western Society.* Oxford and New York: Oxford University Press, 1995.

Murray, Charles, and Louis Cox. *Beyond Probation: Juvenile Corrections and the Chronic Delinquent.* Beverly Hills, Calif.: Sage, 1979.

Nietzsche, Friedrich. *Beyond Good and Evil.* 1886. Buffalo, N.Y.: Prometheus, 1989.

Oshinsky, David. *"Worse Than Slavery": Parchman Farm and the Ordeal of Jim Crow Justice*. New York: Free Press, 1996.

Pace University School of Law. "Prison Reform Revisited: The Unfinished Agenda: A Symposium Held at Pace University School of Law and The New York State Judicial Institute, October 16–18, 2003." *Pace Law Review* 24, no. 2 (2004).

Palmer, Ted. "Martinson Revisited." *Journal of Research in Crime and Delinquency* 12 (1975): 133–52.

Parenti, Christian. *Lockdown America: Police and Prisons in the Age of Crisis*. London and New York: Verso, 1999.

Petersilia, Joan. *When Prisoners Come Home: Parole and Prisoner Reentry*. Oxford and New York: Oxford University Press, 2003.

Renaud, Jorge Antonio. *Behind the Walls: A Guide for Families and Friends of Texas Prison Inmates*. Denton: University of North Texas Press, 2002.

Rhodes, Richard. *Why They Kill: The Discoveries of a Maverick Criminologist*. New York: Knopf, 1999.

Rose, David. *Guantánamo: The War on Human Rights*. New York and London: New Press, 2004.

Ross, Jeffrey, and Stephen Richards. *Behind Bars: Surviving Prison*. Indianapolis: Alpha, 2002.

———. *Convict Criminology*. Belmont, Calif.: Thomson Wadsworth, 2003.

Rothman, David. *Conscience and Convenience: The Asylum and Its Alternatives in Progressive America*. Boston: Little, Brown, 1980.

———. *Discovery of the Asylum: Social Order and Disorder in the New Republic*. Rev. ed. London: Aldine, 2002.

Rusche, Georg, and Otto Kirchheimer. *Punishment and Social Structure*. New York: Columbia University Press, 1939.

Rush, Benjamin. *The Autobiography of Benjamin Rush: His "Travels Through Life" together with his* Commonplace Book *for 1789–1813*. Edited by George Corner. Princeton, N.J.: Princeton University Press, 1948.

———. *The Selected Writings of Benjamin Rush*. Edited by Dagobert Runes. New York: Philosophical Library, 1947.

Schmitt, Carl. *The Crisis of Parliamentary Democracy*. 1923. Cambridge, MA, and London: MIT Press, 1985.

Sechrest, Lee, Susan White, and Elizabeth Brown, eds. *The Rehabilitation of Criminal Offenders: Problems and Prospects*. Washington, D.C.: National Academy of Sciences, 1979.

Smith, Joan, and William Fried. *The Uses of the American Prison: Political Theory and Penal Practice*. Lexington, Mass.: Lexington, 1974.

Spierenburg, Pieter. *The Spectacle of Suffering: Executions and the Evolution of Repression: From a Preindustrial Metropolis to the European Experience*. Cambridge and New York: Cambridge University Press, 1984.

Sullivan, Larry. *The Prison Reform Movement: Forlorn Hope*. Boston: Twayne, 1990.

Sykes, Gresham. *The Society of Captives: A Study of a Maximum Security Prison*. Princeton, N.J.: Princeton University Press, 1958.

Taylor, Ian, Paul Walton, and Jack Young, eds. *Critical Criminology*. London and Boston: Routledge & Kegan Paul, 1975.

Taylor, William Banks. *Brokered Justice: Race, Politics, and Mississippi Prisons, 1798–1992*. Columbus: Ohio State University Press, 1993.

Teeters, Negley K., and John D. Shearer. *The Prison at Philadelphia, Cherry Hill: The Separate System of Penal Discipline: 1829–1913.* New York: Columbia University Press for Temple University Publications, 1957.

Toch, Hans. *Acting Out: Maladaptive Behavior in Confinement.* Washington, D.C.: American Psychological Association, 2002.

———. *Violent Men: An Inquiry Into the Psychology of Violence.* Washington, D.C.: American Psychological Association, 1992.

Tonry, Michael. *Malign Neglect: Race, Crime, and Punishment in America.* Oxford and New York: Oxford University Press, 1995.

Tonry, Michael, and Kate Hamilton. *Intermediate Sanctions in Overcrowded Times.* Boston: Northeastern University Press, 1995.

Trebach, Arnold. *The Great Drug War: And Radical Proposals That Could Make America Safe Again.* New York: Macmillan, 1987.

Walker, Samuel. *Popular Justice: A History of American Criminal Justice.* Oxford and New York: Oxford University Press, 1997.

Wells, Ida B. *Southern Horrors and Other Writings: The Anti-Lynching Campaign of Ida B. Wells, 1892–1900.* Edited by Jacqueline Jones Royster. Boston and New York: Bedford/St. Martin's, 1997.

Wicker, Tom. *A Time to Die.* New York: Quadrangle, 1975.

Wilks, Judith, and Robert Martinson. "Is the Treatment of Criminal Offenders Really Necessary?" *Federal Probation* 40 (1976): 3–8.

Williams, Jack. *Dueling in the Old South: Vignettes of Social History.* College Station, TX, and London: Texas A & M University Press, 1980.

Wilson, James Q. *The Moral Sense.* New York: Free Press, 1993.

———. *Thinking about Crime.* New York: Basic, 1975. Rev. ed. New York: Vintage, 1985.

———, ed. *The Metropolitan Enigma: Inquiries into the Nature and Dimensions of America's Urban Crisis.* Cambridge, MA: Harvard University Press, 1968.

Wilson, James Q., and Joan Petersilia, eds. *Crime.* San Francisco: Institute for Contemporary Studies, 1996.

Wilson, James Q., and Michael Tonry, eds. *Drugs and Crime.* Chicago: University of Chicago Press, 1990.

Wilson, William Julius. *When Work Disappears: The World of the New Urban Poor.* New York: Knopf, 1996.

Wines, Enoch Cobb. *The State of Prisons and of Child-Saving Institutions.* New York: Cambridge University Press, 1880.

Wynn, Jennifer. *Inside Rikers: Stories from the World's Largest Penal Colony.* New York: St. Martin's, 2001.

Yackle, Larry. *Reform and Regret: The Story of Federal Judicial Involvement in the Alabama Prison System.* Oxford and New York: Oxford University Press, 1989.

Young, Jock. *The Exclusive Society: Social Exclusion, Crime and Difference in Late Modernity.* London and Thousand Oaks, Calif.: Sage, 1999.

Zimbardo, Philip. *Stanford Prison Experiment: A Simulation Study of the Psychology of Imprisonment.* Stanford: Philip G. Zimbardo, 1972.

Zimring, Frank, and Gordon Hawkins. *Crime Is Not the Problem: Lethal Violence in America.* Oxford and New York: Oxford University Press, 1997.

Zimring, Frank, Sam Kamin, and Gordon Hawkins. *Crime & Punishment in California: The Impact of Three Strikes and You're Out.* Berkeley: University of California Institute of Governmental Studies Press, 1999.

Zlotnick, David. "Shouting into the Wind: District Court Judges and Federal Sentencing Policy." *Roger Williams University Law Review* 9, no. 2 (2004).

INDEX